MAY

W9-BPL-921

Interviewing

Interviewing Theories, Techniques, and Practices

Fifth Edition

ROBERT A. SHEARER, Ph.D.

College of Criminal Justice
Sam Houston State University

PEARSON

Prentice
Hall

Upper Saddle River, New Jersey 07458

Library of Congress Cataloging-in-Publication Data

Shearer, Robert A.
    Interviewing : theories, techniques, and practices / Robert A. Shearer.— 5th ed.
        p. cm.
    Rev. ed. of: Interviewing in criminal justice. 4th ed.
    ISBN 0-13-119070-9
1. Interviewing in law enforcement.   2. Interviewing in corrections.   I. Shearer, Robert A.
Interviewing in criminal justice.   II. Title.
HV8073.S423 2005
364—dc22

2004017221

Executive Editor: Frank Mortimer, Jr.
Associate Editor: Sarah Holle
Production Editor: Karen Berry, Pine Tree
    Composition
Production Liaison: Barbara Marttine Cappuccio
Director of Manufacturing and Production:
    Bruce Johnson
Managing Editor: Mary Carnis
Manufacturing Buyer: Cathleen Petersen

Creative Director: Cheryl Asherman
Cover Design Coordinator: Miguel Ortiz
Cover Designer: Michael L. Ginsberg
Marketing Manager: Tim Peyton
Editorial Assistant: Jessica Rivchin
Formatting and Interior Design: Pine Tree
    Composition
Printing and Binding: Banta, Harrisonburg,
    Virginia

Pearson Education LTD.
Pearson Education Australia PTY, Limited
Pearson Education Singapore, Pte. Ltd.
Pearson Education North Asia Ltd.
Pearson Education Canada, Ltd.
Pearson Education de Mexico, S.A. de C.V.
Pearson Education—Japan
Pearson Education Malaysia, Pte. Ltd.
Pearson Education Upper Saddle River, New Jersey

10 9 8 7 6 5
ISBN 0-13-119070-9

To Linda,

my significant other,
life mate,
cohabitant,
live-in,
girlfriend,
lover,
best friend,
dance partner,
and wife.

Contents

CHAPTER 2   Preliminary Interviewing Considerations   43

CHAPTER 3   Diversity and Special Needs   87

CHAPTER 4   The Basic Skills Model   115

CHAPTER 5　Skillfully Communicating Accurate Empathy　147

CHAPTER 9   Concreteness Skills   223

CHAPTER 10   Confrontation Skills   255

CHAPTER 11   Assertion Skills   271

CHAPTER 12   Skill Integration   297

Preface

After teaching Interviewing to Criminal Justice students and training professional employees in agencies for thirty years, this text is probably long overdue. After thirty years, it could be thought that all had been seen and all had been said about interviewing, but each new class or training group brings new ideas and new questions about the criminal justice system.

In the early days, there was little available on the subject. Those of us who taught in the late 1960s and early 1970s had to rely on our experience, creativity, and imagination. We borrowed, adapted, and improvised materials for instruction. Fortunately, our students and trainees were not bashful, and they candidly indicated which techniques worked and which didn't. Their honesty and helpful criticism has been a major contribution to the production of this book.

If any generalization could be made about professionals in the criminal justice system, it is that they are very practical. They view an endless parade of quick-fix nostrums proposed by politicians, philosophers, and academics. Consequently, they have a keen eye for practical people. The purpose of this book is to provide a practical interviewing guide for persons who work with people in the criminal justice system. Police officers, correctional officers, probation officers, parole officers, counselors, and social workers are the personnel likely to find this book useful. These individuals are called upon to interview, and their practical needs dictate that this book contain critical theory and research support but not be overburdened with such information. The book has several specific purposes.

First, the book combines for the student the basic concepts of interviewing and criminal justice considerations. This includes the goal of the student being able to discriminate between interviewing, interrogation, and counseling.

Second, the book tries to help the student prepare for interviews in criminal justice through professional development, avoidance of hazards, and recognition of human diversity.

Third, the book tries to help the student develop interviewing skills based on a systematic, theoretical training model. The structural foundations for the book are the fields of police psychology, communications/human relations training, counseling psychology, forensic psychology, and multicultural training.

Fourth, the book approaches interviewing from a scientifically validated research perspective. Hopefully, through this approach, the book will help move the field of interviewing toward greater understanding of human interaction in the criminal justice system.

Many specialists are needed in criminal justice to cope with the problem of crime and associated human problems, but this book is written mainly for nonspecialists. It is designed so they have the understanding, skills, and techniques to meet their day-to-day encounters with people. Therefore, all criminal justice professionals who encounter people as a part of their job will find this book useful. On the other hand, it would be pretentious and foolish to suggest that this book will have immediate practical application to all interviews conducted in the diverse and vast collection of agencies found in our system of criminal justice. An attempt is made in the book to bridge the enormous gap between traditional interviewing practices and criminal justice needs. The needs in criminal justice are great. The challenge to accomplish this task has been exciting and humbling. Hopefully, if the design of the text is followed and the stated objectives are met, a significant degree of success will be evident in the accomplishment of this task. You the reader will ultimately make that judgment.

The objectives of this book are achieved through a combination of "how-to," "hands-on" instruction, illustration, theory, and research support. This book combines the more traditional with the practical and mirrors the development of criminal justice education in this country in the last twenty years.

This book first presents the basic concepts of interviewing and topics related to interviewing and then presents basic interviewing skills. This format allows the reader to progress from general concepts to specific techniques.

Chapters 1, 2, and 3 introduce basic concepts in interviewing in criminal justice. Chapter 4 is a detailed description of the interviewing skills model that provides the basis of learning in this book. Chapters 5 through 11 focus on specific interviewing skills. Chapter 12 concludes the text by drawing together all of the skills and techniques as well as the future of interviewing.

A complete list of references appears at the end of the book. Additionally, several of the interviewing skill chapters contain exercises for additional skill development at the end of the chapter. Each chapter ends with study questions and an interviewing challenge. The text is based on fifteen years of training workshop and undergraduate classroom use. Consequently, the curriculum of the text and supplementary exercises and assessments have been both academically and field tested. A valuable and effective textbook must be current with the discipline. It is my sincere hope that my efforts have led to this result so that the learning and instructional value of this text will not only be a contribution to the field, but also be a source of knowledge to the student or trainee.

Acknowledgments

Several people have made this book possible and they deserve to be recognized. David Epps, Janie Burwick, Delia Frederick, Harriet Brewster, and Kay Billingsley are appreciated for their excellent work in preparing the manuscript. In addition, the staff at Prentice Hall, Frank Mortimer and Sarah Holle, have been very professional, efficient, and enthusiastic.

Robert A. Shearer

1

Introduction to Interviewing

Learning Objectives

Subject.   Introduction to Interviewing

Objectives.   After a period of instruction, the student (trainee) will:
1. Understand the need for and functions of interviews.
2. Be able to distinguish between reliability and validity.
3. Understand the difference between interviewing, counseling, and interrogation.
4. Be able to distinguish between suggestibility and compliance.
5. Identify the purposes of interviewing.
6. Identify the biases and barriers in interviews.
7. Be able to describe the optimum environment for communication.
8. Identify three types of structured interviews.

Learning domain—cognitive.

The three learning domains targeted in this interviewing text were *cognitive, affective,* and *psychomotor* (Bloom, 1956). Some of the subsequent chapters include only one domain. Other chapters include all of the learning domains.

- **Cognitive domain.** This domain includes knowledge, awareness, understanding, and insight of the concepts, theories, principles, practices, and techniques of interviewing.
- **Affective domain.** This domain includes awareness of feelings and emotions, emotional sensitivity, and emotional intelligence.
- **Psychomotor domain.** This domain focuses on the skills, competencies, decision making, and abilities of interviewing that can be demonstrated and assessed.

In the subsequent chapters, the domains will be simply referred to as *cognitive, affective,* and *psychomotor.*

> The distinction between legitimate and illegitimate interrogation techniques is ill-defined.
>
> Charles E. Silberman
> *Criminal Violence,*
> *Criminal Justice* (1978)

1

Interviews play an important role in the operation of the criminal justice system. In law enforcement, the courts, and corrections, information is gathered daily through interviews with offenders, witnesses, and criminal justice professionals. The information gained through these interviews leads to behavioral, legal, and procedural decisions that have consequences for the entire system of justice. Consider the following case:

> Reginald is a 16-year-old youth who has been referred for carrying a prohibited weapon (a handgun) and possession of marijuana. He is an aggressive, hostile youth who has five prior referrals for assault and theft. Reginald claims to be a youth gang member and states he dropped out of school a year ago. His parents are divorced and he lives with his father, a reported alcoholic. His mother has AIDS and is a heroin addict, living on the streets. Reginald is currently in the detention home. Reginald is scared because he has never been in detention before, but he displays a very "tough" image and is difficult to talk to.

Reginald will likely be interviewed by a succession of police officers, mental health workers, social workers, probation officers, juvenile institution case workers, psychologists, and parole officers. If he continues his criminal behavior and moves into the adult system of justice, most of these interviews will be repeated at the adult level. Reginald will be questioned, probed, analyzed, lectured, advised, scolded, referred, and diagnosed by the host of professionals he encounters. The criminal justice system can be face-to-face and one-on-one intensive at any point. Thus, it is important that interviewers be informed about the basic principles and skills of interviewing that will produce the most reliable and valid information needed for good decision making in a diverse society.

Couple this with the fact that many suspects and offenders are high risk for future crimes, including violence, and the importance is magnified. Consequently, the decisions made in criminal justice interviews may have a profound impact not only on the offender, but also on innocent, unsuspecting citizens who may be far removed from the original interview.

The Need

The need for interviewing training in criminal justice is supported by the importance of obtaining complete and accurate information in all components of the system. By improving interview techniques, the functioning of the entire system can be improved since the system relies so heavily on information gathered in face-to-face encounters.

In addition, in-service workshops in law enforcement, varying from hypnosis to nonverbal interviewing techniques, testify to the interest and curiosity of officers in "exotic" procedures (Holmes, 2002). These officers typically have very little formal training in basic interviewing techniques. In other words, they sometimes learn advanced or controversial techniques before they learn basic fundamental techniques.

Finally, research by Fisher, Geiselman, and Raymond (1987) points out the critical need for interviewing training. They found universal problems in police interviews that can easily apply to other components of the criminal justice system. Their research identified the following problems:

- Interviewer interrupting the interviewee
- Excessive use of closed-end questions
- Inappropriate sequencing of questions
- Negative phrasing
- Non-neutral wording
- Inappropriate language
- Distractions
- Judgmental comments
- Lack of follow-up on potential leads
- Underemphasis on auditory cues

The excessive number of difficulties in police interviews seems to be a direct result of the lack of formal training in interviewing. "Police investigators are thereby left to their own intuitions, on-the-job learning (for example, observing more senior partners conduct interviews), and informal comments between colleagues. As a result of the lack of formal training in interviewing, especially memory, police are forced to use their essentially lay knowledge of memory processes and, hence, the lack of scientifically based questioning procedures" (Fisher et al., 1987, p. 182).

This book is designed to meet the critical needs of interviewing training for criminal justice personnel, both pre-service and in-service. It is consistent with the following recommendation: "It is clear to us that a major change must be enacted at the institutional level, namely, to introduce formal training in the science of interviewing cooperative eyewitnesses. This should be done both at the entry level of the uniformed street police officer, and also as in-house training for the more experienced investigator" (Fisher et al., 1987, p. 182).

Finally, basic interviewing skills are one of the required proficiencies for probation officers. Depending on the focus of a particular probation department, a wide variety of specific skills are required for probation work, but basic interviewing skills serve as a foundation for more specialized skills, such as supervision, community development, resource brokerage, and treatment planning (Shearer, 2001). For example, Seiter and West (2003) have identified the activities or functions of probation and parole officers. Several of the activities require interviewing or human relations skills. These include:

- Home visits
- Employment visits
- Conducting assessments
- Counseling offenders

■ Explaining, monitoring, and emphasizing supervision require-
ments
■ Detention hearings
■ Leading offender groups
■ Meeting with significant others
■ Making referrals to community programs

The only activities that seemed to have less need for interviewing or
human relations skills were conducting drug tests, writing reports,
and court appearances. In any case, probation and parole officers
spend a major portion of their time in face-to-face interviewing situations with a variety of individuals associated with the offender.

The Interview

The interview is a conversation between two people with a purpose.
It is a form of dyadic communication that incorporates sharing, purpose, and the asking and answering of questions. Other forms of
dyadic communication such as interrogation, social conversation,
debate, and fight, unlike the interview, do not involve mutual sharing (Stewart & Cash, 1985). An interview is a structured and pur-
poseful method for meeting the needs of two people. In an interview,
one of the two people takes responsibility for the development of the
conversation, but both participants have a need to be in the interview. "A consistent theme in the literature on effective interviewing
is that both parties have something to gain from the interaction between the participants and that both can and will contribute something to the final outcome. In order to be successful in interviewing,
even when the participants strongly disagree, they must be open
and cooperative with each other" (Sincoff & Goyer, 1984, p. 6). Participants come to an interview with motivation based on individual
needs. Interviews can be considered on a continuum, ranging from
those in which one participant has little need to be in the interview,
to interviews where one person has considerable need to be in the
interview. In Figure 1.1, these possibilities can be seen.

The need possibilities are shown as a continuum in Figure 1.1
to indicate that (1) the needs of the interviewee or interviewer can
exist in varying degrees in the interview and that, (2) the needs can
change on the continuum during the course of the interview. This
would constitute a *motivational shift* during the interview. This occurs when one or both of the participants in the interview realize a
different need intensity for participating in the interview. An example familiar to most readers is the situation where you begin to realize you aren't interested in the job you are interviewing for during
the interview. Your motivation shifted from high interviewee need to
low interviewee need during the interview.

In the first continuum, the interviewee has very little need to be
in the interview, but the interviewer has a high need to be in the interview. An extreme example of this is the case of product surveys

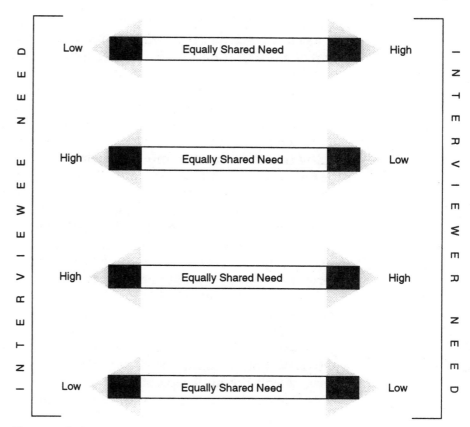

Figure 1.1

in a large shopping center or a census interview. The interviewer needs your responses but you don't care to take too much of your time with the interview because it doesn't provide any direct benefit to you. Many criminal justice interviews also take this form. For example, in interviewing a witness to a crime, the payoff for the interviewee is minimal while the interviewer has a high need to conduct the interview to obtain critical information for the investigation. In fact, with the exception of interviewing crime victims, most criminal justice interviews are not conducted with high interviewee needs in mind. In the second continuum, the interviewer has a low need to be in the interview and the interviewee has a high need. An example of this is a situation where employment interviews are being conducted with hundreds of applicants, each of whom need the job, and the interviewer is quite remote from the actual hiring decision or the job qualifications disqualify most of the applicants. This is also the case of most counseling and social work interviews in and out of criminal justice settings. "While both interviewer and interviewee derive some satisfactions from the interview encounter, the explicit rationale for conducting the interview is heavily weighted in maximizing the payoff for the interviewee. Interviewer satisfactions are incidental" (Kadushin, 1990, p. 5).

This is one of the primary distinctions between *interviewing* and *counseling* or *social work* interviews. In addition to the use of specialized techniques, the primary purpose of counseling and social work interviews is to help the interviewee who has a high need to participate in the interview. Obviously, many interviews are conducted in criminal justice where the purpose is to help the interviewee, but criminal justice interviews, in general, would fall along the continuum at various points from high to low interviewee need.

In the third continuum, both the interviewer and interviewee have a high need to be in the interview. Both are willing and cooperative, making this the optimum interview condition. An example of this is a detective who wants to apprehend a burglar and the victim being interviewed who desperately wants his/her stolen property returned.

In the fourth continuum, neither the interviewer nor interviewee have any desire to participate in the interview, yet for reasons beyond the participants, the interview occurs. Your supervisor, for example, insists on the interview even though you feel it's time wasted and the interviewee is very unmotivated to participate in the interview.

Sincoff and Goyer (1984) identify these as the four *motivational conditions* of interviewing. They point out that if a degree of commonality (continuum three) can't be reached, the preparation of the interviewee, interviewer, or both will be inadequate or time will be wasted. Without a common ground of motivation based on needs, the interview will not succeed.

In the final analysis, even though the interviewer is in charge of the interview, both participants must have a need to be in the interview, and the outcome is dependent on both participants. If these conditions are not met, the interaction ceases to be an interview or becomes less so as it progresses.

Interviewing Skills

Interviewing deals with relatively sophisticated interpersonal verbal and nonverbal communication skills. These skills are the abilities and competencies needed to perform interviews in criminal justice. The position of this text is that lack of interviewer ability leads to poor interviews and high interviewer competency and ability leads to effective interviews, which then leads to reliable and valid decision making in criminal justice.

A skills-based interviewing approach is not new. As early as 1952, Fenlason was advocating a skills approach to interviewing. "Good interviewing comes from the *skill* with which the interviewer uses in the client's behalf: his knowledge, understanding, agency, the time prescribed, and the interaction between persons" (Fenlason, Ferguson, & Abrahamson, 1962, p. 197). What is new is the validation of basic interpersonal skills and the incorporation of these skills, in the last twenty years, into a systematic training model. The state of the art is that we now have available interviewing skills that are clear, behavioral, teachable, and valid. The basic skills model and supporting research studies are presented in Chapter 4.

Interviews as Verbal Communication

Interviews are based on verbal communication. When both of the participants are talking, the process is working and can be successful. If one of the participants is silent, the process begins to break down and the interview will be threatened. This can be viewed as a continuum, as in Figure 1.2.

Aside from the skills and techniques covered later in this book, when the interviewee is silent the interviewer is pretty much at a loss to recover the interview. In other words, the interviewee can leave the interview physically or mentally. In either case, the interview is finished. Even if an interviewee is communicating irrelevant or incorrect information, it is usually preferable to an interviewee who begins the interview very reluctantly or suddenly becomes silent in the course of the interview. At this point the interviewer is left with nonverbal communication, which makes conducting the interview exceedingly and increasingly more difficult.

Interviewing as Instantaneous Response

Interviewing is also characterized as a process involving instantaneous responses. An instantaneous response is one that is made without the benefit of concurrent consultation, thought, or research. The responses are calculated but the interviewer doesn't have the luxury of being able to go to a library for further information, check the laws on a subject, or consult with others during the course of an interview.

The interviewer can hesitate, pause, and avoid a particular subject, but for the most part, they have to respond without the benefit of "time out" or "instant replay." Many interviews in criminal justice are single-contact interviews, so that the importance of instantaneous responses is magnified because the information gathered is final or difficult to verify. The interviewer must respond or initiate at the point of contact with the interviewee because later contacts are too late. An extreme example of this is interviewing potential suicide cases. Because the interviewer is potentially the last one to interview the person, the interviewer's skills become very important.

Interviewing as Influencing

In most criminal justice interviews the goal of the interviewer is not to manipulate or overtly influence the responses of the interviewee. On the other hand, an interviewer subtly influences the interviewee's

Interviewee   ←――――――――――――――――――――→   Interviewee
silent   extremely
talkative

Figure 1.2

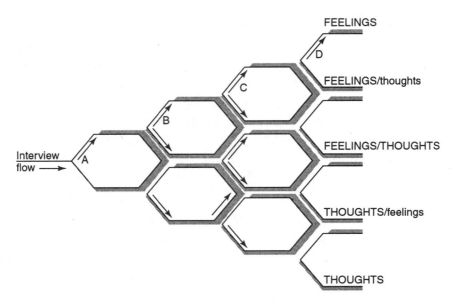

Figure 1.3

responses by making decisions as to what he/she responds to. If the interviewer responds to the feelings of the interviewee, the interview is more likely to stay in affective areas. If the interviewer chooses to respond more to the thoughts the interviewer is communicating, the interview is likely to stay in cognitive areas. The critical point is the interviewer's *choice*. Interviewing is a process of the interviewer choosing initiatives and responses. These choices will in turn subtly influence the direction of the interview. A schematic of critical choices is seen in Figure 1.3.

As can be seen in this schematic, the interviewer chose at point A to respond to affective data and also did so at points B, C, and D, which caused the interview to stay in the affective areas. Had the interviewer chosen to respond differently at point A, or even subsequent points, the interview may have had a completely different outcome with the same interviewee. For example, the interview could take a distinctively different direction if the interviewer had repeatedly responded only to the interviewee's thoughts. The direction and flow of the interview would then tend to stay in the cognitive (thinking) direction. In any interview there are usually several points where these choices can be made.

The key conclusion to be drawn from this is that the competent interviewer is aware of these choices and is flexible to make choices as needed. Consequently, one of the goals of this skill-based interviewing approach is the interviewer's ability to use a specific interviewing skill when the interviewer decides the skill is appropriate in the interview.

Neutrality

Neutrality as an interviewing principle is a difficult notion to understand because, strictly speaking, it is physically and logically impossible to remain absolutely neutral. The moment the interviewer acts, the interviewer is not being neutral with respect to that specific action; the behavior affirms itself. On the other hand, neutrality is an extremely important interviewing guideline. To be neutral in an interview is to adopt a posture in which the interviewer accepts everything as it is taking place in the present and avoids any attraction to, or repulsion from, anything that the interviewee says or does. The interviewer remains open to whatever happens and flows with the stream of spontaneous activity, not against it. At the same time, however, the interviewer avoids being drawn into taking a position for or against any person or issue (Tomm, 1987a, 1987b), or compromising his/her and community standards (Garrett, 1972).

Neutrality can be approached by the interviewer attempting to avoid:

- taking sides in a dispute
- agreeing or disagreeing with an interviewee's views
- being defensive about criminal justice processes, practices, and decisions
- "telegraphing" or cueing their own opinions, values, or attitudes to the interviewee

If an interviewer adopts too much neutrality, and only accepts things as they are, eventually the interviewer stops being an advocate of the criminal justice system and an agent of change in the lives of people. On the other hand, if an interviewer moves away from neutrality and becomes committed to their opinions, values, or attitudes by indicating to the interviewee the "correct" or "right" behaviors or solutions, he/she runs the risk of:

- Violently imposing their values on a resistant interviewee.
- Manipulating others to suit their needs.
- Being blind to the other perspectives of an issue.
- Having interviewees tell them what the interviewee thinks the interviewer wants to hear, rather than what the interviewee actually feels or thinks.

In most cases, when the interviewer cannot maintain a degree of neutrality, the interviewer's bias will defeat the purpose of the interview. If an interviewer is committed to a position of neutrality, then blindness, manipulation, and excessive control will be reduced to the point that the primary purpose of the interview will be realized.

Interviewing as Assessment

Another way to view interviews is as a process of measurement and assessment. The goal of the interview is to quantify behavior, attitudes, experience, knowledge, or opinions. We frequently want to know answers to questions of "how much," "how little," or "how long." We assess police candidates to see how violence-prone they are. We assess other job candidates as to how much knowledge or experience they have for the position. We assess witnesses to a crime as to how much knowledge they have. We interview the general public as to the incremental changes in their opinions about capital punishment. Whether these assessments are accurate is the central question of measurement.

Validity

The first question that we ask about an interview is its *validity*, which "refers to the extent to which you are observing, receiving, or measuring what you think you are observing, receiving, or measuring" (Downs, Smeyak, & Martin, 1980, p. 14). Another way of looking at validity is to question the accuracy of the data you are receiving. We may think we are measuring the offender's likelihood of a successful probation, but we don't really know if we are until the interview is tested by subsequent performance on probation. If the interview does well in picking successful probationers, then we could say it had high predictive validity. This is the degree to which the information obtained in the interview will estimate future performance or behavior (Brown, Amos, & Mink, 1975). Unfortunately, validity is much harder to gauge and document than reliability (Segal & Coolidge, 2003).

Anything that decreases the accuracy of obtaining and receiving data can threaten the validity of the interview. Some of the more common threats to validity are:

- lying, deception, or distortion by the interviewee
- interviewer bias
- cultural, ethnic, or language differences between the interviewer and interviewee
- incomplete or inadequate interview techniques

These threats highlight the importance of interviewers improving their techniques.

Reliability

The second critical question in measurement is *reliability*. "Reliability is the extent to which you would get the same results if you or another interviewer were to conduct a similar interview with the same individual. If two people interview the same person on the same topic and do not get consistent information, something is wrong, and the results of both interviewers would be questioned" (Downs et al., 1980, p. 15). An example familiar to most criminal justice professionals is the case of two psychiatrists who both examine an offender to determine insanity. One psychiatrist says the offender is insane and not fit to stand trial and the other indicates the offender is not insane. This obvious inconsistency questions the reliability of the measurement used to determine insanity. Another example familiar to police officers is the case of interviewing three witnesses to the same crime who each give different versions of the crime. This inconsistency questions the reliability of eyewitness testimony.

It is important to note that even if high reliability is attained, validity is not guaranteed because two interviewers may be in perfect agreement but still incorrect in their conclusions (Segal & Coolidge, 2003).

Since the interviewee's answers and behavior cannot be controlled entirely, the goal of this book is to provide interviewing techniques that will enhance the reliability of your interviews. Without reliability, the measurement becomes random and subject to extreme chance results. Skills and technique are far superior to a coin flip when it comes to working with people.

Interview Styles

Most interviewers use a style that can be characterized by the extent to which they try to control the interviewees' answers. The degree to which this is accomplished determines the interview style. Skopec (1986) has identified four interview styles that are of interest to criminal justice interviewers because they show the possible variations in communication. The interviewer's task is to find a style or styles that will allow the interviewer to do the job.

Talk and Observe

This is an extremely rigid style of interview in which the interviewees hardly have a chance to talk. The interviewee becomes a captive audience. The topics in the interview are mostly of interest to the interviewer and the interviewer tends to control the topics being discussed.

Question-Question

This style is less rigid and allows the interviewee a little more opportunity to control the content of the interview. "Interviewers using this style ask a large number of relatively specific or closed questions for which they expect brief and direct answers" (Skopec, 1986, p. 53).

Question-Probe

In this style of interview, few questions are asked and the interviewer occasionally keeps the interview on relevant topics by making a probe. Only two or three questions may be asked in the entire interview and the interview may seem like a casual conversation.

Nondirective

The interviewer may wish to exercise very little control over the content of the interview. This lack of control tends to produce a nondirective interview approach. Open-ended questions are frequently used to start the interview. The interviewer's intent is to get the interviewee to take control of the conversation while the interviewer listens.

The exact relationships between interviewer and interviewee are difficult to fix according to one of these styles. The interviewer may use a combination of styles or change styles in the course of an interview. Depending on the objectives of the interview, any one of the styles may be appropriate.

Interview Viability

When the motivational conditions discussed earlier in the chapter are combined with Skopec's interview styles, a matrix can be constructed that dramatically illustrates which styles of interviews are viable. Interview viability refers to the degree to which the interview can stay alive, be productive, and be successful. A matrix of these viability combinations appears in Figure 1.4.

A quick inspection of the matrix reveals that of the sixteen combinations of motivation and style, only half (5–12) are viable. The rest are doomed to failure or minimal results. In addition, it can be seen that regardless of the interview style, interviewee motivation has to be high for the interview to be viable (High EE, Low ER or High EE, High ER). As long as these conditions are met, the interview has a strong possibility of being viable. When an interview

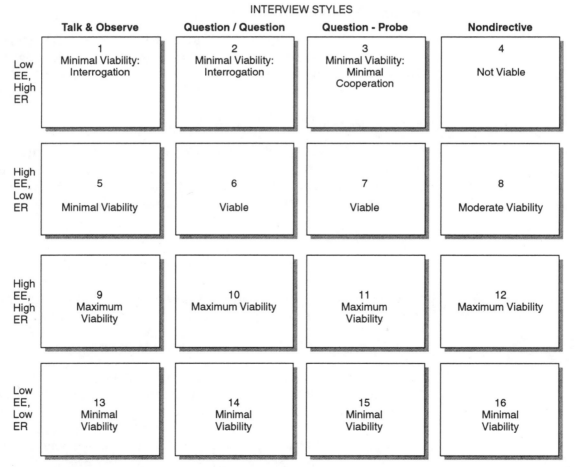

Figure 1.4 Interview Viability Matrix

moves away from these motivational needs conditions, the results are likely to be minimal at best and nonexistent at worst.

Interviewing and Interrogation

Interrogation is a special and problematic case of dyadic communication. In an interrogation, the process is predominantly one-way and is highly controlled by the interviewer (Shuy, 1998; Stewart & Cash, 1985). In an interview, both participants have a need to be in the relationship. An interview is a talk with someone who is friendly and cooperative, who is willing to participate, and who has no apparent reason to lie or conceal information. An interrogation is a talk with someone who is not friendly and cooperative (Rabon, 1992). The person being interrogated has something to conceal even if they appear to be cooperative (Clede, 1990). In an interrogation, one participant needs relief from the relationship. In other words, the interviewee's need on the first continuum in Figure 1.1 is zero—there is no motivation to participate in the interview so the dyadic relationship moves from an interview to an interrogation. Interrogation has an extensive history of use in the criminal justice system and only in recent years has the process been analyzed and discussed.

Knight and Stevenson (1976) have outlined the differences between interviewing and interrogation. These differences appear in Figure 1.5.

The differences between the two forms of communication are such that there is little similarity between them and completely

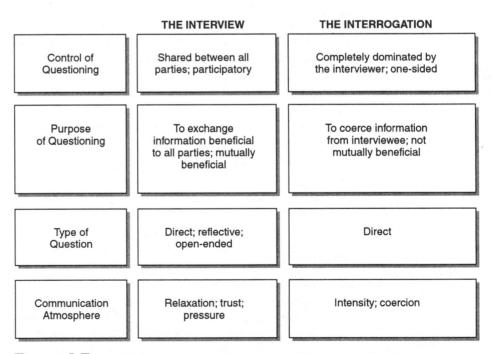

	THE INTERVIEW	THE INTERROGATION
Control of Questioning	Shared between all parties; participatory	Completely dominated by the interviewer; one-sided
Purpose of Questioning	To exchange information beneficial to all parties; mutually beneficial	To coerce information from interviewee; not mutually beneficial
Type of Question	Direct; reflective; open-ended	Direct
Communication Atmosphere	Relaxation; trust; pressure	Intensity; coercion

Figure 1.5 Differences between Interviewing and Interrogation

different atmospheres are created in each. The atmosphere in interrogation is ultimately one of mistrust, deception, defensiveness, and stress. This process is counter to the approach presented in this book and is the central reason why an extensive presentation of interrogation does not appear. In addition, interrogation is not presented for the following reasons:

- Interrogation is not supported by any "validating evidence gained through systematic experimentation" (Bartol, 1983; Gudjonsson, 2003). It is part of the "folklore" of criminal justice. Interrogation practices have been passed from generation to generation and from supervisor to officer as a strong but unsystematic tradition. Within this "folklore" tradition there probably are techniques that work and don't work. We simply do not have any evidence as to which are effective and which are not effective, especially the rate of false or true confessions. All we have in this "folklore" tradition is a specific individual testifying about how a specific technique worked for them. Individual testimony, case studies, or anecdotal evidence tends to ignore or omit techniques that show limited success so that the results of successful techniques may actually be due to chance. Without a systematic and objective comparison that includes random success factors, no evidence exists that is reliable and valid for broad implementation. Nevertheless, anecdotal evidence and training techniques based on individual cases can be very valuable in developing an understanding of the conditions and challenges of actual interviews, rather than laboratory simulated interviews. What anecdotal reports lack is the intense critical analysis of forensic and behavioral scientists who publish the results in a public forum, for all to inspect, before final conclusions are made and published in a textbook. How does a student of interviewing know the difference? The answer to this question isn't easy to find, but an initial guide would be to check references in the book. Anecdotal reports tend to have few references; scientific books tend to have many references.
- Verbal interrogation has, on occasion, in criminal justice agencies, led to physical interrogation and brutality (Wrightsman, 1987). This close association of physical interrogation to forced questioning has led to a strong avoidance of the term "interrogation" by most modern democratic institutions. Some countries in the world still unashamedly advocate physical interrogation. Specifically, in totalitarian, terrorist, or fascist countries, the term "interrogation" is a euphemism for torture and confessions extracted by pain and suffering (Huggins, Haritos-Fatouros, & Zimbardo, 2002; Timerman, 1981).

  In this country, this kind of interrogation has been referred to as use of the "third degree." The practice of the third degree was used to secure confessions from citizens or get information from suspects. In addition to torture, many suspects were questioned for hours or days, deprived of sleep or food, threatened, and beaten. Fortunately, the American public no longer is willing to tolerate these brutal third-degree interrogation practices and they are primarily a relic of the past (Kappeler, Sluder, & Alpert, 1994). The word "interrogation" creates a bad public image for law enforcement, and many officers prefer the more neutral term of "interview" (Shuy, 1998).

The term "interview" could just as easily become a similar euphemism, but at the present time the term is less aversive and doesn't carry the negative baggage that "interrogation" did when it was used at an earlier time in this country and as it is currently used in other countries.

■ Interrogation has led to false confessions and confabulation (i.e., the making up of information) by suspects under intense pressure and stress or who are highly suggestible (Gudjonsson, 2003; Holmes, 2002).

■ Because of the associated legal and procedural problems since *Miranda,* many criminal justice agencies are moving away from interrogation and toward less coercive techniques. Myren and Garcia (1989) have identified the specific types of conduct that the courts will not tolerate during the interviewing of a suspect.

- There should, obviously, be no physical abuse.
- There should be no threat of physical violence, either openly or by implication.
- There should be no warning that dire consequences will follow if the person does not talk.
- There should be no threat to arrest the suspect's significant other if he or she doesn't talk.
- There should be no promise of release or of reducing or dropping charges in return for admissions or confessions.
- There should be no promise to intercede with other authorities for leniency in return for a statement.
- There should be no promise not to prosecute for other known or suspected crimes.
- There should be no use of illegally obtained evidence to break down the person's resistance.
- The subject should not be arrested on some trumped-up charge in order to create an opportunity for questioning.
- The person should not be held incommunicado.
- The questioning should not be prolonged unduly.

Admissions or confessions obtained using these practices may threaten their admissibility at a later trial. Consequently, interviewers are safer if they use noncoercive interviewing techniques. Techniques that treat the interviewee with decency and respect have been found to be more effective and rewarding. "No matter how despicable the crime, a sympathetic and understanding attitude by the interrogator is far more effective than pressure tactics" (Clede, 1990).

■ There is not presently known any scientifically valid interpersonal technique to determine if a person is lying or concealing information even though the criminal justice system perpetuates "folklore" to the contrary (Bartol, 1983). Considerable evidence exists questioning whether an instrument such as the polygraph can reliably, validly, and legally detect lying or deception (Bartol, 1983; Ekman, 1986; Nardini, 1987; Shneour, 1990; Wrightsman, 1987).

The National Research Council (2003) has concluded: First, after a century of scientific research, little basis exists for the expectation that a polygraph test could have extremely high accuracy. Second, theoretical rationale for the polygraph is quite weak. Third, research on the polygraph has not shown much progress in accumulating knowledge or strengthening the scientific support for the test. Finally, estimates of polygraph accuracy, based on existing research, overestimate accuracy in actual practice. The council generally concluded the evidence on the polygraph is scanty and scientifically weak.

- Interrogation practices, when they are aversive, are a form of mental and emotional assault in much the same sense as we view physical assault. In both cases, the person is subject to coercion, force, intimidation, or deceit to do or say something they would rather not do or say. This is also consistent with our understanding of what constitutes mental and emotional abuse as well as physical and sexual abuse of a child or adult. Obviously, abuse and assault can take different forms with equally devastating results. On the other hand, we sometimes fail to recognize these results if the interrogator doesn't physically touch the person being interrogated. A case in point is the traditional reluctance of law enforcement investigators to use hard interrogation tactics on young children. Society views this as mental and emotional abuse of the child. Yet, we have seen these same tactics occasionally employed with adults who are either very mentally unsophisticated or are handicapped by diminished intellectual capacity. In the final analysis, force and intimidation are abusive regardless of the person's age or capacity. The interviewer who uses such tactics must search their ethical standards to justify their use on suspects that are "presumed innocent."

Interviews are similar to interrogation in that they usually involve two people in communication even if the communication by the interviewee is minimal or nonverbal. They both also involve the interviewer asking questions even though in an interrogation the interviewee may resist answering questions. Any additional similarity stops here, even though in the field the terms are sometimes used interchangeably.

The problems created by interrogation far outweigh any possible benefits gained by their use. The field of criminal justice needs valid, reliable, and professional interview techniques based on sound theoretical models and scientific investigation. With the introduction of routine tape-recording, discussed in more detail in Chapter 2, the need for coercive interrogation tactics may be further reduced. It seems that the persuasive interrogation style of the past has been replaced by a confrontational type of questioning that is less manipulative in nature (Gudjonsson, 1989).

Suggestibility and Compliance

Two problems with interrogations that have been studied extensively of interest to prospective criminal justice interviewers are interrogative suggestibility and compliance.

Interrogative Suggestibility

The extent to which, within a closed social interaction (an interrogation), the suspect or witness comes to accept messages communicated during formal questioning, as a result of which they acknowledge their acceptance of the suggested information. Suggestibility has particularly been of concern in cases where mentally handicapped victims or suspects were questioned and where defendants had retracted confessions made during police interviews. It applies to the recollection of past experiences and events and it appears that "leading" questions can increase the likelihood of false information with a highly suggestible interviewee.

Summarizing the work on the role of suggestibility in interrogations, Trowbridge (2003) concluded that children and adolescents and mentally retarded and mentally deficient, highly acquiescent, and highly anxious suspects have shown to have high interrogative suggestibility. He suggests that police interrogators should be very careful to not ask leading or suggestive questions with these types of suspects. Low self-esteem has also been found to be related to decreased resistance to interrogative suggestibility. Baxter, Jackson, and Bain (2003) reported this relationship and also found that higher levels of self-esteem were related to decreased suggestibility. If the interviewer was friendly, high self-esteem interviewees were less suggestible. If the interviewer was abrupt, severe, formal, stern, authoritative, or negative, the high self-esteem interviewees indicated even lower suggestibility. Consequently, interviewers need to be very cautious in identifying witnesses who are perceived as vulnerable to suggestibility. The results could be the opposite of what is intended, particularly if the witness is a person with a high level of self-esteem.

It is also worth noting that much of the suggestibility in an interview is under the control of the interviewer and interviewers can be trained to keep the suggestiveness of an interview to a minimum (Boon & Baxter, 2000).

Compliance

When the individual goes along but does not believe the propositions offered by the interrogator, it is considered compliance rather than suggestibility. This is different from suggestibility, where there is personal acceptance and belief of the proposition offered by the interrogator. The interviewee disagrees with the interrogator but simply acquiesces to the pressure and authority of the situation. Research has also suggested that there may be certain personality types that may be more compliant than others (Gudjonsson, 1992). The "SSP" exercise at the end of this chapter provides a personal exploration into this possibility.

Purposes of Interviewing

Reviewing the basic interview, we need to look at the various purposes that interviews serve. With the diversity of functions in the criminal justice system, we could expect to find a wide variety of interviews with different purposes. Molyneaux and Lane (1982) have identified the following interview goals:

> Getting information
> Giving information
> Expressing and exploring feelings
> Solving problems
> Planning for future action

Using the above goals, we can see how each fits criminal justice interviews by the following examples.

Getting Information

- Completing a presentence investigation to make a sentence recommendation
- Interviewing victims of and witnesses to crimes
- Interviewing juveniles in an institution who have had a fight in order to complete a disciplinary report
- Interviewing suspects in a crime investigation

Giving Information

- Giving a prospective parolee information about halfway houses or drug or alcohol programs
- Giving information to victims about compensation or community support groups
- Explaining the rules and expectations of probation to a probationer

Expressing and Exploring Feelings

- Listening to a fellow officer who has been passed over for promotion
- Listening to a parolee who is expressing anger and embarrassment because you visited her at her workplace
- Exploring feelings with a victim of crime

Solving Problems

- Working with a parolee who wants to tell his boss he's an ex-convict
- Assisting a police officer who is burned out but afraid to leave the profession

■ Working with an inmate who is losing parental rights to his children

Planning for Future Action

■ Identifying the steps for an inmate to obtain his Certificate of General Educational Development (GED)
■ Scheduling activities for a juvenile who is very depressed
■ Planning a release placement for a terminally ill inmate

In addition to the aforementioned purposes of interviews, *personnel interviews* are also conducted in law enforcement, the courts, and in corrections in all of the areas identified by Cinnamon and Matulef (1979):

■ employment
■ selection
■ information gathering
■ career counseling
■ performance evaluation
■ problem solving
■ problem employee
■ termination

Most criminal justice agencies are "personnel-intensive," which means that the primary workload is performed by people instead of robots, machines, or tools. Hence, interviewing is considered the primary method for handling personnel procedures and decisions. Surveys, forms, and computer printouts are valuable sources of information but they cannot substitute for a face-to-face interview in most personnel situations. Because of this, *personnel interviews* serve a wide variety of purposes in the various components of the criminal justice system.

Prediction

One of the fundamental purposes of interviews is to predict future behavior. In an employment interview, the interviewer hopes to gather information to enable him/her to decide the future success of an employee. In interviewing a prospective couple for a foster home, the social worker hopes to find a satisfactory home environment for a child. Prediction is critical and oftentimes risky in criminal justice situations because it can affect life or property of innocent victims if the prediction is in error. For example, the wrong parole prediction can lead to further victims of crime. In order to be as successful as possible, the interviewer in criminal justice is often required to gather information from people in complex and stressful situations. Interviewing techniques that encompass the full range of facts recognized in the behavioral sciences can give the criminal justice interviewer a professional advantage over lay and untrained interviewers.

Maximizing Successful Prediction

Even with a highly trained interviewer there are no guarantees. What any professional interviewer does is maximize success so that the techniques the interviewer uses work more often with more people in more situations. This is their professional edge. This means the interviewer brings to the interview the full range of awareness and skills offered by criminal justice and behavioral science research and practice. Under these conditions, if the prediction is in error, the interviewer should be concerned but not guilty or ashamed.

Random Successes

Some interviewing techniques will work for some interviewers sometimes. Many professionals in criminal justice "play it by ear" and experience chance or random successes. Are there police, corrections, and probation officers who are untrained and highly successful? Of course there are. Some are naturally very good at conducting interviews while others experience chance successes. The approach of this book is that you can always do a better job if you know what you are doing and why you are doing it.

Art or Science?

Is interviewing an art or a science? If interviewing is an art, then it involves research, training, evaluation, and skill development. The answer is that, at present, it is a little of both. The approach of this text is that criminal justice interviewing is moving, and needs to move, closer to a science than an art. The field of criminal justice cannot rely on a few gifted or talented interviewers who may or may not groom new, talented interviewers for the rapidly expanding field of criminal justice. What the field needs is a set of basic skills and techniques based on sound research driven by theory and hypothesis testing. Only by moving in the direction of a science will interviewing maintain a high level of professionalism, integrity, and objectivity. Nevertheless, interviewers are not robots in their activities. They are artful in coordinating, planning, and drawing conclusions from the interviewing process. This artful element is more true in interviews that are in-depth than interviews that consist of standardized or highly structured surveys. In any case, there still is an artful element regardless of the prescribed roles of the participants (Gubrium & Holstein, 2003).

Criminal Justice and the Parent Role

In the criminal justice system, many interview situations are somewhat adversarial due to the obvious fact that so many offenders are held against their will. Most criminal justice positions dictate that the worker perform their duties in an authoritarian and supervisory fashion. In most cases, the worker is a legal extension of the court or state. Their position and duties have much in common with what has been identified as a parental role. Berne (1964), Harris (1969), and Perls (1971) have discussed this role and how it affects interpersonal relations. The parent role is characterized as being punitive, authoritarian, critical, judgmental, and moralistic. The parent role is also characterized as being condescending and rigid. Perls described this parent role with the term "top dog": "The top dog usually is righteous and authoritarian; he knows best. He is sometimes right, but always righteous. The top dog is a bully, and works with 'you should' and 'you should not.' The top dog manipulates with demands and threats of catastrophe, such as, 'if you don't, then'—you won't be loved, you won't get to heaven, you will die," and so on (p. 19).

The authority of the parent role is very seductive for many criminal justice workers and it dominates the interviews they conduct. In my personal experience, I have observed police and corrections management personnel conduct employment interviews in a very authoritarian and condescending manner. In these cases, the parent role was very inappropriate and ineffective, but the interviewers did not seem to be able to abandon the authoritarian role.

In addition, it is common for the interviewee in criminal justice to expect the interviewer to act in a parental role. Wicks and Josephs (1977) identify this as parataxic distortion: "Parataxic distortion comes to bear in an interview situation when the interviewee distorts his impressions of you by equating you with another police officer, correction officer or other individuals that he may have previously encountered" (p. 35). In counseling, similar phenomena are referred to as transference or unfinished business. If parataxic distortion does occur, it is likely to reinforce the parent role and make it difficult for the interviewer to change roles. "For many, police officers symbolize authority in general, and the notion that they are a kind of 'parent figure' should not be readily dismissed" (Parker, Meier, & Monahan, 1989, p. 79).

Authority is a legitimate and sometimes necessary part of criminal justice interviews. Authority provides security for the interviewer in situations where conformity to regulations is necessary, as in correctional institutions. When properly used as part of the parent role, authority can be effective. When authority and the parent role are misused, they can lead to *authoritarianism* in an interview where the interviewee is expected to act in a subordinate, patronizing, or condescending manner. The parent role can also lead to *paternalism* where inmates, parolees, or probationers are managed as if they were children.

What are the behavioral cues that signal the interviewer is operating from a parent role in an interview? In other words, what would the interviewer be doing or saying in the interview as a part of this role? The following provides a partial description.

Sample Words and Phrases

Should, don't, must, ought, never, if I were you, be good, try, come on now, you need to, would be best for you, from now on, one more time, you better be good.

Gestures and Postures

Pointing an accusing or threatening finger, pounding on the table or desk; rolling eyes upward in disgust, face tilted up, looking down nose, arms folded across chest with chin set, furrowed brow, raised eyebrow. (Jongeward & James, 1973)

Rather than issuing any "shoulds" or "oughts" about the parent role, the following observations are presented:

■ The parent role requires a lot of energy for maintenance and it will typically consume a lot of the interviewer's energy. With a heavy load of interviews, the criminal justice interviewer runs a risk of burnout (Edelwich & Brodsky, 1980; Whitehead, 1989).
■ Acceptance of human fallibility and the universality of crime will help interviewers maintain their sanity in a situation where there are demands for the parent role.
■ Even though probationers, parolees, or inmates have been convicted of a crime or many crimes, they are not children.
■ The adult interviewing role presented in this book provides a more viable option to criminal justice interviewers because it is based on reason, personal responsibility, data processing, rationality, and behavior.

If the criminal justice interviewer can interview in the role of a parent when the situation demands the role and at the same time maintain enough flexibility to be able to leave the role, the interviewer stands a very good chance of avoiding some of the emotional liabilities of the parent role. Ultimately, this flexibility will increase their effectiveness and enhance their mental health by keeping intense personal involvement at arm's length so that encounters with victims and offenders do not become emotionally draining.

Barriers to Communication

In order for an interviewer to be effective, the barriers to communication need to be avoided or removed. Gordon (1975) refers to these barriers as *inhibitors* to communication. In his *inhibitor-facilitator model* of communication, inhibitors are factors associated with the *unwillingness* of the interviewee to communicate relevant and valid information and the *ability* to do so.

Barone and Switzer (1995) provide a more detailed description of barriers to communication. They use the term "obstacles" and characterize various types to effective listening as environmental, psychological, and cultural. These obstacles are:

Environmental Obstacles

Obstacles or barriers exist in the setting where the interview is taking place. Environmental obstacles include such elements as poor lighting, uncomfortable seating, crowdedness, room temperature, street noises, telephones ringing, or other employees talking.

Psychological Obstacles

Additional obstacles exist within the mental awareness of the interview participants. Psychological obstacles include resistance, shyness, fear, anxiety, depression, and even a headache or stomachache can be a barrier to effective communication. Psychological obstacles include any mental condition that inhibits communication between the participants.

Cultural Obstacles

Finally, these are barriers to effective communication that exist because of cultural and ethnic differences between the interview participants. Cultural differences include language and meaning differences, verbal and nonverbal differences, and differences in values, expectations, and beliefs. Any one of these differences can hinder or detract from effective communication in an interview (Barone & Switzer, 1995). A further discussion of cultural aspects in interviewing will be presented in Chapter 3 in a discussion of multicultural interviewing.

Interview Biases

Many different types of interviews are conducted in criminal justice, but all interviews are subject to biases. These biases have been identified and studied as they relate, in a general sense, to interviews. Consequently, some interviews are more subject to biases than others. Craig (2003) has identified some of the more accepted biases in interviews that are worthy of note to beginning interviewers.

- **Positive halo.** This occurs when an interviewer's general impression of an interviewee leads to a positive impression of all traits or behaviors (Goffin, Jelly, & Wagner, 2003). The result of the positive halo is that interviewees are judged too positive, honest, sincere, truthful, and so on.
- **Negative halo (devil).** This occurs when an interviewer judges an interviewee too negative on the basis of some obvious negative trait. The result is that the interviewee is judged from an overall negative impression consistent with the negative general evaluation derived from the negative trait.
- **Reliance on first impressions.**
- **Interviewee attractiveness.**
- **Focusing on personal traits (personality) instead of the situation.**
- **Viewing behavior as fixed rather than changing.**

By preparing for the interview, establishing a structure for the interview, and determining a purpose, the influence of biases can be reduced. Reduced bias in an interview can lead to better decision making and prediction by the interviewer.

Optimum Environment for Communication

A key element in developing interviewing or interpersonal communication skills is the importance of establishing an optimum environment for communication (OEC) so that the interpersonal relationship will be productive. In the traditional interviewing literature, this has been referred to as establishing *rapport.* An optimum environment for communication is one that can be described as:

■ Friendly
■ Open
■ Warm
■ Accepting
■ Responsive
■ Supportive
■ Relaxed
■ Comfortable

These interview conditions or elements of rapport are necessary for an interviewer to establish in order to facilitate communication in an interview. Figure 1.6 presents a visual display of the continuum of OEC. Interviewers who establish rapport or an OEC are more likely to have productive interviews than interviewers who do not establish these conditions. Consequently, the task of an interviewer is to establish an OEC, which involves developing rapport or a facilitative interpersonal climate.

The importance of creating an optimum environment for communication (OEC) has not necessarily produced a corresponding level of research supporting the importance of OEC in producing positive interview results. Sharpley, Halat, Rabinowicz, Weiland, and Stafford (2001) found that *postural mirroring* increased perceived rapport in an interview. Postural mirroring means that the interviewer matched the posture of the interviewee. If the interviewee leans forward, the interviewer also leans forward. Interviewers can mirror the total posture, the hands and arms, the legs, or the torso of the interviewee. Butler and colleagues (2003) found that emotional suppression (i.e., keeping their emotions from showing) during an interview disrupted communication, increased blood pressure in the interviewee, and reduced rapport and relationship formation. Ap-

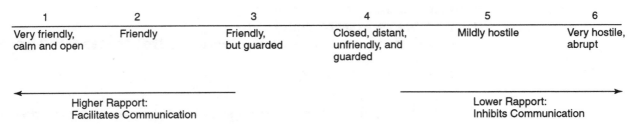

1	2	3	4	5	6
Very friendly, calm and open	Friendly	Friendly, but guarded	Closed, distant, unfriendly, and guarded	Mildly hostile	Very hostile, abrupt

Higher Rapport:
Facilitates Communication

Lower Rapport:
Inhibits Communication

Figure 1.6   Continuum of Conditions for an Optimum
Environment for Communication (OEC): Interviewer Attitude

parently, a lack of rapport cannot only disrupt communication, but can also increase stress in an interview. Consequently, interviewers should be emotionally expressive in an interview.

Finally, Collins, Lincoln, and Frank (2002) found that only five minutes of rapport-building in an interview had a very powerful positive effect on the accuracy of recall. As a result of their study, they strongly recommended that law enforcement administrators should consider including rapport as an aspect of interpersonal communication training for recruits in law enforcement.

Agency-Specific Interviews

The criminal justice system is composed of hundreds of agencies apprehending offenders, hiring employees, assisting victims, and releasing offenders in city, county, state, and federal agencies. In law enforcement and in the courts, corrections interviews are conducted on a daily basis across the country. An interview can, and does, take place on the street at the scene of a crime. Interviews take place in jails, homes, halfway houses, police stations, and squad cars—in many places other than in an office. Each criminal justice agency has specific interviews with predetermined guidelines for conducting an interview. Some are structured, while others are rather loosely structured and informal.

Structured Interviews

Many highly structured interviews are used in the criminal justice system to ensure uniformity and consistency when a variety of individuals are conducting the interviews. The structured interview is particularly useful for inexperienced or minimally trained individuals or employees who do not conduct interviews on a regular basis (Clear, Clear, & Burrell, 1989).

It would not only be impossible but quite cumbersome to present the design and purpose of all of these structured interviews. Nevertheless, it is important for beginning interviewers to gain an understanding of the primary forms of structured interviews used in the criminal justice system. These primary forms tend to be constructed for intake, survey, casework, and investigative purposes.

Intake Interviews

Intake interviews are a traditional part of the intake process for individuals entering correctional programs. Typically, these programs are treatment programs, halfway houses, and other community corrections programs. Excellent examples of intake interviews have been produced by the TCU Institute of Behavioral Research (TCU Institute of Behavioral Research, 2002). They produce the *TCU/Brief Intake Interview* and the *Comprehensive Intake* interview forms for use in treatment programs. The brief version covers the following items:

- Background information
- Psychosocial functioning in the past six months
- Drug use background
- Drug use problems in the past year

These items are investigated by an interviewer that asks 121 questions as a part of the intake process. In addition to a traditional "yes–no" answer form, the brief version uses a "never–sometimes–often" form to elicit answers from the respondent. For example, one of the typical questions asks for the respondent to indicate relationships with family members during the last six months. The individual being interviewed is asked to indicate on items, including whether the family enjoyed being together, got drunk together, had disagreements, and other family occurrences, on the scale of "never–sometimes–often" or "never–monthly–weekly–daily." The result of the brief intake form is a quantification of substance abuse and related problems.

The comprehensive version of the intake interview form covers:

- Sociodemographic background
- Family background
- Peer relations
- Criminal history
- Health and psychological status
- Drug history
- AIDS risk assessment
- Interviewer comments
- Client assessment profile

The comprehensive intake process is accomplished through the use of over 100 questions, many of which contain multiple parts. One of the unique features of the comprehensive intake form is the section devoted to the interviewer's response to the interviewee's participation in the interview. For example, using a "strongly disagree" to "strongly agree" answer form, the interviewer is asked to rate the interviewee on a variety of items, including cooperation, motivation, attention, interest, distraction, memory, and assertion. As in the case of the brief version, this intake version is designed to quantify some very difficult and subjective issues of substance abuse by using an extensive list of structured interview questions.

Investigative Interviews

One of the primary tasks of law enforcement officers is to conduct investigative interviews with victims, witnesses, and suspects. The preferable sequence to follow in an investigation is to interview victims first, then witnesses, and then suspects. The victim should be interviewed first, because he/she will often be the complaining party with firsthand information about the crime. The victim may lead the interviewer to other individuals who have additional information to support or refute the original claims of a criminal offense or information indicating a different offense. After the information from victims and witnesses is obtained, the suspect should be interviewed (Reese, 2003).

There seems to be little disagreement as to the importance of these interviews, but some disagreement about how the interviews should be structured. Regardless of structure, investigative interviews have several goals:

- Obtaining the maximum amount of information that has the highest quality.
- Obtaining information that is not contaminated in a way that affects the witness's memory.
- Following the rules and guidelines of the organization that is conducting the interview.
- Obtaining information in a manner that minimizes personal harm to the witness (Yuille, Marysen, & Cooper, 1999).

Fortunately, several structured investigative interview designs have been used in law enforcement. Three are presented here.

First, the U.S. Department of Justice, Office of Justice Programs (TWGEYEE, 2003) has suggested a sequence for interviewing witnesses in order to obtain the maximum amount of information. The sequence that is recommended in the training of police officers to interview eyewitnesses is:

- Attempt to minimize the witnesses' anxiety.
- Establish and maintain rapport.
- Encourage the witness to take an active role in the interview.
- Request a "free narrative" description of the incident.
- Ask the witness to mentally recreate the circumstances of the incident.
- Ask follow-up questions to elicit additional information related to the witnesses' narration.
- Review your notes and other materials.
- Ask the witness, "Is there anything else I should have asked you?"
- Close the interview.

An earlier report (TWGEYEE, 1999) was more specific in suggesting several different procedures for structuring investigative interviews that are worth noting at this point. They are:

- Ask open-ended questions.
- Caution the witness not to guess.
- Encourage nonverbal communication.
- Avoid leading questions.

Second, Dowling (1979) developed an investigative interview format using six parts described by the acronym "IRONIC," which stands for Identity, Rapport, Opening statement, Narration, Inquiry, and Conclusion.

- **Identity.** Prior to commencing an interview, the investigator should identify himself/herself to the witness by name, rank, and agency. The investigator's official authority to make the inquiry is thereby established as witness cooperation is probably increased—since most persons respond positively to figures of authority. The witness also obtains the name of a person to contact in the future, if necessary.

  - **Exceptions.** This step may be omitted if there is no need for the person to know the officer's identity, or when a pretext encounter is staged to obtain a closer view of the party.

    Example
    An officer need not identify himself/herself in asking a gas station attendant for the location of a particular address.

- **Rapport.** Upon making contact with the witness, the investigator must seek to establish rapport with him/her—since a good interpersonal relationship maximizes the ability to extract information. This affinity may be established by presenting a good appearance, by a cordial and understanding attitude, and by otherwise allaying the witness's fears. In some cases, "small talk" may be necessary in order to calm the witness.

  - A good rapport is especially important when dealing with persons who are contacted on a regular basis—such as license clerks, court personnel, telephone company employees, or law enforcement personnel.
  - The salesmanship of the investigator (referred to previously) is crucial to a good witness–investigator relationship. Reluctance and even hostility can be overcome if the officer establishes a good relationship with the witness.

- **Opening Statement.** At some point in the interview, the investigator will need to indicate why the witness is being contacted. (In some situations, the reason for inquiry will be obvious, such as when the victim teller in a bank robbery is interviewed.)

  - However, the witness should usually be told no more about the reason for contact than fairness requires.

    Example
    Where the former employer of a fugitive is asked for information about the employee's whereabouts, he normally needs to be told only that the police are seeking to locate the employee. Whether the employer is told the nature of the alleged crime charged and the employee's fugitive status is a discretionary decision based on all of the circumstances.

    Example
    On the other hand, the neighbor of a burglary victim will need to be told that a burglary occurred and the approximate time of day it took place. Otherwise, the interviewee cannot meaningfully respond to questions.

- **Narration.** As a rule, the investigator should allow the witness to present whatever information he or she possesses as a narrative in his/her own words. The officer should refrain from injecting questions or comments until the witness has finished his/her story. Interruptions should be made only to keep the witness on track and eliminate nonpertinent information.

Example

The questioning of a homicide complainant might begin, "Tell me the circumstances surrounding your discovery of the deceased's body."

Interviewing officers should also structure their follow-up questions so as to produce this narrative type of response (i.e., the investigator should guide the witness, but not lead him/her).

- **Inquiry.** Once the witness has told his initial story, the investigator may *then* ask specific questions to fill in omitted facts, clarify ambiguous statements, verify names, dates, and other details, and insure that all pertinent information has been extracted.

  - Just as entries in a notepad should contain the who, what, when, where, why, and how of various topics, the interviewing officer should be sure that the same "5 W's and H" are covered with respect to the information that the witness may have seen.
  - In accomplishing this task, the investigative officer should avoid leading or suggestive questions. Specific inquiries generally should require elaboration on a point rather than a mere "yes" or "no" response.

- **Conclusions.** The interview should be concluded when it becomes apparent that the witness has nothing pertinent left to offer. At that time, the officer should orally summarize the witness's statement. This gives the witness an opportunity to correct erroneous information and add additional facts that he/she then recalls. At this stage, the investigator should also insure that he has the witness's correct name and address in the event that further contact is needed. Finally, the witness should be thanked for his/her aid.

Finally, Cherryman and Bull (2001) report a model of investigative interviewing developed in England. This model uses the acronym "PEACE" to identify the component parts of the interview model:

- Preparation and Planning
- Engage and Explain
- The main Account
- Closure
- Evaluation

It is worth noting that the second, third, and fourth items compose the actual investigative interview in the "PEACE" model.

Casework Interviews

Many structured interviews are used in correctional casework with offenders. Some of these structured interviews are developed by a specific agency and some are proprietary interviews that have been adopted and purchased by the correctional agency. Most of these casework interviews include an assessment of the risk and needs levels of the offenders. They also tend to be combinations of face-to-face interview information and information that is part of an offender's permanent record.

One of the widely adopted structured casework interviews is the *Client Management Classification* (CMC) system developed for probation and parole agencies (Lerner, Arling, & Baird, 1986). The CMC is also known as the *Strategies for Case Supervision* (SCS) in some states (CJAD, 1991).

The CMC system uses a structured offender interview and scoring guide to classify offenders according to four groups: selective interventions, environmental structure, casework control, and limit setting. The Client Risk and Need Assessment Survey is part of the Client Management Classification System, and is designed to be used with the interview schedule. The system is designed to assist probation or parole officers in assigning offenders to minimum, medium, or maximum supervision (Walsh, 1997).

Before offenders are released on parole into the community, they are usually interviewed in the institution as a part of their parole petition. The *Institutional Parole Case Summary* is an example of a structured interview (Texas Department of Criminal Justice, 1999). This case summary also combines a face-to-face interview with information from the offender's official records. This interview consists of a risk assessment and information including a victim impact statement, letters protesting the parole, victim restitution summaries, adult probation record, criminal history, and substance abuse history.

One of the most widely recognized and adopted proprietary casework interview systems is the *Level of Service Inventory—Revised* (LSI-R; Andrews & Bonta, 1995). The LSI-R uses information from an offender's file and a semistructured interview to assess a range of criminogenic factors, such as offense record, alcohol and drug use, and personal relationships. The LSI-R provides information relevant to treatment planning and supervision levels. The LSI-R has been found to be effective in screening violent offenders for both need and level of risk of recidivism (Hollin & Palmer, 2003).

Survey Interviews

Many structured surveys are conducted within and between agencies in the criminal justice system. Most of these surveys are conducted for either research, planning, or funding purposes. Whatever the case, most of them are conducted through internal mail systems, traditional mail, or electronic mail. Few are conducted in face-to-face interviews because of the time, cost, and training involved to conduct structured survey interviews. On the other hand, one of the most comprehensive and extensive structured survey programs in the United States uses face-to-face interviews. The *Arrestee Drug Abuse Monitoring Program* (ADAM) surveys adults and juveniles concerning their drug use and abuse. These interviews take place four times a year in a number of cities. The information gathered provides valuable insights into arrestees' attitudes about and reported use of such things as firearms, methamphetamine use patterns and markets, gang-related activities, HIV-related behavior, and domestic violence. At each ADAM site, trained interviewers conduct voluntary and anonymous interviews and collect urine specimens from adult male, adult female, juvenile male, and juvenile female arrestees.

The ADAM structured interview contains a variety of questions about substance use and abuse, but one of the unique features of the ADAM interview is the use of a twelve-month calendar where the respondent is requested to record a variety of events that occurred over the last twelve months. The interviewer is asked to note on the calendar:

- Inpatient stay
- Outpatient stay
- Mental health treatment
- Arrests
- Jail/prison time
- Alcohol use
- Marijuana use
- Crack or crack cocaine use
- Powder cocaine use
- Heroin use
- Methamphetamine use
- Other drug use

The results of the ADAM interviews can assist in national, state, and local policy development on drug-related issues.

Employees usually learn how to conduct interviews in their agency in pre-service or in-service training programs. In some agencies, they learn to conduct interviews through on-the-job training. Consequently, it would be virtually impossible to learn all of these agency-specific interviews and, in many cases, wasteful because in many agencies the procedures change quite often.

On the other hand, several excellent materials have been produced in recent years that focus on specific areas in the criminal justice system (see, e.g., Clear et al., 1989; Gluckstern, Packard, & Wenver, 1989; MacHovec, 1989; Memon, Vrij, & Bull, 2003; Neil, 1980; Parker et al., 1989).

Direction of Training

The interviewing training presented in this book begins with a discussion of preliminary interviewing considerations and then moves to the interviewing model that serves as the foundation for training. Next, a series of interviewing skills are addressed. Finally, in the last chapter, these skills are integrated into a coordinated and smooth interviewing style.

Throughout the book, illustrations, examples, and exercises are provided for the student or trainee to help master the material covered. A key to these exercises is provided in the instructor's manual.

With this in mind, the approach of this interviewing text is to provide basic interviewing principles, techniques, and skills that are applicable to a wide variety of agency demands. These principles, techniques, and skills are directed toward the trainee's main need to communicate effectively with the public and understand basic human relations.

This text is not designed to provide advanced or specialized interviewing skills. Second, it is not designed for preparing individuals to interview people with serious emotional or psychological problems, families in a group, or individuals with serious intellectual handicaps. Also, it is not applicable to hypnotic interviewing, crisis hotline interviewing, child abuse investigations, or employment interviewing. It is applicable to face-to-face interviews with individuals who are functioning in a broadly defined range of acceptable levels of adjustment and may serve as a foundation for many of the special interviews just mentioned.

Finally, the model of training used in this text consists of a seven-phase process (Shearer, 1989). This seven-phase process is similar to multiple stages of training developed by Kohnken (1998) and Chang and Scott (1999), and some of the stages are quite similar. Both models rely on videotape role plays, but the seven-phase model starts with skill acquisition instead of an overview of interviewing. Introduction and overview sections are treated as assigned readings so that there is optimum time in training for skill acquisition. The seven-phase process model is as follows:

Phase 1. Read about the skill.
Phase 2. Discuss the skill with the instructor.
Phase 3. The skill is modeled by the instructor in a role play or a videotape.
Phase 4. Trainees prepare role plays with the instructor coaching role-play construction.
Phase 5. Train on a specific skill or group of skills.
Phase 6. Evaluate skill acquisition in trainees.
Phase 7. Simultaneously provide focused video feedback on skill proficiency.

As the training progresses, skill acquisition can be enhanced by written exercises, interview challenges, and self-evaluations, which are included with each chapter in the text.

Finally, the direction of training in this text follows a microskills training model. The skills are divided into smaller units so that the trainees learn, step by step, how to become competent with the skill. The trainee builds on skill acquisition toward a repertoire of skills. More difficult and complicated skills are designed to be built on basic skills so that the result will be skill competency across all of the skills. There is more empirical research data supporting the effectiveness of the microskills approach than any other skill-building method (Pederson, 2000).

Summary

Interviews play an important role in all phases of the criminal justice system. Training in interviewing skills is needed. Interviews have specific purposes, and they are different than counseling and interrogation. As an assessment tool, interviews can be biased and contaminated. There are optimum conditions for conducting interviews. Many interviews in the field are highly structured. The interviewing training in this text follows a well-accepted model of training.

Now that you have completed Chapter 1, you may want to look forward to the activities at the end of this chapter. Exercises 1.1, 1.2, and 1.3 and an Interview Challenge are provided for an additional and alternative method for looking at some of the ideas and concepts presented in the chapter.

Study Questions

1. What have been some of the problems with police interview techniques?
2. What is the primary distinction between interviewing and counseling?
3. Why is the importance of instantaneous response so great in some criminal justice interviews?
4. How do interviewers influence the interviewing process?
5. Explain the difference between interview reliability and validity.
6. What are the differences between interviewing and interrogation? Similarities?
7. What is the "folklore" of criminal justice?
8. What is the actual meaning of interrogation in some countries?
9. What is parataxic distortion?
10. What are the liabilities of the "parent role" in criminal justice interviews?
11. What are the assets and liabilities of anecdotal evidence?
12. What are the principle types of structured interviews?
13. Explain IRONIC and PEACE.
14. What is ADAM?

Exercise 1.1

Reliability/Validity

Directions: *Assume you are a pro-scout for a baseball team. You are evaluating the potential of a prospective pitcher. In the left column are the pitches and results you observed in a practice session. Indicate the pitcher's effectiveness in the right columns by placing a check under the appropriate headings concerning reliability and validity, keeping in mind the pitcher's goal of preventing the ball from being put in play or a player from reaching a base.*

Reliability

The pitcher is consistently able to throw a certain pitch, particularly the one he wants to throw.

Validity

The pitcher throws the ball over the plate in the strike zone.

Pitch/Result	Reliability		Validity	
	High	Low	High	Low
Three strikes over the plate				
Three balls, high and out of the strike zone				
A wild pitch				
A strike, low and out of the strike zone				
A walk, unintentional				
Three curve balls over the plate for strikes				
First pitch over the plate hit for a home run				
A hit batter				
A change-up over the plate for a strike				
A strike, inside and out of the strike zone				
A change-up out of the strike zone for a strike				
A fast-ball over the plate for a strike				
A foul ball on a low pitch				
A foul ball on a pitch over the plate				
Walk, intentional				

Exercise 1.2

Targets

Directions: *Below appears a series of targets that were retrieved from the police pistol range. Assuming minimal officer error (such as unsteadiness), indicate with a check which weapons were reliable, valid, reliable and valid, or neither reliable nor valid based on target results.*

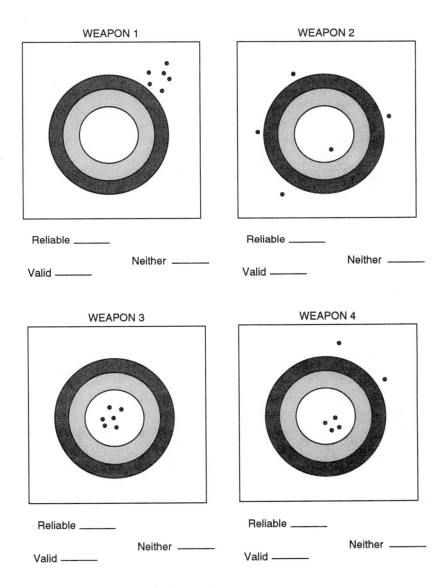

WEAPON 1

Reliable _____

Valid _____   Neither _____

WEAPON 2

Reliable _____

Valid _____   Neither _____

WEAPON 3

Reliable _____

Valid _____   Neither _____

WEAPON 4

Reliable _____

Valid _____   Neither _____

Adapted from Brown, Amos, & Mink, 1975.

Exercise 1.3

Skeptical–Suggestible Profile (SSP)

Directions: *For each of the numbered scales that follow, read the descriptions at the ends of the scales, and the circle the number or the scale that is the closest to how you would describe yourself.*

I tend to believe what people in authority tell me				I tend to doubt what people in authority tell me
5	4	3	2	1
I tend to agree with what important people want me to do				I tend to question what important people want me to do
5	4	3	2	1
I prefer to be agreeable				I don't mind being disagreeable
5	4	3	2	1
With a little persuasion, people can win me over to their viewpoint				I am not easily persuaded
5	4	3	2	1

I prefer to keep quiet when people are voicing opinions I do not agree with				I prefer to speak out if I do not agree with people
5	4	3	2	1

My first inclination is to believe what people say is the truth				My first inclination is to question what people say is the truth
5	4	3	2	1

After you have completed the exercise, connect the numbers to produce a visual profile of your characteristics. Then, average your scores on the six scales. The higher the score, the more suggestible you have indicated you are. The lower the score, the more skeptical you have indicated you are. Above "3" indicates a high score or suggestible and below "3" indicates a low score or skeptical.

Interview Challenge

How would you complete the following encounter? Keep in mind the concerns raised by the questions following the preliminary interview narrative.

You have been assigned to conduct an internal affairs investigation of another officer who is suspected of being involved with a group of officers who are responsible for disappearances of money and drugs in the departmental property room. This is your first interview with one of the officers with whom you have not had a close relationship in the past. The officer begins the interview with the remark, "I sure would like to know how they come up with you people to do these investigations."

1. What skills will you need to get the interview started?

     _____

     _____

     _____

2. What will you want to ideally get accomplished in the interview?

     _____

     _____

     _____

3. How will you divide your interview time between official objectives and personal concerns in the interview (i.e., how closely will you stay with required questions)?

     _____

     _____

     _____

4. What do you anticipate the major segments of the interview to be?

     _____

     _____

     _____

5. What would be the most appropriate interview style to use in this situation?

_____

_____

_____

6. What will be some of the barriers to communication in this interview?

_____

_____

_____

7. What would you need to minimally accomplish in this interview for you to consider the interview successful?

_____

_____

_____

8. How much of this interview will focus on facts? Feelings? Values? Opinions?

_____

_____

_____

2

Preliminary Interviewing Considerations

Learning Objectives

Subject: Preliminary Interviewing Considerations

Objections: After a period of instruction, the student (trainee) will:

1. Understand how to be professionally prepared to conduct interviews.
2. Understand the research on interviewing and interrogation.
3. Understand the cautions, terms, difficulties, and techniques of detecting deception in an interview.
4. Understand the diversions that can occur in an interview.

Learning domain—cognitive

> Years ago a cop probably could have beat the bejesus out of them until he got a confession. You can't anymore.
>
> Mark Baker
> *Cops* (1985)

Before getting started conducting interviews in criminal justice, several preliminary considerations need to be discussed in the areas of professional development, interviewing diversions, and deceptive interviewees. Getting started is considerably easier if the interviewer has a map of the territory that will anticipate some of the features that lay ahead. In addition, interviewers can incorporate some specific procedures into their own professional development.

Professional Development

The first thing you can do is take specific steps in professional development. Professional development involves: (1) preparing for interviews, (2) note taking, (3) electronic documentation, (4) role playing, (5) video and audio feedback, (6) unfreezing and refreezing,

43

(7) legal and ethical standards, (8) research in dyadic communication, and (9) interviewing with time constraints.

Preparing for Interviews

Most interviews in criminal justice are initiated by the interviewer, which gives the interviewer an opportunity to prepare for the interview. This preparation depends on whether the interview is going to be unstructured or highly structured. The unstructured interview usually consists of a list of topics to be covered. Highly structured interviews are thoroughly planned with all questions and answer options predetermined. The questions and answer options do not vary from one interviewee to the other. Presentence investigation forms are an example of a highly structured probation interview.

Finally, criminal justice workers sometimes encounter spontaneous, interviewee-initiated interviews. This type of interview can occur almost anytime and anywhere. An example of this is an inmate who stops you in the hallway to consult you about a letter he received from his wife. You weren't expecting the interview and you don't have time to prepare your responses but you have to conduct the interview anyway. The most extreme form of this impromptu interview is in crises resolution. This is one of the most difficult interviews to conduct and the interviewer needs to be skilled and competent. The skills covered in the following chapters will provide a basis for this type of interview.

In general, the following guidelines will assist in preparing for interviews:

- Anticipate the interviewee's emotional state. Is the interviewee likely to be angry, despondent, or confused?
- Formulate questions you wish to ask. How these questions are to be asked will be covered in a later chapter.
- Anticipate areas to be emphasized. Which one of the probationer's rules will you need to spend a lot of time on to emphasize its importance?
- Consider how much of the interview is going to have to be recorded in a report after the interview has ended. Are you going to make a detailed report or a brief synopsis?

"Careful planning sets the interviewer on a definite course and makes her or him more aware of options. The interviewer then becomes a better master of the situation" (Downs et al., 1980, p. 39).

Note Taking

In criminal justice agencies, as much as in any place, documentation of the interview or conversation is the rule more than the exception. How can this documentation or written report be accomplished without disrupting the interview? How can the interviewer take notes that may be requested by the court and still concentrate on the interviewee? There aren't any specific rules about note taking in an interview that can answer these questions. Schubert (1971) presents a general guideline: "Follow a procedure that does the least to interfere with your attention to what the client is saying and to the feeling he is expressing about the events he is recounting; further follow a procedure that gives the client some confidence that you are making a serious attempt to understand accurately what he is trying to tell you" (p. 29).

If you take notes during an interview, guidelines suggested by Stewart and Cash (1985) may help you to take notes effectively:

- To avoid interfering with the communication climate of the interview, maintain eye contact while taking notes, be as inconspicuous as possible, and use abbreviations or shorthand to speed note taking; to avoid gaps in the interview while writing, learn to remember materials so all information will not have to be written down.

- To avoid communicating to the respondent what we think is important, do not begin to take notes frantically during or immediately after an answer, take notes throughout the interview (even if we must pretend to do so at times), or delay note taking on an answer until the respondent is answering another question.

- To avoid excessive respondent curiosity or concern about what we are writing, ask permission before taking notes, explain why note taking is necessary, show notes occasionally, or ask interviewees to check our notes for accuracy.

- To avoid respondent concern about how we will use the information, agree to follow ground rules for the interview, explain how and when we will use the material, or agree to let the respondent see the results of the study, report, or article before it is made public.

- To ensure accurate reporting from notes, review notes as soon after the interview as possible.

If you don't take notes in an interview, it is advisable to write a detailed summary immediately after the interview is finished. Most interviewers who have put off the summary until later have found it very difficult to remember the interview with any accuracy.

In conclusion, note taking in interviews follows a hierarchy of preferences from most desirable to least desirable:

Most desirable.   Focusing your undivided attention on the interviewee without taking notes; maximum eye contact.

Desirable.   Focusing most of your attention on the interviewee with occasional breaks for note taking that the interviewee can observe.

Undesirable.   Focusing occasional attention on the interviewee with extensive note taking that the interviewee cannot observe.

Least desirable.   Extensive note taking during the interview that cannot be observed by the interviewee with very little focus on the interviewee; minimum eye contact.

Interviews in some agencies are highly structured and fit the least desirable category. This is understood as being the way the job is done. The challenge for a professional interviewer is to combine the most desirable note-taking arrangement with the agency's specific situational demands.

Electronic Documentation

The use of video technology is well known and widely used to document interrogations and confessions. Agencies that videotape suspects' statements do so for the following reasons:

- To avoid defense attorneys' challenges of the accuracy of audiotapes and the completeness of written confessions
- To help reduce doubts about the voluntary nature of confessions
- To jog detectives' memories when testifying
- To counter defense criticism of "nice" or "softening up" techniques for interrogating suspects.

Videotaping appears to be a distinctly useful tool and most police agencies use video technology in some way. Police agencies who do not use videotape cite financial concerns as the main reason they don't use the technology. Financial concerns include the cost of the equipment, remodeling interview rooms, storing tapes, and maintaining the equipment.

Three issues concerning videotaping interviews have emerged and some police departments are sharply divided on these issues.

Issue 1: Selective versus nonselective taping.   Should a police department tape some suspects' statements in serious felony cases or should the department videotape all confessions? Evidence exists both for and against the prediction that a police department that tapes *any* serious felony will have to tape *most* or *all* interrogations or confessions.

Issue 2: Overt versus covert taping.   Nearly all police agencies videotape openly, either telling suspects they are being taped or leaving the camera or microphone visible during the session. On the other hand, agencies that tape covertly are strongly in favor of the procedure. Covert taping is done to portray a suspect talking willingly, who might, if aware of it, object to a video record being made.

Issue 3: Full interrogations versus recaps.   Police departments are sharply divided between taping an entire confession or interrogation or just highlights of the interview. A recap could include both incriminating statements and the actual confession. As a rule, defense attorneys strongly prefer entire interviews to "sound bites." Departments that tape entire interviews feel that recaps lose potentially useful information. On the other hand, departments who use recaps cannot understand how departments who use the entire interview can obtain any useful information from suspects amidst discussions full of "tangents and exculpatory claims" (Geller, 1993). They also can't understand how agencies can afford the time and cost of video-taping interviews that last an average of two to four hours.

Overall, videotaping has led to better preparation for interviews since the interviewers' techniques and performance may be viewed by the public and supervisors. There are still some critical issues to be resolved in electronic documentation of interviews, but practitioners with firsthand knowledge of videotaping clearly favor videotaping for certain felonies (Geller, 1993).

It is important to point out, however, that videotaped interviews are not foolproof. Research by Handby, Weiland, and Munhall (2002) underscores this caution. They determined that a simple change in camera perspective can alter a verdict in a simulated trial. They also indicated that the best camera perspective to use is one that focuses on the interrogator because this could help detect coercive influences, which in turn could improve assessments of the reliability of a particular videotaped confession.

Role Playing

Role playing is the primary training technique presented in ensuing chapters to learn interviewing. Role playing involves a fellow trainee assuming a hypothetical and realistic character in an imaginary criminal justice encounter. "Role-playing is reality practice and action learning; it involves realistic behavior under unrealistic conditions" (Shaw et al., 1980, p. 7). The trainee is asked to "be" the other person and communicate their thoughts, feelings, and concerns. They are asked to express not only the character's thoughts but the full range of emotions this person might be experiencing. "One important aspect of role-playing is that it *provides a simulated reality experience in which one can practice complex skills without hurting oneself or anyone else through failure*" (Shaw et al., 1980, p. 2). Through role playing, criminal justice interviews can be practiced on a trial-and-error basis in a safe learning environment.

Parker and colleagues (1989) have presented a comprehensive study of role playing in criminal justice. They concluded that role playing "is particularly appropriate as an interpersonal learning tool with police and corrections personnel" (p. 74). The authors' experience of teaching interviewing using role playing for three decades supports their conclusions. Role playing provides an effective training device by simulating face-to-face encounters in criminal justice.

The major concerns that students frequently have in anticipation of role playing in interviewing are realism, transfer of learning, and heightened emotionality.

Realism. The challenge of role playing criminal justice encounters is to make them realistic enough so that they simulate actual situations in the field. Justifiably, students are frequently concerned about realism in training because they realize they have had very little contact with agency situations. In addition, role playing calm, businesslike, middle-class situations misses the mark in criminal justice and doesn't provide readiness for the student. This dilemma can be resolved by instructor coaching and a little research by the students. This can also be accomplished by completing an assignment of researching three roles in-depth, such as a victim, a prostitute, a drug addict, and so on.

Transfer of Learning. We haven't begun training very long before students inevitably make the statement, "I'm not sure I can do this in class but I know I can when the real thing comes along" or ask the question, "Will this help me in the real world [of criminal justice]?" These are legitimate concerns and involve the issue of whether what is learned in training will transfer to actual employment situations. Despite the extensive use of role playing, there seem to be few studies that have tested its success rate. What can be said is that the method has been employed extensively and it appears to be more successful than listening to a lecture or viewing a demonstration, due to its similarity to actual interviewing situations.

In further support of the use of role playing, it has been found in training that probation officers and students usually cannot distinguish one from the other when they view videotapes of an interviewer and an unseen role player. Criminal justice students thought the probation role players were real. Probation officers thought the student interviews were real. Third-party, uninvolved observers thought both were real. Obviously, the quality of the role playing enhances realism and transfer of learning.

Heightened Emotionality. Another challenge in conducting role playing is avoidance of or running from emotional issues. Banaka (1971) indicates the interviewer "tends to change the topic or shift the logical level from personal exposure to more impersonal, factual questions. The effect is to get away from embarrassment, and the potential involvement in EE's (interviewee's) affective state" (p. 41). This avoidance of heightened emotionality can be changed by:

- The instructor setting the tone by "pushing" trainees' role plays into emotional concerns.
- The instructor modeling role playing with heightened emotionality.
- Starting the interview training in affective areas and excluding cognitive areas at the beginning of the training.

Beginning criminal justice students in interviewing training who have limited or no experience in the field usually find it difficult to role play criminal justice situations. With this in mind, the following stimulus situations are presented:

Law Enforcement

- A rookie female police officer explaining to her supervisor, male or female, her reactions to intense sexual harassment by male officers.

- A rookie police officer approaching her superior officer with concern about major undocumented disappearances of items in the police property room.
- A police officer revealing to his partner a serious fight with his spouse the evening before.
- A police officer explaining to a personnel officer his recent symptoms of posttraumatic stress reaction following a violent shooting.
- A police officer complaining to his superior about being passed over for promotion.
- A police officer indicating he is "burned out" on police work.
- A minority police officer indicating racism in the department.
- A police officer indicating a conflict about whether to leave policing for a higher-paying job.
- A police officer whose spouse has been arrested for shoplifting.
- A police officer whose teenage son or daughter has been picked up for stealing a car.

Parole

- A parolee who can't find a job in order to stay on parole.
- A parolee who wants out of a halfway house because of a weak program at the house.
- A parolee who is angry and embarrassed because his parole officer visited his place of employment.
- A parolee who, after being told she was hired for a job, was fired when it was found she had been in prison.
- A parolee who can't decide whether to reveal being an ex-convict to prospective employers.

Institutional Corrections

- An inmate who has just received a letter indicating her ex-husband has filed in court for her to lose parental rights to her children.
- An inmate who has been approached by a gang member to join the gang but who is reluctant to get involved.
- An inmate who is very despondent and depressed because she was denied parole for the third time.
- An inmate whose wife appeared at yesterday's visitation with a boyfriend.
- An inmate who has been writing to a lady in a foreign country (not revealing he was an inmate) has just received a letter she is on her way to the U.S. to see him.
- A correctional officer who has been absent from work lately because of an impending divorce.
- A correctional officer whose wife and child fled to a shelter for abused women.

Probation

- A probationer whose urine analysis was dirty because someone slipped something into his drink at a party.
- A probationer who wants to leave the state for a family reunion.

- A probationer who wants out of their required attendance at AA meetings.
- A probationer wants to go into the car wash business with his brother who is a convicted felon.
- A probationer who needs occupational skills training.

Victims

- A victim of rape or sexual assault.
- A man or woman whose ex-spouse has kidnapped their only child.
- An elderly grandmother whose grandson physically beat her and took her social security check.

Regardless of the situation used in a role play, two guidelines may be helpful in constructing role-play situations. First, the emotional intensity in a role-play situation is likely to decline quickly unless the role player is trained in acting. In a later chapter, we will see that the emotional intensity may escalate rapidly in many real-life situations. A rapid decline will make it increasingly more difficult for the trainee to have emotionally relevant statements to respond to. Second, role-playing situations with a person suspected of a crime who chooses to remain silent or uncooperative does not work well in a training situation, because, again, few emotional or cognitive statements will be presented for the trainee to demonstrate proficiency. Consequently, lively role-play exchanges, punctuated with periods of silence, tend to provide trainees with the best opportunity to demonstrate skill proficiency.

Unfreezing and Refreezing

Shaw and colleagues (1980) have presented a model that serves as the goal of role playing. We have looked at the technique of role playing and now we need to focus on what the technique is designed to accomplish. The goal is divided into three parts: (1) unfreezing current behavior, beliefs, and stereotypes about criminal justice interviews; (2) changing to new interviewing behaviors; and (3) refreezing the new interviewing behaviors into place.

The first part involves unfreezing the behaviors, beliefs, and preconceived notions that the trainee brings to training. Students tend to have certain automatic assumptions about interviewing or they may have a routine way of doing something. For example, they assume interviews are conducted like they are on television "cop" shows. They also tend to bring to training a "quick-fix" attitude to interpersonal relations. These preconceived notions can be unfrozen through role playing. Students, for example, become self-consciously aware of their authoritarianism in the interview. "The period of unfreezing is not comfortable. Anxiety is generated when old styles of behavior are labeled unsatisfactory. The reasons for such tensions are clear, for this represents a period of 'unlearning' what is already known but no longer is appropriate" (Shaw et al., 1980, p. 25).

The second part involves experimenting with new interviewing behaviors. The sequence of skills presented later in this text can be tried and tested to see how other individuals react to new behaviors.

> Role-playing also gives people the opportunity to try out new behaviors in a "safe" setting. One can discover—surprisingly well—how comfortable new behaviors are and which of several alternative actions "fits" best. One can practice, trying out minor variations repeatedly. Thus weeks, months, and even years of real-life experience can be simulated in a few role-play sessions. Although the learning may not be quite as powerful as in a real setting, this lack is more than compensated for the ease, safety, and creative learning potential of the role-play situation. (Shaw et al., 1980, p. 25).

The third part of the goal is refreezing new behaviors into firmly established patterns of interviewing behavior. This refreezing typically occurs in actual on-the-job interviews. Role playing does not apply to any great extent in this part. What is critical at this point is that the new behaviors are socially supported in actual interview situations. "This kind of social support is crucial for re-freezing new patterns of behavior and making the new patterns last" (Shaw et al., 1980, p. 25).

This third goal of role playing underscores the need for communication and coordination between criminal justice education—specifically interviewing—and criminal justice agency practices. It is important that interviewing training reflects the needs of criminal justice agencies and that acquired skills are supported in agencies.

Focused Audio or Video Feedback

The use of audio and videotapes in interviewing training has been invaluable to the interviewing student and instructor. Videotape can be an invaluable tool in learning to interview and it is preferable to audiotape because it adds sight to sound. Focused feedback refers to stopping or replaying a tape in order to concentrate on or review a particular aspect of an interviewer's behavior.

For the student, videotape provides the following advantages:

- Nonverbal as well as verbal behavior can be studied.
- Students can see how others see them.
- Verification can be made by seeing behavior over and over.
- Other trainees can note behaviors they wish to avoid, initiate, or reinforce.

For the instructor, videotape provides the following advantages:

- The instructor can model interviewing skills that can be replayed in order to focus on specific behaviors.
- In critiquing interviews, the videotape eliminates some of the threat of personal criticism since the critique is of the tape and not the student directly.

■ The videotape gives the instructor more objectivity in evaluating a student's skill level because of the advantage of replay. This is particularly advantageous where multiple or simultaneous skills are involved.

Now that videotaping is accessible to almost any training program, it is an indispensable method for learning how to interview. Without it, a trainee is missing the learning that takes place through observation and feedback.

Legal and Ethical Standards

The general practice of interviewing is not supported by specific legal guidelines or ethical standards. Furthermore, the diversity of the criminal justice system makes it unlikely that a specific set of guidelines could apply to all situations in law enforcement, the courts, or corrections.

Legal Considerations.   Most criminal justice professionals perform their day-to-day job tasks, including interviews, within the boundaries of legal rights, responsibilities, and liabilities. In today's legally charged atmosphere, police, probation, parole, and correctional officers are being sued for a variety of wrongs, real and imagined. In order for officers to reduce the risk of liability incurred through interviews, they need to pay particular attention to legal rules and regulations.

Fortunately, in recent years, some very good materials have been prepared for criminal justice professionals on legal concerns, so that they no longer have to work in a legal vacuum. Specifically, the works of del Carmen (2001); Gilbert (2004); Silver (1986); and Wolf, Mesloh, and Cherry (2002) are recommended.

The interviewing model presented in subsequent chapters supports most requirements for legal considerations in conducting interviews. Specifically, it provides the following advantages:

■ It follows a specific verifiable process that is supported by empirical research.
■ It facilitates record keeping and documentation of information obtained in interviews.
■ It focuses more on behavior and less on complex interpretations of motives, attitudes, or values.

Ethical Standards.   Ethical standards in criminal justice interviewing are likely to be covered by the published statements of one of the following organizations:

■ National Association of Social Workers—*Code of Ethics*
■ American Psychological Association—*Ethical Principles of Psychologists*
■ American Association for Counseling and Development—*Ethical Standards*

- American Correctional Association—*Code of Ethics*
- International Association of Chiefs of Police—*Law Enforcement Code of Ethics*

Each of these professional organizations function with detailed ethical standards that vary on certain specific items. Even with this variation, four common principles seem to stand out as being relevant to interviewing in general. These four are:

- The interviewer proceeds from a philosophical assumption of the worth and dignity of the individual.
- The interviewer strives to use those methods and techniques that have the greatest evidence of scientific reliability and validity.
- The interviewer strives to maintain a high level of honesty and openness consistent with general guidelines concerning assessment of human subjects.
- The interviewer recognizes the need for continuous professional renewal and upgrading of interviewing skills and techniques.

"The ethics of interviewing is seen as the interviewer's choice of actions in which his moral obligations to the larger society, to science, to the research organization, and to the respondent must all be taken into consideration to find the best short-run and long-run effects. There is no way the interviewer can avoid making ethical choices, whether or not he is aware of them" (Gordon, 1975, p. 173).

Specifically, an interviewer in criminal justice is risking ethical conflict if they:

- Deliberately suppress information obtained in an interview.
- Intentionally bias the results of an interview.
- Intentionally bias an interpretation of interview results.
- Falsify the results of an interview.
- Take shortcuts in an interview because of boredom, fatigue, or disinterest.
- Deliberately obtain information in an interview in order to harm the interviewee or others.
- Break confidentiality when confidentiality is assumed or guaranteed.
- Deliberately deceive an interviewee (Gordon, 1975).

The final item of the list presents a particularly difficult decision for interviewers who interview suspects in criminal investigations. Inbau, Reid, and Buckley (1986) approve of "psychological tactics and techniques as trickery and deceit that are not only helpful but frequently indispensable in order to secure incriminating information from the guilty or to obtain investigative leads from otherwise uncooperative witnesses or informants" (p. xiv).

They also provide legal support for the use of deceit and trickery by pointing out court cases that have consistently supported the use of such methods. The courts have upheld the use of deceit and trickery as long as the methods are not too extreme.

Inbau and colleagues (1986, p. xvii, emphasis added) support the ethical use of trickery and deceit with the following reasons:

- In dealing with criminal offenders, and consequently also with criminal suspects who may actually be innocent, the interrogator must of necessity employ *less refined methods* than are considered appropriate for the transaction of ordinary, everyday affairs by and between law-abiding citizens.
- Interrogators must deal with criminal suspects on a somewhat *lower moral plane* than that upon which ethical, law-abiding citizens are expected to conduct their everyday affairs.

The support for their point of view is that the end justifies the mean. "How else would the murderer's guilt have been established" if an "unethical" practice had not been employed?

On the other hand, Zulawski and Wicklander (1993) take the high road on ethics in interrogation:

The interrogator who believes that it is okay to "Lie to a liar" or that "he is just getting what he deserves" soon becomes no better than the criminals with whom he is dealing and, the interrogator should recognize that little separates the honest from the guilty. Often, it is merely the honest individual's adherence to the legal, ethical and moral guidelines that separate the two parties. (p. 319)

This position leaves the interviewer, who we assume is very concerned about law and ethics, in a professional and procedural quandary. Trickery and deceit are unethical, but legal. One source maintains that it is necessary to be unethical when dealing with some suspects. Obviously, each interviewer will have to make their own ethical decision concerning the use of trickery and deceit, but a few points are offered to assist in the decision:

- Regardless of the outcome of an interview, the interviewer is personally responsible for the methods employed. The interviewer doesn't *have* to employ certain techniques. They *choose* to employ the techniques.
- Once an unethical technique has been employed, there is a tendency to rationalize or make up acceptable excuses for employing the technique.
- Operating on a "lower moral plane" with "less refined" methods places the interviewer on a "slippery slope" of ethics. The question immediately is one of "How low is acceptable?" or "How less refined can we tolerate?" In addition, the "slippery slope" introduces the potential that our techniques will be slightly less ethical next time and then slightly less refined the next, and so on.
- Regardless of the offense committed or how unsavory the character of the suspect, the interviewer can still choose to follow

the highest ethical standards. The interviewer controls his/her behavior; it is not controlled by the suspect, the system, or the situation.

As a precaution, the interviewer should be well versed in the employing agency's guidelines concerning ethical and legal standards. For example, questions of privacy and confidentiality should be clearly understood by the employee before interviews are conducted.

Nevertheless, several conclusions can be drawn from the dilemma of ethics in criminal justice interviewing, particularly as the dilemma relates to police interviews:

- The law enforcement field needs to adopt a coherent "professional ethic," which would encompass a body of knowledge with a clear assertion of the priority of certain values, principles, and rules that protect those values in practice (Newton, 1998; Yeschke, 2003).
- Most police officers believe trickery and deceit are not only appropriate tools for law enforcement, but also are ethical and professional (Ruffin, 2002).
- Even though some techniques of trickery and deceit are lawful, particularly those involving jailhouse informants, draconian use of police trickery and deception is unlikely to materialize into overzealous and systemic police practice, because of the increased professionalism in law enforcement and the enhanced civil liability among criminal justice personnel (Vaughn, 1992).

Confidentiality. Of specific concern to criminal justice interviewers is the degree to which information obtained in the interview is available to a wider public. Confidentiality refers to the anonymity and right to privacy of the interviewee.

On one hand, the assurance of confidentiality facilitates the disclosure of information by the interviewee, but on the other hand, in many cases, information concerning law violations may be vital to the public welfare and therefore not subject to confidentiality. The criminal justice interviewer may have to walk a fine line between these two concerns.

Because there are so many diverse agencies in the criminal justice system, it is difficult to make a general statement about confidentiality. Each agency and department has special considerations in the area of privileged communication. For example, the fields of social work (see Kadushin, 1990) and probation (see Clear et al., 1989) have explored the dimensions of confidentiality in interviews.

Confidentiality is not always required in interview situations, particularly when:

- The interviewee makes or is a threat to themselves.
- The interviewee makes or is a threat to others.
- The interviewee discloses major law violations.
- The interviewee has been or is violating the laws of child abuse or neglect.

Court decisions have consistently limited confidentiality and dictated a "duty to warn" a person in danger of harm in cases where an interviewee has made serious threats of harm to someone else.

Interviewing and Interrogation Research

Interviews tend to be used in specific fields; the people who conduct the interviews tend to be very practical and research is often not their primary concern. Consequently, research on interviewing is field-specific and quite limited, especially in criminal justice. The irony of this is that so many important criminal justice decisions are based on a process on which we have so little research.

On the other hand, it is not an exaggeration to state that it would require an entire book to review all of the literature related to interviewing across all of the specific fields that use interviews—business, medicine, psychotherapy, research, journalism, and criminal justice. In this section an attempt is made to introduce the main areas of research that focus on specific criminal justice concerns that appear in the subsequent section.

Another factor that limits interviewing research related to criminal justice is the extreme variability of the interviews conducted in criminal justice. Professionals in law enforcement, corrections, and the courts conduct interviews that range from personnel selection to interrogation of crime suspects. With such variability, research findings concerning one type of interview are likely to have little application to any of the other types.

Fortunately, there is a significant overlap between interviewing research and research done with regard to psychotherapy. This is fortuitous for criminal justice because it provides a foundation of interpersonal and relationship skills in working with the public in one-on-one encounters. This foundation serves as the design and structure of the interviewing training program in this text.

On the other hand, many criminal justice interviews don't have the same goals and objectives as counseling or therapy. As research in criminal justice interviewing increases, differences will likely become more apparent; less borrowing and blending from other disciplines will be needed. Since most criminal justice professionals deal directly with the public on a daily basis, basic human relations skills originating in counseling and therapy, whose use has been validated by research, will continue to be of significant value to interviewers in criminal justice.

One comprehensive study on dyadic communication, conducted by Siegman and Pope (1972), provides useful information for beginning interviewers. Based on their work, the following conclusions can be drawn:

- The higher the stress in an interview, the lower the facilitation of self-disclosure.
- A warm interviewer increases the productivity and fluency of the interviewee.
- A high status interviewer increases the productivity of the interviewee.

- The use of gestures as an aid to the interviewer's speech facilitates communication.
- High interviewee stress will result in rapid or flustered speech.
- If the interviewer initially monopolizes the interview, the interviewee will be predisposed to remain silent later in the interview.

Another interesting research question concerns the determination of what actually occurs in an interrogation. What are the techniques used and what is the process of interrogation? In a very unique study conducted by Leo (1996) and summarized by Gudjonsson (2003), these questions were answered by analyzing interrogations of 182 suspects in three police departments. Leo identified twelve interrogation techniques and the percentage of the cases where the technique was used for each tactic. Two of the twelve techniques were used over 85% of the time. The two used were: (1) appeal to the suspect's self-interest and (2) confront the suspect with existing evidence of guilt. The additional ten techniques were used less than half the time, but the average number of tactics per interrogation was 5.6. These tactics produced self-incriminating statements, which could be used against them in court, in 64% of the suspects. Which of the tactics were most successful in obtaining a confession? Leo concluded that the following tactics were successful more than 90% of the time:

- Appeal to the suspect's conscience.
- Identify contradictions in the suspect's story.
- Use praise or flattery.
- Offer moral justification/psychological excuses.

In addition, Leo (1996) found that the greater the number of tactics used and the longer the time length of the interrogation, the more likely the suspect was to confess to the crime. Second, most of the interviewers lasted only one hour. Finally, he found that coercion was present in only four of the 182 interviews, which was inconsistent with recommended practices in some of the more accepted interrogation training programs.

Stereotypical Interrogation Beliefs

Many interviewers hold beliefs about detecting deception that do not match the results of scientific research studies. This mismatch creates a technology transfer gap and a discrepancy between believed cues to deception and actual cues to deception. The result of misinterpretations of the cues can lead to a wrongful conviction.

> **Stereotypical belief #1.** There is a strong relationship between deceptive behavior and gaze aversion.
> **Research indication.** Not supported. Eye contact is likely to increase during deception.

Stereotypical belief #2. There is a strong relationship between deception and an increase in body movements.
Research indication. Not supported. Body movements decrease during deception.

Stereotypical belief #3. Consecutive statements from liars are less consistent than consecutive statements from individuals telling the truth.
Research indication. The opposite is true.

Stereotypical belief #4. Legal professionals (police officers, prosecutors, and judges) know a great deal about scientific research on deception.
Research indication. Presumed experts have admitted to knowing close to nothing about the subject (Stromwall & Granhag, 2003)

Stereotypical belief #5. Training and prior experience can improve performance in detecting deception.
Research indication. Neither factor influences accuracy. Training and experience increase response bias in the direction of indicating deceit instead of truth (Meissner & Kassin, 2002). Furthermore, evidence shows that police become more confident that they are correct with the on-the-job experience, but they don't increase their accuracy in detecting deception (Frank & Feeley, 2003; Kassin & Fong, 1999; Porter, Woodworth, & Birt, 2000).

Stereotypical belief #6. Suspects tend to deny involvement in crimes or prefer to remain silent and police interrogations last a long time.
Research indication. Confession rates are between 50% and 60%. Only 5% of suspects remain completely silent and most interviews are short (Vrij, 2003).

Stereotypical belief #7. Suspects make admissions to crimes because police officers use skilled questioning techniques.
Research indication. In the interviews that have been analyzed, the offenses were minor, the evidence was substantial, and the suspects were willing to talk. No special questioning techniques were needed. Furthermore, most suspects do not change their "story" regardless of how interviews were conducted (Vrij, 2003). Deceptive and truthful consecutive statements are equally consistent over repeated interrogations (Granhag & Stromwall, 2002).

Stereotypical belief #8. The statements produced by two liars in collusion will be more inconsistent than individuals telling the truth, and consecutive statements given by a single liar will be more inconsistent than statements given by individuals telling the truth.

Research indication. First, statements made by liars are more consistent than consecutive statements given by single liars and truth tellers are equally consistent (Granhag, Stromwall, & Jonsson, 2003). Deceptive and truthful consecutive statements are equally consistent over repeated interrogations (Granhag & Stromwall, 2002).

Interviewing with Time Constraints

A primary consideration that affects many criminal justice interviews is limited time to conduct the interview. Police officers often have to hurry interviews with witnesses because of subsequent emergency calls. Probation officers have caseloads that shrink the time available for any single probation interview. Very few criminal justice interviewers have the luxury of lengthy interview contact.

Some rather superficial, obvious, simple, or direct information or decisions can be handled in short or quick interviews. On the other hand, decisions to be made from complex information obtained from interviewees usually require much longer interviews. These range from determining whether a prison inmate is likely to be successful on parole to whether a police cadet is likely to be violent or overly aggressive as an officer. Information of this nature is extremely complex and requires lengthy interview exposure. If the interview is hurried in these situations, then decisions based on information obtained in the interview are likely to be less reliable.

How can an interviewer conserve valuable time? The first principle that answers this question is *do not use an interview to accomplish a task that can be more efficiently handled in some other manner.* For example, do not use valuable interview time asking a person background information (i.e., name, address, date of birth) if this information can be obtained with a written questionnaire. One of the most wasteful practices in criminal justice is that of having well-paid professionals asking biographical information in interviews. (An exception to this is the case of interviewees with language, reading, or writing difficulties who would have difficulty in responding to a written questionnaire.) If a written questionnaire will accomplish the interview task without any loss of effectiveness, then it should be used to conserve valuable time for tasks that can only be accomplished in a face-to-face interview.

The second principle that answers the question of time conservation is to *prioritize your interview contacts by level of effectiveness.* Unless you have specific departmental or legal directives to the contrary, you should spend the maximum interview time with the interviewees with whom you will be most effective. For example, instead of seeing all of your probationers for ten minutes, you may want to schedule a few for longer periods of time. Valuable time can be conserved by fitting your interviewing skills to interviews where they can be most effective.

Nonverbal Communication

Another major area of concern for criminal justice interviewers is nonverbal communication. It is generally recognized by experts that a wealth of information is available to the interviewer if nonverbal communication is correctly interpreted.

Nonverbal communication has been of considerable interest to psychologists, therapists, sociologists, and linguists in recent years. Almost every aspect of nonverbal communication has been described and classified (Cormier & Cormier, 1979). The importance of nonverbal communication in interviews is underscored by the fact that almost two-thirds of the meaning in an interviewer's message is conveyed nonverbally.

In recent years, this enthusiasm for nonverbal communication has led to a focus in criminal justice, specifically in law enforcement, on training police interviewers, interrogators, and investigators in nonverbal interrogation techniques with a particular emphasis on detecting lying or deception in an interview.

Nonverbal behavior plays several roles in interpersonal communication:

- **Communication.** Nonverbal behavior serves as a method of emotional expression, dramatic presentation, and a form of rhetoric that helps in impressing, beguiling, or deceiving another person.
- **Style.** Nonverbal behavior serves as a personal style to make the person's communication whole, consistent, and unique. It is like your signature, voice characteristics, or fingerprint.
- **Skill.** Nonverbal behavior is an acquired skill. It involves expressing or sending a message and the subsequent interpretation or receiving aspects of a nonverbal exchange. The skill can be learned, practiced, and used in interpersonal communication (Rozelle, Druckman, & Baxter, 2003).

A particularly useful training technique to learn the effective use of nonverbal communication is to focus on the nonverbal technique used by certain television personalities. Late-night talk show hosts, televangalists, and comedians are typically masters of the communication, style, and skills of nonverbal behaviors. Trainees can readily access these sources in order to gain an impression of the effectiveness of nonverbal communication.

Types of Nonverbal Communication

There are various types of nonverbal communication, which can best be separated into three areas known as proxemics, kinesics, and paralanguage.

Proxemics.   Nonverbal communication involves space and distance in an interview. Proxemics focuses on the distance between the interviewer and interviewee. Also of concern is the change in interpersonal space and how the interviewee takes up space in an interview. Areas that the interviewer would be concerned with is the comfortable distance between themselves and the interviewee. Has the interviewee moved back or forward in the interview? Is the interviewee constricted and taking up less space or are they gesturing with open arms and taking up more space? Answers to these questions may provide clues to the type and level of communication in the interview.

Kinesics. Kinesics focuses on the body in movement, including movements of the torso, head, limbs, face, and eyes as well as the impact of posture. This is popularly referred to as "body language." In making a note of nonverbal communication, the interviewer should focus on eye contact, hand-to-face movements, foot activity, fidgeting, looking at a watch, and grooming.

Paralanguage. Another source of nonverbal data is called paralanguage. It focuses on how messages are delivered, including elements such as tone, loudness, pitch, and fluency of speech (Cormier & Cormier, 1979). The interviewer should focus on the interviewee's pauses and hesitations. Does the interviewee answer quickly? Do they mumble or speak loudly at particular times in the conversation?

Several very important and frequent types of criminal justice interviews are conducted where nonverbal behavior is not available for decision making: telephone interviews, depositions, and electronic messages.

In telephone interviews, such as crisis or crime "hotlines," the interviewer is receiving information with the possibility of assessing the urgency of the verbal and nonverbal behavior of the interviewee. Obviously, conclusions drawn from these interviews are at a high risk for misinterpretation or error.

Legal depositions and interrogations are taken from witnesses, victims, and suspects. A deposition is an oral statement by a potential court witness, given under oath in the presence of a court reporter and attorneys from both sides. It is taken in question-and-answer form with cross-examination by opposing attorneys. Written interrogatories may also be taken, but these do not permit cross-examination (Wrightsman, 1991).

In either case, nonverbal behavior is not recorded so that the subtleties of the communication are lost and what is recorded in writing is taken at face value.

In order to successfully interpret and include nonverbal behavior in decision making, the interviewer needs to be able to fully observe the interviewee. If the interviewee is unseen or shielded by furniture, little nonverbal behavior will be visible and much valuable information will be lost.

What are the specific kinds of nonverbal behaviors that an interviewer should be observing? Burgoon and Buller (1994) studied several nonverbal behaviors:

- Vagueness/uncertainty in answering questions
- Brevity in answering questions
- Gaze avoidance while answering questions
- Negative emotions/unpleasantness while answering
- Nervousness, fidgety and uncomfortable while answering questions
- Poor impression while answering questions

Burgoon and Buller examined these nonverbal behaviors as an interpersonal communication event and as a method of incorporating interpersonal communication theory in the study of deception in an interview.

Risks in the Use of Nonverbal Information

In using nonverbal information, both the novice and expert interviewer sometimes confuse descriptions, interpretations, and confidence levels. A clear distinction among them is presented in the following hierarchy:

- *Low Risk:* Descriptions based on observation ("I saw the interviewee break eye contact"); descriptions of nonverbal behavior are supported by extensive classification and observation.
- *Medium Risk:* Interpretations and decoding from what has been seen to be based on conjecture, speculation, and some scientific data ("Breaking eye contact means the interviewee is nervous, which in turn means they are deceiving the interviewer"); there is much contradictory evidence in this interpretation.
- *High Risk:* Claims made concerning overall interviewing or interrogation effectiveness based on interpretations derived from descriptions ("If you use this technique your arrest clearance rate will improve" or "You obtain more confessions than when you don't use the technique"); these are completely unsupported assertions that range somewhere between gross error and outright fraud.

Anytime an interviewer moves away from scientifically validated techniques, the risk factor increases because nonverbal communication is not an area with extensive research conclusions. In simpler terms, there is a lot of rhetoric about nonverbal communication but few scientific conclusions.

Nonverbal Interviewing Techniques

Interviewing techniques based largely on nonverbal communication have been developed and presented to thousands of participants in an extensive series of training seminars. Public and private security and law enforcement personnel have been trained using the *Reid Technique of Interviewing and Interrogation* (Reid & Associates, 2000) and *The Kinesic Interviewing Technique* (Link & Foster, 1989). Both of these extensive training programs have been developed in the nonverbal communication tradition and both programs report high popularity with law enforcement participants.

Both of these training programs are extensive and detailed and it would be both impractical and imprudent to attempt to present their entirety in this text. However, these training programs contain interesting and unique approaches to learning nonverbal interviewing techniques. The definition of interrogation using the Reid (2000) technique is: "Interrogation is an art whereby through the use of questioning and observation the truth is elicited from a suspect by sound reasoning and understanding without the use of threats or promises" (p. 5).

This technique uses nine steps of interrogation: direct positive confrontation, theme development, handling denials, overcoming objections, procurement and retention of suspects' attention, handling passive moods, presenting an alternative question, suspect orally relating details, and converting an oral confession into a written confession (Reid & Associates, 2000).

The kinesic technique is based on stress forces that the developers of the technique believe will appear as nonverbal behavior when the person interrogated is not truthful. The focus of this technique is the "art of diagnosing internal states from external behaviors and appearances" (Link & Foster, 1989). Some limitations are provided with the use of the technique:

> The Kinesic Interview Technique does not have adequate validity in some situations. This includes cases in which the person being interviewed is schizophrenic, a chronic alcoholic, or has been using hallucinogens or other hard drugs. It is also true that persons fifteen and younger often can convince themselves that they are innocent when they are not. Therefore, often no meaningful kinesic information can be obtained from them. (Link & Foster, 1989, p. 11)

While it is not the intent to conduct an intensive evaluation of these interviewing techniques, they do present an interesting methodological paradox. This paradox seems to be divided into three critical concerns:

■ Each of the previously mentioned training techniques claims to be an "art" and not a science. On the other hand, each technique ostensibly draws heavily on the scientific research results of physiological stress reactions, but results of this research do not support the generalizations of specific kinesic cues to deception.

■ Neither of the techniques is supported by research data to substantiate the effectiveness and validity of the technique other than antedotal reports or "field testing." On the other hand, the popularity of the techniques is widespread. For example, Reid and Associates (1992, p. 2) indicate that "more than 55,000 persons in the law enforcement and security fields have attended these seminars since they were first offered in 1974" and that

75,000 people have admitted guilt to the Reid staff of interrogators (Reid & Associates, 1995).

■ Finally, very unlikely or extraordinary claims should be met
with extreme care and built-in suspicion and must be supported
by extraordinary evidence (DeJager, 1992). Note the claims
made in a promotional brochure for the *Reid Technique, 1992
Seminar Schedule:*

> In trying to maintain a structure of verbal lies, however, that sus-
> pect most often develops internal conflicts and tensions which man-
> ifest themselves in nonverbal behavior. Thus, body indicators can
> also be used to determine whether the suspect under interrogation
> is listening, maintaining a defiant attitude, or is ready to confess.

This is a rather extraordinary claim that would seemingly be supported by more than the personal testimony of the individuals marketing the technique. It is not. There is not any supportive data
from carefully controlled, impartial scientific studies supporting the
truth as to whether "internal conflicts manifest themselves in nonverbal behavior." Furthermore, if these nonverbal behaviors did
exist, there is not any research to support what they mean or how
to interpret them.

On the contrary, convincing experimental evidence provided by
Kassin and McNall (1991) raises serious questions about the effectiveness of the Reid techniques. Based on experimental research,
they argue that the techniques proposed by Reid have the potential
to coax innocent people into confessing to crimes they did not commit. Where does this leave the criminal justice professional concerning interviewing or interrogation practices based on nonverbal
communication? The most that can be said is that these are highly
successful training techniques whose theoretical and methodological research support remains enigmatic.

Detecting Deception in an Interview

Can an interviewer determine when someone is lying in an interview? Are there clues that can be spotted when an interviewee is
lying? These questions are of serious concern to criminal justice interviewers. "The ability to detect deception would obviously be of
great value in interrogation since it would enable an officer to evaluate the veracity of responses thus saving time otherwise wasted
following false leads and instead focusing on honest responses"
(Waltman, 1983, p. 166).

Both of the training programs mentioned in the previous section
are directed toward determining if the subject being questioned is
telling the truth. The need in law enforcement for this ability is great,
even desperate. This need is juxtaposed with a very complex and
misunderstood area of research on lying and deception.

Where the stakes for a mistake are the highest, attempts already are
being made to spot nonverbal clues to deceit. "Experts" unfamiliar
with all the evidence and arguments are offering their services as lie

spotters in jury selection and employment interviews. Some police-men and professional polygraphers using the "lie detector" are taught about the nonverbal clues to deceit. About half the information in the training materials I have seen is wrong. (Ekman, 1986, p. 22)

For example, notice the following statements made by Zulawski and Wicklander (1993) in their discussion of the possibility of an in-dividual faking truthful behavior:

> It is also difficult for the guilty to fake behavior successfully because the subconscious mind acts independently of the conscious mind. Be-cause of this, the non-verbal behavior is often in stark contrast to the words that portray innocence. (p. 54)

Several observations can be made regarding these assertions that cast serious doubts about the interviewing techniques based on them.

- No documentation is provided to support the assertions about the subconscious and conscious mind. These relationships are key to the authors development of the role of leakage in detect-ing deception. It would seem that such key theoretical notions would be accompanied by some form of theoretical, philosoph-ical, or scientific documentation to support the assertions.
- The notion of a subconscious is theoretical, not factual. The un-sophisticated reader is likely to take these assumptions as fact rather than theory.
- The use of the term "subconscious" is also problematic. If the authors mean "preconscious," then the statement doesn't make any sense since the preconscious is simply a transition zone between the conscious and the unconscious where many mem-ories are stored that can be retrieved without special techniques. On the other hand, if the authors mean "unconscious," the as-sertion is flatly incorrect since the unconscious does not act in-dependently of the conscious. Most students in an introductory psychology class learn that the unconscious influences the con-scious and they are in continuous conflict.
- In either case, the relationship between the subconscious and the conscious is theoretical, not factual. The extraordinary as-sertion of this relationship by the authors would seemingly need to be supported by extraordinary evidence.

A more recent approach to interviewing using kinesic techniques has been developed by Walters (2003). This kinesic approach is a scientific and theoretical improvement over earlier kinesic ap-proaches because it does incorporate some information about re-search evidence concerning detecting deception. Nevertheless, this newer approach is still very troublesome for several reasons. First, the foundation for the kinesic technique is based on four stress–response states: anger, depression, denial, and bargaining. Walters does not present any support for the stress–response states or why the particular states were chosen over emotional responses such as fear, embarrassment, or anxiety. In addition, including denial as a stress–response state further confuses the theory, because denial has traditionally been considered a defense mechanism or cognitive thinking error.

Fortunately, Walters (2003) does indicate that kinesic interviewing is not as reliable with some groups, including people who are mentally deficient, children and adolescents, psychotics, and subjects under the influence of alcohol or drugs. Because they are not mentioned, we must assume that women, members of various cultural groups, and psychopaths are part of the general population and the kinesic techniques will be effective with them.

Finally, Walters (2003) does provide cautions in the risk of a false confession when kinesic techniques are misused and the rights of citizens are violated. Overall, this kinesic approach provides a blend of the experience and knowledge of field investigation with the scientific research on detecting deception by using nonverbal clues. In conclusion, it appears that some writers in the field of interrogation play fast and loose with facts and theory to support a particular set of techniques.

Basic Terms

In order to understand the confusing field of detecting deception, several basic concepts are presented in the following sections.

Norming.   This term refers to the need for the interviewer to establish a behavioral baseline of nonverbal communication that is normal for the interviewee before beginning a discussion of the critical areas to determine how the person reacts to being in an interview situation. The goal is to determine the interviewee's normal body movements so that they can be distinguished from body movements created by deception.

Leakage.   "The nonverbal clues one can read in detecting deception are called leakage because these nonverbal signals can escape from a person despite his or her attempts at control during deception" (Waltman, 1983, p. 166). Leakage is a theoretical construct, not a scientific process. Leakage and clues to deception do not always happen nor do they always have a singular or meaningful interpretation.

Types of Lying.   "There are two major forms of lying: concealment, leaving out true information; and falsification, or presenting false information as if it were true" (Ekman, 1985, p. 28).

False Positive.   One of the two kinds of mistakes that are made in detecting deceit in an interview is a false positive. A false positive mistake is disbelieving the truth.

False Negative.   This is the second type of mistake made in detecting deceit. False negative refers to believing a lie.

Brokaw Hazard. A few people happen to be evasive or convoluted in their speech. "Any behavior that is a useful clue to deceit will for some few people be a usual part of their behavior" (Ekman, 1985, p. 91). The possibility of misjudging these people as lying is called the "Brokaw Hazard."

Othello Error. "This error occurs when the lie catcher fails to consider that a truthful person who is under stress may appear to be lying" (Ekman, 1985, p. 94). This means anxiety may increase before the interviewee relates a perfectly true story if they know it sounds too improbable to be believed. Apparently, the ability to differentiate between cues driven by anxiety related to true deception and cues driven by anxiety related to being suspected of deceiving has not been established. The state of the art in lie detection would not support any contentions to this effect.

Stanislavski Technique. When an interviewee is reexperiencing an emotion to cover a lie, there may not be any signs that the behavior is false. "The line between false and true becomes fuzzy when emotions are produced by the Stanislavski Technique" (Ekman, 1985, p. 117).

Sample Bias. When a particular trait or group of traits is overrepresented and not randomly distributed in a sample, the sample is considered biased (E.S. Johnson, 1981). Conclusions or generalizations made from the biased sample will be in error if the particular bias influences these conclusions or generalizations. Sample bias is relevant to detecting deception because the sample of people that police officers interview is not typically randomly composed of liars and nonliars. The sample is likely to be overrepresented by liars. Laboratory research experiments, which tend to use random samples, have shown that the ability to detect deception is not better than chance. On the other hand, police investigators are likely on a daily basis to be interviewing suspects that are more often likely to be lying. Thus, we can understand why so many investigators testify as to their ability to detect liars: Most of the people they interview are likely to be lying. This is due to the fact that the investigators obviously don't spend a lot of time and effort questioning suspects who aren't under suspicion and who don't have any motivation to lie to police officers. The sample of people that police officers interview is probably biased by overly representing deceivers.

The Boy Who Cried Wolf Effect. Even liars tell the truth sometimes, and even honest people lie on occasion (O'Sullivan, 2003).

Fundamental Attribution Error. This is the tendency when forming impressions of others to overestimate the importance of traits (internal factors) in the person being judged and to underestimate the importance of the situation (external factors). This is one of the reasons why lie catchers are so inaccurate (Ainsworth, 2002; O'Sullivan,

2003). They have a cognitive bias toward rating others as lying who they perceive as having negative traits, such as untrustworthiness.

Nixon Effect.   This refers to former President Richard Nixon, who blinked over 50 times per minute during his resignation address when discussing his being forced from the presidency. Research has shown that nervousness results in an increase in blinking. The popular belief that liars behave nervously by fidgeting and avoiding eye contact has been shown to not be true. In fact, Mann, Vrij, and Bull (2002) found that suspects blinked less and paused longer while lying.

White Lies.   These are polite lies with very little emotional attachment. Detecting these types of lies is probably not very important and most difficult because of the low emotional intensity associated with them (Frank & Feeley, 2003).

High-Stakes Lies.   These are lies with considerable emotional attachment. Fear of getting caught, going to jail, or getting punished can evoke strong emotions. Theoretically, these strong emotions can result in leakage, despite the efforts of the person to hide them. Training officers to detect these types of lies to catch individuals deceiving the authorities is very important. Training should focus on detecting high-stakes liars (Frank & Feeley, 2003; Vrij & Mann, 2001).

Pinocchio's Nose.   There are no giveaway cues in lie detection, like Pinocchio's nose, which grew larger the more he lied. Consequently, there is nothing the lie detector can rely on. This means that police officers who have been taught to look for behavioral indicators of deception have been taught the wrong cues (Memon et al., 2003).

Duping Delight.   A person might experience excitement at the prospect of telling a successful lie and the opportunity of fooling someone. This excitement could be confused with other forms of emotional arousal such as fear, stress, or guilt (Gozna, Vrij, & Bull, 2001; Vrij, Edward, Roberts, & Bull, 2000).

Ekman, who has previously been referred to in this section, has devoted considerable time to the nonverbal constituents of the act of lying (Ekman, 1986, 2001). He supports the development of training in how to spot the clues to deceit so that criminal justice personnel would be more accurate, "decreasing both disbelieving-the-truth and believing-a-lie mistakes." The information to support such programs would take a great deal more research than is available today, so that what the student learning to detect deception has available is hints and cautions about when clues are useless or misleading.

With these ideas in mind, a synopsis of Ekman's research is presented as an introduction to the complexity of detecting deception. This introduction is not meant to take the place of a thorough reading of the research on deception and any criminal justice professional or student who is involved in training or interviewing should make a thorough investigation of the research findings. The following points will guide both the student and professional into the area of detecting deception:

- When there is a choice about how to lie, liars usually prefer concealing to falsifying.
- Criminal psychopaths fool the experts.
- There is no sign of deceit itself—no gesture, facial expression, or muscle twitch that in itself means the person is lying.
- It is not a simple matter to catch lies.
- The best clues to deception are in facial expressions.
- The body is a good source of leakage and deception.
- The voice is a good source of clues to emotional arousal.
- Innocents are also sometimes emotionally aroused, not just liars (the Othello Error).
- No clue to deceit is reliable for all human beings.
- Shifting posture is unrelated to truthfulness, even though people believe it is.
- It is only liars who know they are lying when they lie who are likely to get caught.
- Few people do better than chance in judging whether someone is lying or truthful.
- Most people think they are making accurate judgments even though they are not.
- Lie catchers should strive to become aware of their own preconceptions about the suspect.
- Many behaviors are signs of more than one emotion.
- Differences in national and cultural background can obscure the interpretation of vocal, facial, and bodily clues to deceit.
- Consider the possibility that a sign of an emotion is not a clue to deceit but a clue to how a truthful person feels about being suspected of lying.
- Most liars fool most people most of the time.
- First meetings are especially vulnerable to error in judgment (no baseline or norm for behavior).
- Evaluating behavioral clues to deceit is hazardous (Ekman, 1985).

More recently, Ekman has devoted research attention to the study of facial expression of emotion (Ekman, 2003; Keltner & Ekman, 2000; Keltner, Ekman, Gonzaga, & Beer, 2003). He has identified the facial signs that betray a lie. He has identified, specifically, what is termed micro expressions, which are very fast facial movements (one-fifth of a second) that reveal leakage of an emotion a person is trying to conceal. False expressions can betray an individual in a number of ways:

- The expression is slightly asymmetrical.
- The expression lacks smoothness in the way it flows on the face.
- The expression lacks smoothness in the way it flows off the face (Ekman, 2003).

His study of facial expression of emotion has also focused on cultural variations. The results of these research findings are covered in more detail in Chapter 4.

Notes of Caution

Nonverbal communication has been a fascinating and confusing area of dyadic communication. Detecting deception from nonverbal clues has been particularly fascinating for law enforcement interviewers and interrogators. The potential of these areas needs to be explored through legitimate research and until we know more about these areas, so that our training and practical applications don't far outrun valid information, we need to be cautious.

First, the validity and reliability of nonverbal communication has not been established. Most of what we know is based on theory at most and erroneous speculation at least. "It is especially foolhardy to accept the prevailing folklore in the area. If anything, the cues associated with deception may be better indicators of stress and anxiety than they are signs of lying" (Bartol, 1983).

Second, much of the literature of nonverbal communication is vague, imprecise, and ambiguous. Discussions of "leakage," for example, are filled with words such as "usually," maybe," "might," "most," "few," "could be," and "generally." Quantification is rare so caution is in order when making any conclusions from the literature.

Third, distinctions between nonverbal behavior for men and women are practically nonexistent in the literature. Assuming that men and women respond the same nonverbally is very risky in the absence of any data to support a hypothesis in either direction. The issue of deception in diverse populations will be discussed in greater detail in Chapter 4.

Fourth, the issue of decoding nonverbal cues raises the concept of cross-cultural differences with regard to interpretation of nonverbal behavior. Ekman noted the effect cultural differences can have on nonverbal communication but neither of the nonverbal communication training programs mentioned earlier qualify techniques in the area of multicultural applications.

Fifth, caution should be exercised in accepting exaggerated claims concerning what nonverbal communication techniques will do for job performance, such as "you can save investigative man hours, increase recovery rates, and increase the number of guilty pleas." The state of the art is simply not refined to the point that these claims can be substantiated. As Ekman (1985) points out, you should "worry about 'experts' who go unchallenged by public scrutiny and the carping critics of the scientific community" (p. 23). Some experts who make these claims may be guilty of concealment.

Sixth, falsely calling attention to a nonverbal cue is likely to cause the cue to appear. If the interviewer draws an inference of guilt from it or asks the suspect to account for the fact that the cue appeared, the interviewee may interpret the otherwise inexplicable behavior as evidence of their own guilty conscience, particularly since the suspect does not know that simply calling attention to a part of one's body can elicit a response there (Cohn & Udolf, 1979).

Seventh, it is a well-known fact that people confess falsely to crimes they did not commit, despite the fact that legitimate law enforcement sources are convinced that "human beings ordinarily do not utter unsolicited, spontaneous confessions" (Tousignant, 1991, p. 14). Some people have a neurotic need for punishment. Others confess because they feel guilty due to imaginary acts that may or may not be related to the crime in question. Inbau and colleagues (1986) caution against the "conscience-stricken" confession as having a likelihood of being false. This type, they point out, may be the result of a mentally ill person or a normal person wanting to gain publicity or wanting to manipulate the police for some personal reason, such as evading police investigation or suspicion of a much more serious crime. "One method for checking the authenticity of a conscience-stricken confession, or one that seems to be the result of mental illness, is to refer to some fictitious aspects of the crime and test whether the suspect will accept them as actual facts relating to the occurrence" (Inbau et al., 1986, p. 216).

In any case, in the absence of corroborating evidence or information, the interviewer would do well to remember that every time a major crime is reported in the papers, dozens of people come forward to confess to it (Cohn & Udolf, 1979). The question remains: Who is likely to confess to a crime? Pearse, Gudjonsson, Clare, and Rutler (1998) found that younger suspects, suspects who had no experience with prison or jail, and suspects who had consumed an illicit drug in the last 24-hour period were more likely to confess. They did not find that psychologically vulnerable suspects were particularly likely to confess. Four types of false confessions have been identified:

- **Voluntary false** is elicited without any external pressure. The person may simply go to the police after a reported crime and confess, commonly due to a morbid desire for notoriety.
- **Coerced-compliant** is commonly elicited during persuasive interrogation where the person perceives there is some immediate gain from confessing falsely, such as being released from custody or escaping the stress of the interrogation. The person is fully aware of not having committed the crime.
- **Coerced-internalized** is elicited by persuasive questioning. The suspect is gradually persuaded that they have committed a crime of which they have no memory, or they have become so confused that they don't trust their own memory and accept a false scenario suggested by the police. This type of confession is associated with high suggestibility and a tendency toward confabulation.
- **Coerced-reactive** confessions occur when a person is pressured to confess by somebody other than the police, such as a spouse (Gudjonsson, 2001).

Eighth, criminal justice professionals need to become more aware of their own preconceived notions about guilt and deception. For example, law enforcement investigators have been notoriously guilty of being biased in assuming a suspect is guilty. One source defines interrogation as "the questioning of a person suspected of having committed a crime." This definition seems relatively unbiased. The writer goes on to identify one of the goals of interrogation as "to obtain an admission of guilt from the suspect" or "to secure a confession" (Tousignant, 1991). No mention is made in the goals of interrogation of also determining innocence; an assumption of guilt is a foregone conclusion of the interrogation. This bias is further reinforced by the fact that many suspects are obviously guilty, but all are not. The obvious danger of a biased interviewer is making errors by perceiving nonverbal cues to support the bias. If the interviewer is aware of these preconceptions, they may be able to realize that they should be cautious in trusting their judgments about whether or not a suspect is lying. The danger is that police interrogations founded upon an interview-based presumption of guilt can set into motion a biased chain of events, such as a more guilt-presumptive question, a more aggressive interview style, and the tendency to steer nuetral observers into judging the suspect to be guilty (Kassin, Goldstein, & Savitsky, 2003).

Ninth, the presence of prescription or illegal drugs in the system of the interviewee, even in small amounts, may affect nonverbal cues in the interview. Consequently, nonverbal cues may either be exaggerated or muted by the presence of drugs that act on emotional responses.

Tenth, Ofshe (1992) and Loftus and Ketcham (1994) have identified the phenomenon known as "grade 5 syndrome," which describes 5–10% of the population who are so suggestible and hypnotizable that they can produce false information during police interrogations. This syndrome uses "trance logic" to incorporate illogical or contradictory material into their memory systems so that they believe their memories are real. They compulsively fill in the blanks in their memories, and accept incongruent, unlikely, or even impossible information as real and valid (Loftus & Ketcham, 1994). Grade 5 syndrome adds to the caution criminal justice interviewers need when relying on confessions based on memories—the memories may be pseudomemories.

Finally, detecting deception has recently moved into the area of popular culture. In addition to the polygraph becoming a theatrical prop for daytime television talk shows, several pop-psychology self-help books have been published (e.g., Benson, 2000; Lieberman, 1998; Nance, 2001; Walters, 2000).

Most of these publications are further extensions of exaggerated claims based on dubious or scant evidence to support the claims. In addition, the theoretical foundations for the claims are also poorly developed. The success of these popular trends in detecting deception testifies to the apparent intrigue, fascination, and seductiveness of the prospect of determining if a person is lying. It may also be a comment on the lack of quantity and quality of science instruction and critical thinking in the U.S. education system.

Why Is It So Difficult to Detect Deception?

- People underutilize the nonverbal behaviors involved in the emotional and cognitive reactions to lying. They are more likely to pay attention to the cues when judging honest behavior than when judging deceptive behavior.
- People overrely on the content of speech.
- Many people have a truthfulness (Halo Effect) or deception bias. Law enforcement officers frequently rate other people as lying.
- People believe incorrect paradigms about the clues to deception. Most Americans believe that averting eye gaze is one of the signs of deception. Research suggests that most liars actually increase eye gaze when they lie. In addition, the Othello Error is not considered so that a truthful person's fear of being disbelieved is misinterpreted as evidence of lying.
- Physiogonomic, personality, cultural, and behavioral characteristics of the liar or truth teller mislead the observer. Observers tend to misinterpret deviations from the norm as signs of deception.
- There are inadequate samples of the contexts in which lies occur. People lie in different situations and these lies may involve different kinds of detection clues.
- There are variabilities in social/emotional intelligence and these differences are likely to affect lie detection ability.
- There may be a lack of evolutionary selection for lie detection. The cost may have been too severe.
- Most societies discourage deception yet encourage pretending to believe white lies. This may undermine the skills needed to detect deception.
- Accusing someone of lying is an assertive social act that may be dangerous to the accuser. This has been termed "accusatory reluctance."
- Some people are in collusion with liars, while others are self-deceptive by not wanting to detect the truth (O'Sullivan, 2003).

How to Catch a Liar

It is generally accepted by people who study how to detect deception that there are three ways to catch a liar: First, by observing nonverbal behavior; second, by listening to what they say and analyzing the content of their speech; and third, by measuring their physiological responses (Vrij et al., 2000). The third method mentioned above is obviously not a practical one for interviewers, because they would need a physiological recording device in each interview.

With all of the cautions and skepticism of the previous discussions, a few guidelines have emerged from research on detecting deception from verbal and nonverbal behavior. Ekman, O'Sullivan, and Frank (1999) showed that it is possible for some people to make highly accurate judgments about lying and truthfulness without the aid of special techniques or repeated viewing. This ability is not confined to law enforcement groups, but can also be accomplished by psychologists. They caution that we should remain skeptical in our ability to detect deception. The important aspects of verbal and nonverbal behavior in detecting deception are:

- Be suspicious and distrust what people are saying.
- Probe and keep on asking questions about the topic as soon as you detect a liar.
- Do not reveal important information.
- Be informed about the topic of the lie, especially the details.
- Ask liars to repeat what they have said before.
- Watch and listen carefully and abandon stereotypes in order to judge each case individually.
- Compare liars' behavior with their natural behavior. This means you should compare outside the interview situation and not casual conversation at the beginning of the interview (Vrij, 2000).

Finally, Vrij and colleagues (2000) suggest that interviewers are more likely to be successful if they focus on both verbal and nonverbal cues. By using information from the two sources, they may be able to detect truth and lies over 75% of the time. However, they caution that nonverbal behaviors in addition to speech disturbances should be taken into account, such as arm and hand movements, hand and finger movements, and the length of time taken by the interviewee to answer the question.

The overall conclusions that can be made about catching liars are: (1) catching liars is not an easy task and (2) specific verbal and nonverbal behaviors must be observed. The interviewer must be very proficient at observing verbal and nonverbal behavior while at the same time conducting an interview that may or may not be focused on detecting deceit.

Diversions

Interviewers are frequently side-tracked and diverted from central interview techniques. With the variety of things that can happen in a conversation, this can easily occur to even the most experienced interviewers. Diversions in an interview all have the common characteristic of having major negative elements. At first glance they may seem the appropriate way to proceed in an interview. The end results are frequently less than what is expected or needed. A review of some of the more common forms may assist the beginning interviewer in avoiding these diversions unless a specific interview contraindicates.

Advice

Interviewers frequently get diverted by feeling compelled to tell the interviewee how to behave, what to do or not to do. It involves the frequently unstated antecedent phrase, "If I were you."

Giving an interviewee advice can be useful, but it is recommended that it be handled with caution (Brammer, 1979; Dillard & Reilly, 1988; D. W. Johnson, 1981). In making a decision as to whether to use advice, the following points may be useful:

- If the recommended course of action backfires, fails, or turns sour, the advice giver assumes some of the responsibility.
- Giving advice frequently deteriorates to the game of "Yes, but." Note the following example:

  > "Have you tried talking to her?"
  > "Yes, but she won't listen."
  > "My advice to you would be to apologize to her."
  > "Well, yes, I've tried that before but she wouldn't listen to that either."

- Giving advice robs the interviewee of making choices, independence, and personal responsibility. "When you give advice, you tell other people what to do with the information and thereby take away their freedom to determine for themselves what is for them the most appropriate course of action" (D.W. Johnson, 1981, p. 24).
- Giving advice may foster dependency on the interviewer.
- Giving advice may foster dominance by the interviewer.
- If the interviewee is genuinely handicapped so that their ability to reason and make rational decisions is impaired, then giving advice or directions would be increasingly more appropriate.
- In the place of giving advice, other forms of information have been used very effectively, such as explaining the interviewee's options, identifying logical consequences, and outlining alternative courses of action.

The central question the interviewer needs to ask is whether the advice fully covers the needs of the situation so that it will be ultimately facilitative with positive outcomes.

Aversive Language

The particular words or phrases that an interviewer uses can be emotionally charged, ambiguous, inaccurate, or overly technical. Therefore, it is important for the interviewer to be precise or to avoid aversive terms that will confuse or sidetrack the interviewee.

Aversive language tends to be one of two kinds: emotionally charged words or aversive labels.

Emotionally Charged Words.   Words that are emotionally charged usually have a built-in bias or unwanted surplus meanings. Words such as "defensive," as in "He was acting very defensive," should be avoided. Another is the word "hostile," as in "She was very hostile in the interview." It is very difficult to use these words without also making a negative or patronizing judgment.

Indicating the interviewee has a problem, as in "What is your problem?", has a tendency to be aversive. Benjamin (1981) supports this: "The word 'problem' is heavy, loaded, almost something to shy away from rather than to confront. I am not suggesting that people do not have problems. They may have them and not know it or wish to face the fact that they exist. But I feel that to use the word 'problem' at the very beginning, out of context and without knowing how the interviewee reacts to the word, will hinder rather than help" (p. 13).

Aversive Labels.   Many aversive labels should be avoided in criminal justice interviews so that confusion, misunderstanding, and negative feelings are not a by-product of the conversation. Consistent with the guidelines and principles offered by Hadley and Brodwin (1988), the following suggestions are offered as concrete ways to avoid aversive labels:

INSTEAD OF	USE
mental patient	is being treated for a mental condition
retarded	is academically challenged
is blind	is visually challenged
neurotic	has some adjustment difficulties
is deaf	is hearing or audio challenged
is crippled	is physically challenged
is a stutterer	is speech challenged
psycho	has exhibited extreme behavior
is emotionally disturbed	has some emotional challenges

In making these conversions, aversive labels can be avoided, as well as the potential for misunderstanding and confusion. The point is that professionals should choose a vocabulary that accurately reflects his or her meaning in terms comprehensible to the client (Schubert, 1971).

Gossip

Excessive use of gossip in an interview involves the interviewee discussing others not present rather than themselves. Sometimes the interview must be conducted this way, but it can evolve into the game "Let's you and I discuss someone who isn't present." In this game, the interviewee diverts focus from themselves by leading the interviewer into the diversion.

The interviewer can minimize gossip and avoid getting diverted by focusing on the interviewee and not the absent person. The following questions illustrate how the conversation can be brought back to the interviewee:

"You've mentioned your son's difficulties with the police, but what are you doing about the situation?"

"You've said your daughter is out of control. I'm wondering how this makes you feel."

Red-Crossing or Band-Aiding

Red-crossing is a method to minimize a crisis or avoid a confrontation. It has also been referred to as super-mothering. Although red-crossing is done in an apparent effort to be helpful, it is actually highly manipulative and patronizing. Probably few interviewers recognize their interventions as motivated by their own inability to confront these emotions. Observe the following examples:

Interviewee: I feel betrayed. I believed him and now I know he lied to me. I guess I'm partly angry because I see myself as being taken advantage of and made a fool of.

Interviewer: Well, we all have felt that way at times. I think everybody is made a fool at one time or another. I remember once when my friend . . .

OR

Interviewee: When my mother shakes her finger at me I get all tight inside.

Interviewer: She doesn't mean anything by it. She's just making a point.

Reassuring, consoling, excusing, and sympathizing may sound nice and be well intentioned, but they are usually not helpful. Unless the interviewer can predict the future and know that "everything will work out okay or for the best," it is not beneficial to be reassuring. It is best to avoid some of the following phrases:

- No one is ever given more than they can handle.
- Don't worry about it.
- It can't be that bad.
- You are in a bad situation, but it will all eventually be okay.

Saying things like these, that sound consoling or reassuring but are impossible to do, is not an effective or constructive interviewing skill (Chang & Scott, 1999).

Mind Raping

Mind raping occurs when an interviewer makes assumptions about what the interviewee is thinking or feeling. Excessive use of interpretation can be a form of mind raping. Examples of mind raping are:

Interviewee: When I'm here for my probation visit I always have a feeling of wanting to get away from this place.

Interviewer: That's because you think I'm judging you . . .

OR

Interviewee: When I'm with you, I feel . . .

Interviewer: Mm-huh, uneasy, uptight, like you would not want to be here, anxious.

Becoming an effective interviewer in criminal justice will depend a great deal on the professional's willingness to examine the diversions of advice, gossip, red-crossing, and mind raping. To become proficient, the professional may need to abandon some old ways of communicating and acquire new ways that are more effective and less problematic.

Summary

Several aspects of interviewing need to be considered before conducting interviews. Interviewers need to be well grounded in a professional approach to conducting interviews. They need to be aware of the theory and research of nonverbal communication. Preliminary considerations need to be made of the difficulty and techniques of detecting deception in an interview. Finally, interviewers should be aware of the communication techniques that can divert an interviewer from conducting effective interviews.

Now that you have completed Chapter 2, you may want to look forward to the activities at the end of the chapter. Exercises 2.1 and 2.2 and the Interview Challenge provide an additional and alternative method for looking at some of the ideas and concepts presented in the chapter.

Study Questions

1. What are some of the steps that can be taken to develop professionalism in interviewing?
2. What are some of the steps you can take to prepare for an interview?
3. Identify three issues concerning videotaping.
4. What are some of the advantages of role playing?
5. Why is unfreezing uncomfortable?
6. What are some common ethical principles of interviewing?
7. How can an interviewer risk ethical conflicts?
8. What are the arguments for and against trickery and deceit in an interview?
9. What is the "slippery slope" of ethics?
10. Why do agencies videotape suspects' statements?
11. What are some of the traditional threats to confidentiality in an interview?
12. What are the types of nonverbal communication?
13. What is norming in the field of detecting deception?
14. What are the problems associated with using the "subconscious" to explain deception.

15. What is "leakage" and what evidence is there for its existence?
16. What are the major forms of lying?
17. Explain the difference between false positives and false negatives.
18. What is the Brokaw Hazard and Othello Error?
19. What is the Stanislavski technique?
20. Explain sample bias in detecting deception.
21. What do we know about detecting deception in an interview?
22. Identify several cautions of relying on nonverbal communication in criminal justice interviews.
23. Explain Grade 5 syndrome.
24. What are some of the liabilities of giving advice?
25. What is "red-crossing"?
26. What are the interrogation techniques that were not successful in obtaining a confession?
27. Identify eight stereotypical beliefs about interrogation.
28. Identify three roles that nonverbal behavior plays in interpersonal communication.
29. What nonverbal behaviors should an interviewer be observing?
30. What is the fundamental attribution error?
31. Identify the types of false confessions.
32. Why is it difficult to detect deception?
33. How can you catch a liar?
34. What is the Nixon Effect?

Exercise 2.1

Aversive and Technical Language

Many words and phrases that criminal justice interviewers use are either too technical or aversive so that they either don't make sense or threaten the interviewee. Effective interviewers communicate in a way that is understandable to the interviewee. The following exercise involves the translation of common criminal justice language into language the interviewee can understand.

Directions: *Rewrite the words and phrases into simpler forms that the average interviewee is likely to understand.*

Technical/Aversive	*Understandable/Nonthreatening*
1. adjudicated	_____
2. adjustment disorder	_____
3. institutionalized	_____
4. subculture of violence	_____
5. socioeconomic standing	_____
6. social roles	_____
7. plea bargain	_____
8. reintegration	_____
9. recidivism	_____
10. occupational history	_____
11. mitigating circumstances	_____
12. lifestyle	_____
13. incorrigible	_____
14. arrest discretion	_____
15. psychopath	_____
16. resistant to authority	_____

(continued)

Technical/Aversive	*Understandable/Nonthreatening*
17. retarded	_____
18. pedophile	_____
19. restitution	_____
20. moral turpitude	_____

Exercise 2.2

Extended Role Plays/Psychodrama

Directions: *After reading about Reginald, who was mentioned on the first page of the first chapter, write what each of the following individuals would say in an interview with Reginald's juvenile probation officer. Remember, he is a 16-year-old youth who has been placed on probation for carrying a handgun and possession of marijuana. He is aggressive and hostile. He is a gang member and dropped out of school a year ago. His parents are divorced, and he lives with his father, who is an alcoholic. His mother has AIDS and is a heroin addict, living on the streets.*

Reginald's father: _____

_____

_____

_____

_____

Reginald's mother: _____

_____

_____

_____

_____

Reginald's father's girlfriend: _____

_____

_____

Reginald's school counselor: _____

_____

_____

Reginald's maternal grandmother: _____

_____

_____

Reginald's fraternal grandmother: _____

_____

_____

Reginald's cousin (a licensed nurse): _____

_____

_____

One of Reginald's victims from whom he stole electronic equipment:

_____

_____

Reginald's drug counselor: _____

_____

_____

Reginald's social worker: _____

_____

_____

Processing Directions: *After students have completed the exercise, role plays should follow with each student rotating into one or more of the various role plays for the individuals working with or related to Reginald.*

Interview Challenge

How would you complete the following encounter? Keep in mind the concerns raised by the questions following the preliminary interview narrative.

You are dispatched to the emergency room of the hospital to interview an elderly African American lady who is a victim of a rape. Respond to the following questions as a male officer and then as a female officer.

1. What skills will you need to get the interview started?

   _____

   _____

   _____

2. What will you want to get accomplished in the interview?

   _____

   _____

   _____

3. How will you divide your interview time between official objectives and personal concerns in the interview (i.e., how closely will you stay with required questions)?

   _____

   _____

   _____

4. What do you anticipate the major segments of the interview to be?

   _____

   _____

   _____

5. What would be the most appropriate interview style to use in this situation?

   _____

   _____

   _____

6. What will be some of the barriers to communication in this interview?

_____

_____

_____

7. What would you need to minimally accomplish in this interview for you to consider the interview successful?

_____

_____

_____

3

Diversity and Special Needs

Learning Objectives

Subject.   Diversity and special needs.

Objectives.   At the end of a period of instruction, the student (trainee) will:
1. Understand the range of the types of diverse interviewees.
2. Understand the types of special needs interviewees.
3. Understand the techniques for interviewing special needs interviewees.
4. Understand the basic concepts in multiculturalism.
5. Understand the techniques for interviewing in multicultural settings.

Learning domain—cognitive.

> The next morning they would be "hunting and confronting"; the put-up or shut-up phase of the investigation, the point where theories and hunches culminated in hard evidence and charges. Or they disintegrated.
>
> Michael Connelly
> *Angels Flight* (2001)

Another consideration that diverts interviewers from what is done in a typical interview is interviewees with special needs, conditions, or characteristics. The vastness and all-encompassing nature of the criminal justice system practically ensures this. A look at any prison population will reveal inmates with the following special needs:

Hearing challenged   Learning challenged
Vision challenged   Emotionally challenged
Speech challenged   Physically challenged

Any one, or a combination, of these challenges can present the need for unique interviewing skills. The same is also true for interviews in probation, parole, juvenile corrections, and the courts. While individuals with special needs have made major gains toward full citizenship through accessibility and antidiscrimination legislation, they are not immune from crime and delinquent behavior.

A Framework for Multiculturalism and Diversity

The first question that needs to be addressed is: What are the characteristics or factors that are included in the broad canopy of multiculturalism and diversity? Hays (1996) has developed a unique model of cultural and diversity characteristics that uses a clever mnemonic device. Her model is the *ADRESSING* model and it consists of:

- Age
- Disability
- Religion
- Ethnicity
- Social status
- Sexual orientation
- Indigenous background
- Natural origin
- Gender

The *ADRESSING* model can give interviewers awareness of the variety of multicultural identities that people have who are interviewed in the criminal justice system. It can also raise awareness of the multiple influences on interviewees. Finally, it can raise awareness of interviewers' biases and the forms of oppression experienced by a diverse population in our society and in the criminal justice system.

It would be beyond the scope of this book to cover each special need in detail, but as an introduction, traumatized, handicapped, very young, adolescent, interviewees under the influence, antisocial, undercover, and culturally diverse interviewees will be discussed. Specialized techniques used with these special needs groups will be left to advanced interviewing training, usually conducted at the agency level.

Traumatized Interviewees

Interviewees can be traumatized by (a) an event occurring prior to the interview such as an assault or witnessing violence or (b) the conditions surrounding the interview, such as the chaos and confusion typical of agencies where interviews take place. In the second case, it is important for the interviewer to recognize that many children and adults can experience a mild state of shock when they enter the chaotic world of computers, telephones, and office confusion, a world the interviewer doesn't give a second thought. Children are particularly susceptible to this strange world. In either case, the following suggestions can help reduce difficulties in the interview:

- Don't rush the interview. Traumatized interviewees may require twice the time to complete an interview.
- Interview children in surroundings that are familiar to them so that they can pay attention to you rather than be distracted by unfamiliar surroundings.

- Recognize the symptoms of posttraumatic stress including:
  - problems with concentration
  - confusion
  - loss of memory
  - disorientation
  - separateness from others
- Be prepared to change the communications medium. You may want to suggest the interviewee write their responses or draw pictures or diagrams.

Finally, many victims are traumatized so they have special needs. Reynolds and Mariani (2002) suggest the following guidelines when interviews are conducted with victims:

- Be professional
- Minimize unnecessary questions
- Avoid blame and criticism
- Listen patiently with compassion
- Offer reassurance and protection
- Recommend professional help and make referrals

Being the victim of a crime can be very stressful and traumatic. If many crimes are going to be solved, the cooperation of a victim may be critical. The interviewer can help to alleviate some of the stress and trauma by using appropriate interviewing skills.

Interviewees with Special Challenges

Hearing, vision, speech, and learning handicaps may pose problems in interviews. Schubert (1971) makes the following points about the various handicaps:

Vision Challenged Interviewee

- Don't shout at the interviewee or treat him "as if he were mentally as well as physically inadequate" (p. 31).
- "Be particularly alert to the points at which the client has misunderstood what is said" (p. 31).

Hearing Challenged Interviewee

- Don't shout at the interviewee.
- "The interviewer should avoid covering his mouth with his hand or murmuring in an undertone" (p. 31).
- Conduct the interview in a reasonably quiet room.
- "Be particularly alert to the points at which the client has misunderstood what is said" (p. 31).

Schubert (1971) further asserts that "all of the physical and mental states mentioned above and all of the handicaps noted may impose a good deal of strain upon the client and may be fatiguing. This should be taken into account in planning the length of the interview" (p. 31). In addition, it is important to not confuse a variety of gestures that may be used by hearing-challenged offenders in the institutional or free world. Three types of gestures are easily confused:

- Street or gang signs that do not have origins in American Sign Language (ASL).
- Signs and gestures used by correctional officers and hearing offenders.
- American Sign Language (ASL) representative of the prison setting (Miller, 2001).

The world of offenders in "street" settings and institutional settings is unique and potentially confusing in an interview. Becoming familiar with these three types of gestures used by hearing-challenged offenders can help reduce some of the misunderstandings.

Finally, Vernon, Raifman, Greenberg, and Monteiro (2001) have identified several critical issues in interviewing deaf suspects.

- Deaf persons are very likely to have not achieved a high level of development in reading and writing.
- Most deaf people have and use sign language but sign language primarily covers everyday words referring to life processes. It does not include special legal terminology or technical subjects.
- Many deaf people will sign legal documents such as Waiver of Miranda Warnings and confessions that they do not understand. They do this because they are accustomed to signing papers they do not understand and they do not want to appear ignorant. They also fear being held in custody and by signing papers, they think they will be released.

Interviewing witnesses or suspects who are hearing challenged creates some unique problems for interviewers because of the need for qualified interpreters, the basic competencies for the interviewee to understand the criminal justice system, and the difficulty in assessing a deaf witness or suspect's communication skills. The risk is that guilty defendants will be released or innocent defendants will be convicted if certain procedures are not followed when interviewing deaf or hearing-challenged citizens.

Interviewees with Special Learning Challenges

Frequently we must interview offenders or witnesses who have special learning needs. In the past, these people were labeled "borderline," "slow learners," or "mildly retarded" but the labels don't provide much help to an interviewer unless they fully explain or prescribe the unique considerations necessary to conduct the interview.

Aiding People in Conflict: A Manual for Law Enforcement (1988), produced by the National Mental Health Association, is a simple-to-follow, practical guide for helping people with special emotional or mental problems. In relation to interviewing the mentally retarded, this manual points out that "If you ask a mentally retarded person snappy questions, one after another, you may notice a peculiar reticence—an almost suspicious reluctance to answer your questions. On the other hand, the person may appear as if he wants to talk, and actually begin to talk, only to fall strangely silent without getting anything said" (p. 39). In addition, the manual goes on to point out the discomfort many retarded people feel in the presence of an officer. Their fear can lead to silence. "If this happens, be patient—tell the retarded person not to rush, to take his time to think over your question, and to answer when he is prepared to do so" (p. 39).

Additional materials, such as the *Mentally Handicapped Offender Project* (Kercher, Shaddock, Barrum, & Shearer, 1978), provide complete training programs for police, probation, and parole officers to work with handicapped offenders. From this and other programs the following general guidelines seem to provide the best information for working with interviewees with learning handicaps:

- Avoid abstractions and intellectualizations. Instead of saying to a young prostitute that she has violated cultural mores and norms, indicate that prostitution can cause pain, sickness, and death. Use concrete examples and reasoning.
- Don't assume the handicapped interviewee is not "street smart." This kind of ability is termed "social adaptation skills" or "social survival skills." Most learning handicapped interviewees have compensated for their lack of school-related skills by being very proficient at survival. They are also adept at hiding their handicap.
- Don't assume the handicapped interviewee can perform simple tasks, such as telling time, making change, and knowing the date or the year.
- Don't rush the interview and check frequently for understanding. Periodically, stop the interview and politely quiz the interviewee for details. A more in-depth discussion of this skill is presented in Chapter 6.
- Be very cautious about giving interviewees reading material. With the illiteracy rate among adults in this country as high as 25–30%, it is very likely the interviewee in criminal justice can't read. Many of those who can't read are also very clever at hiding it. Consequently, court-mandated rules of probation or parole are beyond the reading ability of many offenders.
- Avoid "leading" questions because research has demonstrated that individuals with intelligence levels well below average, such as those who are borderline or mentally handicapped, tend to be markedly more suggestible (Gudjonsson, 1992).

Why is it difficult to identify persons with a mild mental handicap? Gudjonsson (1992, p. 325) identifies the following reasons:

- Some persons with a mental handicap appear superficially to have satisfactory social functioning, which disguises their vulnerabilities.
- Persons with a mental handicap see their vulnerabilities as being private and personal. As a consequence, many would not inform the police of their limitations and they may even deliberately attempt to hide them.
- Many police officers do not seem knowledgeable about the "signs" that should alert them to the possibility that they are interviewing a person with a mental handicap.
- Even when police officers are aware of certain background information that should alert them to a person's vulnerabilities (e.g., hospital admissions, "special schooling"), they may fail to appreciate the importance of that information.

Across the criminal justice system, people fail to identify persons with a mental handicap. It is sometimes very difficult to do, since symptoms may not be obvious. Even the most qualified miss the signs of a handicap. Criminal justice workers from police officers to probation officers need specialized training in the interviewing of special groups such as those with learning handicaps. Unfortunately, most police officers are not formally trained to recognize, access, and treat persons with mental illness. Most of what they know and can do has been acquired through on-the-job experience (Green, 1997). In addition, Green (1997) points out:

- Most police officers feel the solution to the problem of mentally ill persons should be addressed by the mental health system.
- For many mentally ill people, access to the mental health system only occurs when the person is processed by the police and the courts.
- Most police encounters with individuals who have a mental health problem do not involve any violations.
- Police officers have a great deal of discretion in dealing with persons with a serious mental illness.
- Most police officers view arrest as a last resort.
- Police officers should be more aware of departmental policy in the use of discretion with seriously mentally ill individuals.

Fortunately, a few law enforcement agencies do have specialized approaches to respond to a person with a mental illness (PwMI). Some agencies use specialized mental health response teams such as *mobile crisis teams* (MCTs) that are based at the local mental health center. Other agencies use police-based specialized mental health teams such as *Crisis Intervention Teams* (CITs). These specialized approaches can potentially reduce unnecessary arrests and uses of force with minimum departmental disruptions and costs to the department (Hails & Borum, 2003; Reuland & Margolis, 2003).

As Perske (2000) points out, deceiving a person with mental retardation and other developmental disabilities can be tragic. Without appropriate safeguards, adult and juvenile suspects undergoing police interviews may lead to miscarriages of justice. These individuals may have limited understanding of their rights, may be incapable of understanding questions, may provide unreliable information, or may be unduly influenced by short-term gains such as promises of release from custody or the interviewer's suggestions (Medford, Gudjonsson, & Pearse, 2003). In any case, extreme care needs to be exercised when interviews and interrogations are conducted with handicapped suspects so that an innocent person is not arrested and convicted.

Children

With greater criminal justice involvement in family violence and child abuse, children are being increasingly interviewed in the criminal justice system. Hughes (1988) indicates that only certain types of information are best obtained from interviewing children and the validity of information from children is dependent on the child's stage of development (see Hughes, 1988, and Wilson & Powell, 2003, for a comprehensive review).

Geiselman and Padilla (1988) tested the cognitive interview to be discussed in detail in Chapter 9 with children. They wanted to assess the usefulness of the cognitive interview (which has shown significant success with adults) with child witnesses. With some modifications, the cognitive interview improved the overall accuracy of recall in comparison to standard procedures.

The critical concerns in interviewing children where the legal system is involved are:

■ **Confabulation.** This involves making up information and mixing it with the facts. Care must be taken when the interviewer is trying to enhance the child's memory to avoid the inclusion of false information. For example, the terms "pretend" and "imagine" should not be used in order to avoid encouraging the child's fantasy world.

■ **Hypersuggestiblity.** This involves the controversial issue of "putting words in a child's mouth." Children seem to be susceptible to suggestion depending on their age so the interviewer needs to use nonsuggestive techniques and review their interview to eliminate any words or phrases that could be suggestive to the child.

■ **Post-Disclosure Trauma.** A particularly important consideration when interviewing child crime victims, particularly abused children, is the effect the interview will have on the victim. Further traumatization can occur if the child has disclosed information that may lead to a family member being arrested or removed from the family. The child will, because of their disclosure, then have to face guilt, worry, and pain because they have played a direct role (either real or perceived) in adversely affecting family unity or relationships (Williams, 1989).

Increasing communication in an interview with children can be accomplished by altering the medium. Some of the alternate mediums that have successfully been used with children are noted:

- drawings and painting
- games and play activities
- puppets and dolls
- projective pictures and drawings

In each of these methods the interviewer is interested in getting the child to relate what is occurring or to tell a story. From the child's stories and descriptions the interviewer may be able to make inferences about the child's thoughts, feelings, conflicts, or concerns.

The primary decision that needs to be made when interviewing children is whether the interviewer uses therapeutic or forensic techniques (Steinmetz, 1995).

Forensic Interviews

If the way the information is obtained from children is strictly governed, then the interview tends to be a forensic interview. In addition, if details are very important and alternative explanations are explored, the interview is forensic. Finally, if the interviewer has a neutral stand in the interview, the interview leans in the forensic direction.

Therapeutic Interviews

On the other hand, if the way information is obtained is not as important and neither are the details, then the interview is more of a therapeutic type. In addition, if the subjective reality of the child is accepted and it is assumed the child is telling the truth, it tends to be a therapeutic interview. Finally, in a therapeutic interview, the interviewer is an advocate for the child rather than maintaining a neutral position.

"These techniques differ in approach and have traditionally been thought of as incompatible, but one factor they should have in common is empathy" (Steinmetz, 1995). This emphasis on empathy in both therapeutic and forensic interviewing techniques with children is consistent with and reinforces the model of interviewing skills in this text, which is anchored by empathy skills presented in Chapter 5.

Adolescents

Adolescents are frequently involved with the criminal justice system and conducting interviews with them can be quite rewarding but difficult. Much of the information in the previous section on interviewing children also applies to adolescents.

If an interviewer anticipates that they will be interviewing juveniles on a regular basis, they would be well advised to spend additional time studying the developmental characteristics of adolescents so that the interviewer can:

- anticipate age-appropriate behavior in adolescents
- distinguish between what is within the range of expected behavior and serious maladjustment or abnormality
- predict how an adolescent might behave in an interview
- anticipate some of the common problems associated with adolescence that could affect the interview.

Most in-service or pre-service training programs for professionals who work with juveniles, such as detention workers, case workers, and probation officers, cover the developmental characteristics of adolescents. There are also many books that deal with adolescent development.

Offenders

By sheer numbers and frequency, interviews with offenders in the criminal justice system constitute the majority of interviews conducted. As offenders are processed through the courts and corrections, after initial police and legal interviews, they are interviewed many times before they are eventually released.

If the offender commits another crime, the process starts over with interviews conducted at each point in the system. The majority of the interviews conducted in the system occur at the point of institutionalization, such as a prison or correctional facility. Once in custody, the offender is interviewed by a variety of professionals, such as diagnosticians, educators, counselors, attorneys, and parole officers. In most cases, offenders are interviewed to determine whether they are ready to be released to the free world or to a community placement.

Each of these interviews in the system has specific goals and objectives that don't typically require advanced interviewing training beyond the scope of this text. In addition, special types of offenders do not usually require special types of interviewing skills. Two exceptions are worth mentioning because of the unique difficulties they present to the beginning interviewer: sociopaths and sexual aggressors.

Sociopaths

Interviewers may be called on to interview offenders who are guiltless and manipulative—con artists. In the technical literature these offenders are referred to as sociopaths, psychopaths, or as having antisocial personalities.

Considerable controversy exists in research literature as to whether psychopaths or sociopaths actually exist. The position of this interviewing program is that there is enough evidence supporting the existence of guiltless, manipulative criminals to warrant suggestions on working with them in an interview.

Before we look at any specific suggestions, the following points can provide the first stage in the development of techniques for working with interviewees who may have sociopathic tendencies:

- Most inmates and offenders are not sociopaths. The incidence of the phenomenon has been greatly exaggerated and stereotyped in the media. "Crazed, sociopathic killers on the loose" does not characterize most public offenders or inmates of prisons. For example, in a study conducted by Shearer and Moore (1978), it was found, in a sample of 441 probated felons, that no significant differences existed between probated felons and nonfelon college students on manipulative tendencies. It was suggested in this study that observed manipulative behaviors in probated felons were a product of the situation in probation contacts rather than personality factors.
- Most sociopaths are not criminals or prisoners. Successful businessmen or politicians may have sociopathic tendencies. The reasons that cause the differences between free-world and criminal sociopaths are largely unknown.
- There appears to be very little relationship between intelligence and manipulative tendencies (Christie & Geis, 1970). Consequently, some con artists are quite bright, clever, and intelligent while others, being just as determined to be guiltless and manipulative, are not the least bit clever in their scams and schemes. Theoretically, the most intelligent sociopaths go undetected because they are clever enough to avoid apprehension. On the other hand, the less capable sociopaths in interviews evoke reactions from others ranging from amusement to disgust.

With these guidelines in mind, the following suggestions will help the beginning interviewer prepare for a possible encounter with a sociopathic interviewee.

- Focus on personal responsibility by making *choices*. Create a situation in the interview that places responsibility on the interviewee for making conscious choices (Kierulff, 1988).
- Be wary and firm and offer the possibility of acceptance. "We must not allow ourselves to be seen as fools; we must not allow ourselves to be conned" (Kierulff, 1988).
- Confront errors in the interviewee's thinking. Without a firm stand, being courteous and friendly may be inadequate for avoiding manipulation (Kierulff, 1988).
- Avoid attempts that the interviewee makes to gain sympathy through the PDLM—"poor, dear, little me"—excuse (Kierulff, 1988).
- Watch for *malignant pseudo identification*. It is the process by which the psychopath consciously or unconsciously simulates a certain behavior to increase the interviewer's identification with the individual, thus increasing the interviewer's vulnera-

bility to exploitation. The more impressed the interviewer is with their professional skills and abilities, the more likely the psychopath is to exploit this narcissism. The psychopath will manipulate the interviewer by (a) complimenting the professional competency or knowledge of the interviewer or (b) simulating the affects and mannerisms of the interviewer. This can lead the interviewer to assume a level of identification and bonding that does not exist, which can lead to the interviewer being conned, manipulated, or expoited (Meloy, 1992).

- Personal responsibility for behavior can be facilitated in an interview by *redirecting, reframing,* and *reversals.*

  - *Redirecting* can be used to get the offender to focus attention on the task at hand when he or she is not focused, is argumentative, or is not focusing on immediate realities.
  - *Reframing* can be used to convey the true meaning of what the offender has said when he or she tends to distort the true meaning of a statement.
  - *Reversals* can be used when the offender is avoiding personal responsibility. The interviewers can reflect back to the offender in a manner that the offender assumes responsibility. This is particularly useful when the offender is blaming others for his or her misfortune (Elliott, 2002).

Speaking directly about the skill of *reframing,* Haney and Leibsohn (1999) indicate that the skill is designed to give another view on experiences, thoughts, behaviors, or the current situation. The idea is to offer a different viewpoint. Hopefully, with offenders, the goal is to offer a viewpoint that supports personal responsibility. Reframing lead-ins that can be used are:

- Another way of looking at this is _____
- The way I see what you are saying is _____
- Putting your behavior into a different context _____
- Looking at your experiences from a different viewpoint would look something like _____

The skills that follow in this training program are designed to be consistent with these suggestions. The skills of empathy (as opposed to sympathy), confrontation, and assertion will help the interviewer in encounters with sociopathic interviewees. "Behold I send you forth as sheep in the midst of wolves: be ye therefore wary as serpents and harmless as doves" (Matthew 10:16).

Sexual Aggressors

Offenders who commit sexually aggressive acts are becoming an increasing proportion of the interviews conducted in the nation's courts, probation departments, prisons, and parole agencies. Interviews with sexual aggressors are particularly difficult to conduct and require advanced interviewing skills that are beyond the scope of this text. However, McGrath (1990) has outlined some practical interviewing strategies for interviewing sexual aggressors in clinical assessments that could be helpful to beginning interviewers. For example, beginning interviewers need to note the following points, which have been extracted from McGrath's recommendations:

- Sexual aggressors have a marked propensity to lie about, deny, and minimize information concerning their deviant sexual behavior. Beginning interviewers are not likely to encounter an offender who is completely honest about his sex offense. Most sex offenses evoke extreme condemnation from society and it takes deeply entrenched defenses for the offender to guard against the threat of exposure.
- Most sexual aggressors began their deviant sexual behavior as teenagers.
- Most sexual offenders engage in a variety of deviant sexual behaviors.

Interviewing in the area of human sexuality is a difficult task that requires advanced skills and knowledge. The skills presented in this text are consistent with most of McGrath's recommendations for interviewing sexual aggressors, but beginning interviewers would need advanced skills to conduct in-depth assessments or evaluations with this type of offender.

Zones of Questioning

Figure 3.1 presents a visual representation of three primary zones of questioning for interviewing offenders. The *X-Zone* represents an area for potential questions where self-disclosure is likely to be min-

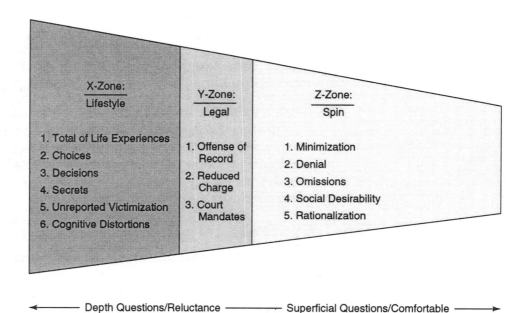

Figure 3.1 Interviewing Offenders: Zones of Questioning and Self-Disclosure

imal and the offender is likely to be reluctant to discuss or answer questions in this area. This reluctance is a product of painful or difficult life experiences, choices, and decisions, such as *seemingly unimportant decisions* (SUDs) that have turned out to be very important. There may also be other victims that have gone undisclosed for some time. Questions directed at this zone would have to be constructed to probe into these areas that, taken as a whole, represent the person's total life experience. This zone is probably a more accurate picture of the complex forces that led to contact with the criminal justice system.

The *Y-Zone* represents a more restricted area for questioning the offender. This zone is a legal zone containing the offense record or history, reduced charges, and specific court mandates, such as probation or parole restrictions. Most of the information in this zone can be matched to official records. Most offenders are likely to be mildly reluctant to discuss these areas, unless the questioning takes place in a public forum. They know that officials know about the particulars in the offender's criminal history reports.

The *Z-Zone* represents a potential area of questioning and self-disclosure where the offender has utilized tactics to defend against the pain and reality of the material in the previous two zones. The result is that a "spin" or distortion emerges if the questioning is superficial by the interviewer. The *Z-Zone* contains denials, omissions, rationalizations, and other attempts to create a socially desirable impression during the interview. Most offenders have a high comfort level in relating information about themselves when questions are asked. If the questions asked are superficial, the information received is likely to be highly unreliable and uncorrelated to the information in the *X-Zone.*

The zones of questioning only represent a conceptual model so some of the zones may overlap, may play a greater role, or may alternate in the focus of the questioning. In any case, appreciation of the three zones can give interviewers a greater awareness of how and where to direct questions and how much self-disclosure to expect from interviewees.

Confidential Informants

One of the types of interviews that is unique to criminal justice, specifically criminal investigation, is the interviewing of confidential informants. An informant is someone with access to information about a crime and a willingness to provide the information about a crime and a willingness to provide the information to an investigator. Whether in an interview room or on the street, an interview takes place and the goal is always the same. The interviewer wants to learn what the informant knows and the validity of the information.

The unique features of the interviewing of confidential informants are that there is no need for hostile questioning, rapport-building, and cooperation is expected. Madinger (2000) has identified several standard interviewing procedures for interviewing informants that might not be used in interrogation of suspects or questioning of victims:

- Ask open-ended questions.
- Move from the general to the specific.
- Make the informant commit to how they know the information.
- Verify the answers against known information or previous statements.
- Train the informant to provide the information in a preferred form, to be more observant, or to focus on specific interests.
- Deal effectively with discrepancies.
- Use the power of association to improve memory.
- Be respectful of a person who is taking large risks.

In interviews with confidential informants, the information is communicated to the officer by the informant. It is then communicated to law enforcement supervisors and the prosecutor, and ultimately to a jury. The importance of effective interviewing skills can make this transfer of information more effective and reliable.

Addicted Offenders

Many offenders in the criminal justice system are involved in heavy alcohol and drug use. In addition, many witnesses to a crime may have been intoxicated at the time they witnessed a crime or at the time of information acquisition.

Based on various studies that have been conducted investigating the adverse effects of drugs on memory, the following few results have emerged:

- Moderate quantities of alcohol impair the process of forming new memories.
- Marijuana impairs the process of forming new memories and short-term retention may also be impaired.
- Information retrieval is facilitated when witnesses are interviewed very soon after the event.
- Information retrieval is facilitated even when mildly intoxicated witnesses are interviewed very soon after the event (Gudjonsson, 1989).

Overall, there is very little research available on the effects of moderate drug use on the memory of offenders or witnesses to a crime. Ample evidence does exist concerning the chronic ingestion of drugs and the effect on mental processes. Extensive psychoactive substance abuse leads to cognitive impairments including decreased speed and efficiency of information processing, increased distractibility, and difficulties with problem solving (Fals-Stewart, 1993). These impairments may result in the interviewee missing much of what transpires in an interview or the interviewee being very difficult to interview because of irritability, impulsiveness, and lack of self-control. As a result, it may be difficult for an interviewer to conduct an effective interview with chronic substance abusers.

Interviewees Under the Influence (IUI)

Drugs, both legal and illegal, are very much a part of the lifestyle of many individuals involved with the criminal justice system. Occasionally, interviewers in criminal justice encounter an interviewee under the influence or withdrawing from either legal or illegal drugs, influencing the outcome of the interview.

In criminal justice interviews, the person being interviewed may be under the influence of drugs or alcohol in a variety of ways, which *may* affect the interviewee's behavior in an interview. The interviewer may or may not be able to detect the effects of the substance, but an awareness of the different alcohol and drug disorders may be helpful in an interviewing situation. These disorders are:

> **Intoxication.** A state of being under the influence of alcohol or other drugs so that thoughts, feelings, and/or behaviors are affected.
>
> **Dependence.** A recurrent or ongoing need to use alcohol or other drugs. This includes both psychological and/or physical dependence.
>
> **Withdrawal.** The physical and psychological effects that occur when a drug- or alcohol-dependent individual discontinues use (Fisher & Harrison, 2000). These effects can range from sweating, tremors, and anxiety to seizures, hallucinations, and delirium (Jung, 2001).

In any case, interviewers need to be alert to either historical or behavioral indicators that the interviewee's behavior is affected by one of these conditions. Considering the high correlation between crime and substance abuse in criminal justice populations, it is probably prudent to err on the conservative side by assuming the interviewee is affected, in some fashion, by alcohol or drugs. At the same time, interviewers should hope that alcohol or drug use has not achieved the level where it has contributed to unacceptable or unlawful behavior.

Illegal Drugs

Criminal suspects, witnesses, and victims may appear in an interview while under the influence of illegal drugs. In these cases, it is recommended that the interview be postponed or rescheduled until the interviewee is not significantly under the influence of illegal drugs.

Alcohol

In addition, suspects, witnesses, and victims may appear for an interview while intoxicated by alcohol. The previous recommendation fits this case also.

Prescription Drugs

Many interviewees in criminal justice may be taking prescription drugs for a variety of mental and physical conditions such as anxiety or depression. If the person's medication is properly regulated, there should not be any need for serious concern as to the effect the medication might have on an interview. On the other hand, if either the interviewee's behavior, medical history, or self-disclosure indicates a difficulty in this area, the interviewer would be advised to wait to conduct the interview at a later date when the medication has stabilized the person. Prescription medications are quite common and they usually will not affect an interview. If a probationer, for example, has too much or too little of a medication, it can affect their behavior and an interview is not recommended until their medication has been properly adjusted by a supervising physician.

Polydrug Abuse

Many drugs are frequently used in combination with other drugs. Alcohol is frequently consumed in conjunction with marijuana, cocaine, amphetamines, and heroin. Cocaine is often combined with heroin or methamphetamines (Jung, 2001). In addition, individuals also mix illicit drugs or legal drugs, such as alcohol, with legal prescription drugs. These "pharmacological cocktails" can also affect the behavior of an interviewer in a criminal justice setting.

Illegal Prescriptions

The illegal use of pain medications and other prescription drugs is on the rise in the United States. Consequently, this constitutes another interviewing consideration that may influence the responses of a person being interviewed.

Research Findings

Several studies have been conducted to investigate the effects of alcohol and drugs on the validity of answers provided in an interview. Some of the most relevant findings are:

- Thirty-six percent of a group of inmates indicated they were under the influence of alcohol or drugs during the police interview.
- Thirty-nine percent of the inmates indicated they were experiencing withdrawal symptoms during the police interview.
- Withdrawal symptoms from opiates do not impair memory recall.
- Alcohol intoxication may reduce the level of suggestibility in a suspect under interrogation.

- Alcohol withdrawal significantly impairs the ability of a suspect to cope with the pressure of an interrogation (Gudjonsson, 2003).
- In addition, offenders tend to be deceptive in their self-reports of substance abuse (Richards & Pai, 2003).

The research on the effects of intoxication and withdrawal is not complete. For example, the effects of prescription drugs have not been studied and the effects of marijuana on eyewitness memory are inconclusive (Yuille, Tollestrup, Marxsen, & Herve, 1998). Until further research results are available, the conclusions concerning the drug, alcohol, and interviewing relationships should remain tentative.

Multicultural Interviewing

The cultural diversification of the United States is clearly reflected in all phases of the criminal justice system. This multicultural movement is challenging all professionals who conduct interviews to consider the cultural perspectives of the many diverse groups in our society. Consequently, the traditionally accepted policies and practices of criminal justice interviews are giving way to interviewing techniques and strategies that are consistent with the life experiences and cultural values of a diverse population of individuals who pass through the criminal justice system.

Conducting interviews from a multicultural perspective is not easy. Evidence continues to accumulate indicating that self-disclosure in an interview may be incompatible with cultural values of Asian Americans, Mexican Americans, and American Indians. Economically disadvantaged, educationally deprived, and developmentally disabled may not be oriented toward "sitting down and talking" in an interview.

Basic Concepts in Multiculturalism

Several basic concepts need to be understood before interviewing diverse populations in the criminal justice system.

- **Race.** This is a category of groups of people based on genetic traits that differentiate physical characteristics. Hair type, skin color, and bone structure would be some of these traits.
- **Ethnicity.** This term refers to a person's family heritage. It is common in the United States for families to have ethnic mixtures in individual families. For example, many families have an ethnic mixture of Mexican or Native American heritage and mixtures of several European groups.
- **Culture.** This is the learned and shared behavior of a certain people together that is learned, transmitted socially, and shared by whole or parts of the population.

■ **Nationality.** This is the country of a person's citizenship, either native born or naturalized.

■ **Cultural Diversity/Multiculturalism.** This term refers to the ways that cultures differ.

■ **Diversity.** All the ways in which people are different is termed diversity. This includes gender and cultural differences; consequently, diversity is a broader category than multiculturalism.

■ **Diversity/Multicultural Competencies.** This term refers to the awareness, knowledge, and skills needed to interview and communicate with individuals from a variety of cultural backgrounds and gender preferences (Tarver, Walker, & Wallace, 2002). Several multicultural training curricula and manuals have been developed for increasing multicultural competencies. Materials developed by Arnoff (1999) for psychologists, Pederson (2000) and Kim and Lyons (2003) for counselors, King (2003), King and Shearer (2004), and Shearer and King (2004) for probation officers, Wong (2003) for health sciences workers, and Palmiotto, Birzer, and Unnithan (2000) and Tarver and Colleagues (2002) for law enforcement/criminal justice are available for diversity or multicultural competency training. Finally, training in interpersonal skills for working with diverse populations is part of the required training for law enforcement officers in several states. Effective communication is a critical element of policing in a multicultural society (Wright, 2000).

■ **Cultural Empathy.** The culturally empathic interviewer retains his or her separate cultural identity and simultaneously is aware of and accepts the cultural values and beliefs of the interviewee (Chung & Bemak, 2002). This interviewing skill has the potential of contributing to the communication process when interviewing across cultures.

Interviewing and Worldview Dimensions

There are many ways to view diversity and multiculturalism, but the view that has intrigued social scientists for several centuries is the one of individualism and collectivism (Garcia, Winston, Borzuchowska, & Cartwright, 2003; Graham & Miller, 1995; Pederson & Ivey, 1993; Williams, 2003). While it would be very difficult, and beyond the scope of most interviews, to determine either the personality type or details about the person's cultural tendencies, it may be of value to assess his or her interactive preference style. How would an interviewer know? To begin, about three-fourths of the cultures of the world are collectivistic and the primary individualistic cultures are Northern European and the United States. This would be the first clue, but it would have to be considered in the context of a diverse United States culture that is a blending of many world cultures. Other clues could be detected by noticing some of the following differences:

INDIVIDUALISTIC (LOW CONTEXT)	**COLLECTIVISTIC (HIGH CONTEXT)**
assertive	indirect
independent	affiliated
competitive	team oriented
impatient	respectful
time conscious	strong community
results oriented	emotions important
strong willed	good listener

The primary interviewing consideration is that interviewers who have profiles of high or low context will be able to communicate well with interviewees with similar characteristics but not with interviewees with different worldviews. The challenge of learning interviewing skills that apply to multicultural (high or low context) interviewees is to become proficient at interviewing in all diverse cultural and gender interview situations. How difficult is this task? Research by Pekerti and Thomas (2003) provides some clues to the answer to this question and some implications of interviewing in intercultural situations. They explored, for example, whether an interviewer should adapt their communication style (low context vs. high context) to that of the other culture. They identified the two styles of communication consistent with the way they were explained in the previous discussion, but with an emphasis on communication:

LOW CONTEXT	**HIGH CONTEXT**
explicit	inexplicit
unambiguous	ambiguous
task oriented	implicit
say what you mean	harmony oriented
words convey the message	words convey only part of the message

Their results are worthy of note and they could be helpful to interviewers working in intercultural situations. Specifically, they found:

- Individuals faced with communicating across cultures can predict the probable communication behavior of others based on whether the communication is high context or low context. A culturally based style of communication emerges in communication situations.
- Individuals are likely to exaggerate their cultural style, not adapt, in intercultural situations.
- A second language is even more demanding and time consuming in communication situations.
- Training individuals in the communication style of others, or training them to adapt their style, may be counterproductive. This is because the new behavioral style may be seen as either unnatural or insincere.

The conclusion to be made based on these results is that it is very difficult to overcome barriers across cultures by adapting a communication style. Consequently, the course of action may be to maintain proficiency in your cultural style while attempting to understand other cultural styles.

A critical understanding of several barriers to effective communication can assist an interviewer in conducting more effective interviews in multicultural settings.

Social Distance

In an interview, social distance is the degree that the interviewer is willing to associate with the interviewee. It represents a comfort level in the relationship. On a primary level, it represents a specific contact level in an interview when an offender is involved since the particular offense in question may be particularly abhorrent or repulsive to the interviewer. On a secondary level, it represents a general comfort level because of different cultural values, beliefs, realities, and social roles. For example, the interviewer may feel very uncomfortable in interviewing an offender convicted of incest because the offense is very disgusting to them. In addition, the offender may be a member of a specific cultural group, which may also make communication difficult.

Sapir-Whorf Hypothesis

This is the theory that, to a certain extent, language determines a culture's definition of reality (Whorf, 1956). This means that the criminal justice interviewer needs to be aware that the language used in an interview may communicate a different cultural reality to the interviewee. The language used may reflect the interviewer's values and beliefs, particularly those regarding law and social conformity.

Ethnocentrism

The belief in the natural superiority of one's own culture is known as ethnocentrism. In a broader sense, it applies to one's cultural, racial, or ethnic group. In whatever form it appears, ethnocentrism limits our ability to see and accept the reality and value of interviewees from other cultural groups. This limitation can seriously limit the accuracy of the interviewer's perceptions in an interview if they discount much of the interviewee's culture as inferior and not worth listening to (Barone & Switzer, 1995).

Stereotyping

An interviewer in criminal justice might also have a tendency to judge all people in a given culture on the basis of one member or a few members. This is referred to as "stereotyping," which reduces the likelihood an interviewee is going to be assessed on their particular qualities. If the interviewee is perceived inaccurately, then the effectiveness of the communication is bound to be affected (Barone & Switzer, 1995).

Interviewers must be able to shift their interviewing strategies to meet not just the communication abilities of interviewees but also the cultural factors that influence communication in an interview. Failure to incorporate the cultural perspective of the interviewee may lead to erroneous information, judgments, decisions, and conclusions. For example, a probation officer may get very frustrated with a probationer who is not verbally, emotionally, or behaviorally expressive. Yet, valuing expressiveness, often a key to successful interviews, can clash with the cultural values or behaviors of various racial and ethnic minorities.

Clearly, criminal justice interviewers have to use culturally appropriate interviewing strategies. This involves developing individual interviewing skills. It also involves using intrinsic interviewing approaches of culturally diverse groups (Sue, 1992).

Specifically, Barone and Switzer (1995) suggest four steps the interviewer can take to assume that we are conducting an interview in an open and not distant, stereotypical or ethnocentric manner.

- Define the interview. Be very clear about the purpose and needs of the interview. Have a clear set of expectations.
- Learn the culture of the person being interviewed. If you know in advance the culture of the person being interviewed, find out the cultural values, traditions, customs, and practices.
- Seek clarification of meanings. The use of paraphrasing, perception checking, and tactful probing questions are particularly essential when the shared cultural experiences of the interviewer and interviewee are limited.
- Utilize multiple assessments. Bias in an interview can be minimized by using different interviewers who share their observations and multiple contacts with the same interviewee in order to expand your knowledge about the interviewee (Barone & Switzer, 1995).

Language and Cultural Differences

Communicating in an unfamiliar language or with a person from a different culture can be a barrier. Language and cultural symbols can be very different when we are trying to communicate with people from a diverse cultural background. Bucher (2004) indicates that poor listening skills make it much harder to communicate across cultural boundaries. Active listening helps to overcome misunderstandings. In addition, Bucher identifies eleven strategies for communicating inclusively:

1. Address people the way they want to be addressed.
2. Keep an open mind.
3. Listen actively.
4. Check understanding.
5. Do some research on unfamiliar cultural backgrounds.
6. Think through what you are going to say before you say it.
7. Avoid slang words and phrases.
8. Do not share ethnic jokes.
9. Use a variety of styles of communication.

10. Do not assume that you should ignore differences.
11. Be conscious of how fast you are talking.

By using these techniques, the interviewer can minimize some of the distortions and biases from their observations. There is not any way to eliminate all of these biases and distortions created by ethnocentrism and stereotyping, but these specific steps can provide the professional edge that will go a long way to improve communication in the interview.

Hot Buttons

Interviewing in a diverse society that is reflected by the diversity in the criminal justice system requires that interviewers recognize there is language that is considered very inflammatory. These are referred to as "hot buttons," and they represent words and phrases that trigger negative reactions from people who view the language as insulting and derogatory (Bucher, 2004). Setting political correctness aside, interviewers need to be particularly sensitive to these hot button issues so that an interview is not jeopardized by needlessly creating mistrust and hostility in the interview. Typically, these hot buttons focus on issues of gender, race, ethnicity, culture, or political affiliation. In addition to being sensitive to these issues, interviewers need to be vigilant to changes in these issues, because in a rapidly changing national and international scene, the issues change quickly.

Multiculturalism and Emotions

A very important consideration for interviewing across cultures is the universality of emotions. In other words, what is the evidence for answers to the following questions: Are there universal emotions? Are facial expressions of emotion universal? Some intriguing research findings give interviewers clues to the answers to these questions.

■ The emotions of anger, fear, sadness, agony, surprise, disgust, and enjoyment are universal (Ekman, 2003).
■ Facial expressions relate to the experience of emotion (Keltner et al., 2003).
■ Individuals from different cultures vary in the inferences they draw from facial expressions of emotion (Keltner & Ekman, 2000).
■ Very different events elicit similar facial expressions of emotion. One cultural group may show negative emotions to a situation that another shows positive emotions (Keltner & Ekman, 2000).
■ Different cultures vary little in their facial expressions of emotion. The response time, range, and meaning of the expressions may vary, but the actual facial expressions are quite similar (Keltner & Ekman, 2000).

The implications of these findings are that interviewers can rely on facial expressions to determine emotions and facial expressions of emotion are somewhat consistent across cultural groups. Consequently, focusing on facial expressions in an interview should be an important interviewing task for multicultural competency.

Diversity and Deception

In a discussion of interviewing individuals with diverse characteristics or various cultural affiliations, the question of detecting deception in these diverse groups has been studied. Although there is not much information on the subject of deception in diverse groups of people, the research conducted and summarized by Vrij (2000) is worthy of noting at this point:

- Women are superior to men in interpreting nonverbal messages, but they are not better than men at detecting lies.
- It is not easier to detect lies in friends and lovers than in strangers.
- It is more difficult to detect lies when the liar and lie detector do not share the same ethnic background.
- Cross-cultural nonverbal communication errors do occur during cross-cultural police interviews.
- Nonverbal behavioral patterns that are typical of black people are interpreted by white observers as signs of deception.
- Even though some children are skilled in telling lies, lying is a skill that generally improves with age.

Detecting deception from behavioral cues is not a simple task. Apparently, interviewing across cultures, with various age and gender types, makes the task more difficult.

Multicultural Interviewing Skills

After considering the basic concepts and barriers associated with multicultural communicating, the question remains as to what the critical skills are for multicultural interviewing. Pederson and Ivey (1993) developed a practical guide to skill development that included the following skills:

- *Attending skills*
- Paraphrasing, *summarizing,* and encouraging
- *Question asking*
- *Reflecting feelings and meaning*
- *Confrontation* and mediation
- Focusing, directing, and interpreting

The interviewing skills presented in the following chapters are consistent with the italicized skills in the above list. Consequently, the basic skills model contains the appropriate skills for multicultural interviewing competency. When the basic skills model is combined with an awareness of biases, assumptions, behaviors, values, and stereotypes, effective communication in law enforcement and corrections can be increased (Coderoni, 2002; Sanders, 2003).

Finally, the foundation for effective communication is active listening and human relations training. This foundation is the primary component of many community-oriented policing and corrections training programs. The principle goal of these programs is positive public contact (Tarver et al., 2002).

Summary

Interviewers are very likely to be conducting interviews with a very diverse population of individuals. This diversity ranges from individuals with special challenges to individuals representing several different racial, ethnic, or cultural groups. Diversity or multicultural training is a vital component of most training programs in criminal justice. The foundation for these training programs is effective communication and human relations.

Now that you have completed Chapter 3, you may want to look forward to the activities at the end of this chapter. Exercise 3.1 and the Interview Challenge are provided for additional learning activities.

Study Questions

1. Explain the diversity characteristics identified by the *ADRESSING* model.
2. What are the three types of gestures easily confused when interviewing hearing challenged individuals?
3. Why is it difficult to identify persons with a mild mental handicap?
4. What is confabulation?
5. How can you prepare to interview manipulative interviewees?
6. What are some of the effects of drugs on memory?
7. Explain the Sapir-Whorf hypothesis.
8. What are the steps an interviewer can take to conduct an interview in an unstereotypical or ethnocentric manner?
9. What is the difference between forensic and therapeutic interviews with children?
10. What is malignant pseudo identification?
11. Explain the material likely to be discussed in the X-, Y-, and Z-Zones of questioning.
12. What are SUDs?
13. What are the unique features of interviewing confidential informants?
14. What are the different disorders of alcohol or drug abuse that may affect an interview situation?
15. Distinguish between race, ethnicity, and culture.
16. What is cultural empathy?
17. Explain the difference between individualistic and collectivistic worldviews.
18. Identify several barriers to conducting effective interviews in multicultural settings.
19. What are hot buttons?
20. What are the universal emotions?
21. What do we know about diversity and deception?
22. Identify several strategies for communicating inclusively.

Exercise 3.1

Multicultural Interviewing Competency and Knowledge Inventory (MICKI)

Directions: *Respond to the following statements as to whether you agree, are not sure, or disagree with the statement by circling the corresponding number. Indicate how the statement applies to you.*

<u>0</u>	<u>1</u>	<u>2</u>
Agree	Not Sure	Disagree

1. I know the communication skills necessary to use if an interviewee gets too close to me or "in my face."

    0   1   2

2. It would make me uncomfortable if an interviewee took a long time to answer my questions.

    0   1   2

3. It would be disrespectful to me if an interviewee didn't maintain direct eye contact during the interview.

    0   1   2

4. I assume in an interview that all people should deal with problems directly.

    0   1   2

5. When people get into trouble with the law, they should expect to have to talk with strangers about private matters.

    0   1   2

6. When I interview individuals, I expect them to not waste my time with informal visiting and "small talk."

    0   1   2

7. I would be frustrated in an interview if a person said "yes" to me and they really meant "no."

    0   1   2

8. I would not be pleased if an interviewee verbally challenged me in an interview.

    0   1   2

9. If I am interviewing an individual, I wouldn't like the prospect of having to get the person's family involved if a problem arose.

    0   1   2

10. I would find it very difficult to interview individuals who believe that personal change primarily happens by chance.

0   1   2

11. Missing scheduled interviews or arriving late for an interview by another person would be very frustrating for me.

0   1   2

12. I don't worry a lot about embarrassing an individual in an interview.

0   1   2

13. I would rely on "common sense" if I was trying to communicate with a person from a different cultural background.

0   1   2

14. I would get impatient in an interview with a person who had an obvious accent or dialect.

0   1   2

15. It would be difficult for me to interview people who are having personal problems if I couldn't say to them what I think they need to do to solve a problem.

0   1   2

16. I have little patience when I am working with an interviewee who has no interest in self-improvement.

0   1   2

17. Using animated hand or arm gestures in an interview would not be my style of interviewing.

0   1   2

18. A difficult interview for me would be one where the interviewee wandered off the topic too much.

0   1   2

Interview Challenge

How would you complete the following encounter? Keep in mind the concerns raised by the questions following the preliminary interview narrative.

You are a parole officer with the state. Your parolee is a man in his late twenties who has recently been released from state prison and has been looking for a job. He says: "The foreman told me I had a job in construction last week. I showed up for work today at 8:00 and his supervisor told me I didn't have the job. He saw I had a record. Nobody will give you a chance once they see you have a record. I was qualified for that job too."

1. What skills will you need to get the interview started?

   _____

   _____

   _____

2. What will you want to get accomplished in the interview?

   _____

   _____

   _____

3. How will you divide your interview time between official objectives and personal concerns in the interview (i.e., how closely will you stay with required questions)?

   _____

   _____

   _____

4. What do you anticipate the major segments of the interview to be?

   _____

   _____

   _____

5. What would be the most appropriate interview style to use in this situation?

_____

_____

_____

6. What will be some of the barriers to communication in this interview?

_____

_____

_____

7. What would you need to minimally accomplish in this interview for you to consider the interview successful?

_____

_____

_____

4

The Basic Skills Model

Learning Objectives

Subject. The Basic Skills Model

Objectives. After a period of instruction, the student (trainee) will:
1. Identify and explain the components of the model.
2. Identify support for the model.
3. Identify the primary theories of communication.
4. Identify the differences between basic and specialized interviewing skills.
5. Identify the primary interviewing skills.

Learning domain—cognitive.

> I always try to teach the rookies to keep their mouths shut and learn to listen. They usually give more information than they get when they're interrogating somebody.
>
> Joseph Wambaugh
> *The Blue Knight* (1972)

The criminal justice system in this country is one of the most all-encompassing and complex collections of service delivery agencies in the history of mankind. Training and educating professionals to work in this system has become a major task. The particular training model in this text is constructed from a well-established tradition of interpersonal skills acquisition in the behavioral sciences and integrated with the general needs of professionals who interview in the various components of the criminal justice system: law enforcement, the courts, and corrections. By putting the two together, criminal justice professionals can feel confident that their interviewing training is well proven and tested. On the other hand, working with people in criminal justice is not exactly like other social or educational systems in our society; modifications have been made in the training to more closely meet the needs of interviewers in criminal justice.

115

Introduction to the Basic Skills Model

In discussing the basic skills model it is helpful to look at the need for, components of, and assumptions of a basic skills model.

Support for a Skills Model

Why do we need a model of communication in interviewing? The answer is so that we know where we are going and whether what we are doing will get us there. A model for an interviewer is like a road map for a driver. The driver needs to know where they are going and whether their vehicle will get them there.

In addition, a model holds our technique up for public inspection so that it can be tested, critiqued, and refined. In this way we can be more proficient in the future by improving the model or discarding all or parts of the model.

The following questions are frequently asked about communication in interviewing training:

Question: Why can't we just use common sense in communicating with people?

Answer: We can, and many times we do, but we have to be very careful with common sense because much of it isn't common to many people. An example is the proverb "look before you leap," which makes common sense but so does "he who hesitates is lost."

Question: I've been communicating for years. Does this mean that I've been doing it wrong for all these years?

Answer: No. You've probably been doing very well and you have your own personal theory about communication, but usually we are not aware of what we are doing because we haven't looked at it very closely. This training allows you to modify what you have been doing, expand your capabilities, and retain what you've been doing well.

Question: Are police officers, probation officers, and correctional officers who haven't had any formal interviewing training completely ineffective?

Answer: No. Most experienced officers in these areas do very well, but they also recognize the need for interviewing training and thrive on in-service interviewing programs to refine their skills. We are not born with the innate ability to conduct interviews (Yeschke, 2003).

Components of the Model

The primary components of the interviewing skills model are:

UNDERSTANDING–PREDICTION–ACTION

These three components and their relationship are as follows:

■ *Understanding.* The interviewer accurately identifies the facts, feelings, experiences, behaviors, and intentions of the interviewee. This complete and accurate accumulation of information leads to:

■ *Prediction.* The interviewer makes an estimate or speculation as to the most appropriate course of action to be taken during or concluding the interview. This prediction may involve:

- what the interviewer will do next
- what the interviewee will do next
- what the interviewer and interviewee have agreed to do
- what others are likely to do next
- a decision about the interviewee

This prediction leads to:

■ *Action.* The interviewer initiates a course of action that reflects accurate understanding and realistic predictions. Only when the action is based on the two previous components will the action be most effective or successful.

Assumptions of a Skills-Based Model

The skills-based model is supported by several critical assumptions that validate the process of skill acquisition.

■ *Interpersonal Skills.* The approach of this training program assumes that effective communication is facilitated between two people when the interviewer is skilled in interpersonal communication. "The interviewee will be more open, expressive, and receptive to questions if the officer first or concurrently establishes a base of high interpersonal functioning" (Parker et al., 1989).

■ *Behavior.* The approach assumes a focus on interviewee behavior as opposed to motivation or causation for behavior. The interviewer focuses on the feelings and thoughts that lead to specific behaviors. The interviewer is also concerned with action and what the interviewee is doing as opposed to why they are doing it. Finally, the interviewer attends to the antecedents and consequences of behavior—what happened before the behavior and what is likely to happen after the behavior.

■ *Personal Responsibility.* The approach assumes a focus on personal responsibility, both interviewer and interviewee. This means:

- The interviewer is responsible for their behavior in the interview so that they don't violate the interviewees wealth and dignity, that is, treat them as an object rather than a person.
- The interviewer encourages the interviewee to take personal responsibility for their behavior by using the skills that focus on the interviewee's decisions and behaviors.
- The interviewer provides a model of personal responsibility to the interviewer by interviewing in a skilled, objective, and professional manner.

- The interviewer refusing to let the interviewee violate the interviewers rights and dignity in any manner (i.e., derogatory comments or improper behavior in the interview).

■ *Verbal and Nonverbal Information.* The approach assumes the importance of verbal and nonverbal information as it affects understanding and prediction, especially emotional information (Ainsworth, 2002). Some important nonverbal behaviors to look for in training are:
  - Vagueness/uncertainty in the interviewee's responses
  - Brief answers or responses
  - Gaze avoidance
  - Negative affect (emotions)
  - Nervousness/fidgeting
  - Poor impression (Burgoon & Buller, 1994)

■ *Competency.* The approach assumes a goal of interviewer competency. Talking about, discussing, or writing about the skill is helpful but not sufficient. Wishes, desires, or good intentions are helpful but not sufficient. The interviewer can either perform the skill or not. They can either perform at a predetermined level of competency or not. The assumption is that interviewing training is based on how to do something as opposed to learning about something.

Validation of a Skills-Based Model

The skills-based model in this text draws heavily from a tradition of approaches that has been developed in the last thirty years. Training materials and programs developed by Carkhuff (1969, 1971, 1987) and Carkhuff and Berenson (1977) provide the primary support for this skills-based approach and draw heavily from this tradition.

Carkhuff (1987) reports the results of twenty years of research with the skills-based approach. He reports a level of 96% effectiveness "with over 160 studies of over 150,000 people" in a variety of settings and with different populations. Carkhuff's skills approach is largely focused on helping skills for human service delivery, but the core of the program is basic interpersonal skills.

In addition, training materials and programs developed by Evans, Hearn, Uhlemann, and Ivey (1988), Ivey (1971, 1988), Ivey and Authier (1978), Ivey and Gluckstern (1982), and Ivey and Litterer (1979) also provide support for the interpersonal skills approach and this training program draws heavily from Ivey's work.

"Over 250 data based studies have been completed on the microtraining model (Daniels, 1985; Kasdorf & Gustafson, 1978). To these studies should be added more than 20 years of clinical testing with trainees in counseling, business, and many other settings" (Ivey, 1988, p. 17). The results indicate that "microskills hierarchy have been shown again and again to be clear and teachable and show consistent construct validity."

Also, the materials and programs developed by Brammer (1979), Danish and Hauer (1973), Egan (1976a, 1990), and Neil (1980) further support the interpersonal skills training tradition and are consistent with the approach of this book. This particular interviewing training in criminal justice will hopefully add to the previously established validity of the approach.

The communication technology developed by earlier writers, like Carkhuff, has been expanded to include training in developing questions and statements in an interview to capture the dominant theme of the interview. This helps trainees know what to ask and respond to in an interview so that basic communication skills are integrated with interviewing approaches that stress questioning, interpreting, or behavioral interventions (Baumgarten & Roffers, 2003).

In a study of police interviews, Holmberg (2002) found that suspects perceived the attitudes of the interviewers as being characterized by either dominance or humanity. Police interviews marked by dominance were mainly associated with a higher proportion of denials, whereas an approach marked by humanity was associated with admissions to the crime. Holmberg hypothesized that when suspects feel respected and acknowledged, this tended to lend them to gain more confidence and mental space, allowing them to admit criminal behavior.

What interviewing skills are most important according to police officers who conduct investigative interviews? The answer to this question was the focus of a study conducted by Cherryman and Bull (2001). They wanted to know how police officers rated a variety of interviewing skills. They found that police officers rated "listening," "preparation," and "questioning" as the most important skills. Empathy was rated as being important, but also missing in police work, even though when compared to other skills, it was rated lowest. This was a particularly interesting finding, since Cherryman and Bull also found the skill to be significantly more present in skilled compared to less-skilled interviews with suspects.

Finally, the validation of a skills-based model has been further supported by a study by Carter (1997). Using a video-based self-instructional interview training package, he found that a group of inexperienced trainees could achieve a high level of interviewing proficiency from basic interviewing skills. These skills were: asking open-ended questions, paraphrasing, reflecting feelings, and confrontation. These skills are not only similar to the ones in this text, but also consistent with other training programs. In addition, Carter used a five-point scale with a criterion level of three or higher to indicate interviewing proficiency. This criteria level is also similar to this training text. As a result of the training package in Carter's study, 86% of subjects in the training group scored at a level of three or higher.

After thirty years, research support for a basic skills model continues to accumulate, so beginning interviewees can have a degree of confidence that the skills, in one form or another, are based on evidence produced by research findings. An additional consideration is the various theories supporting communication, memory retrieval, confessions, deception, and performance under stress.

Interviewing Communication Theory

The theory and conceptualization that supports the basic skills model is based on the work by Schramm (1960) and Erb and Hooker (1967). Every person formulates and expresses or *encodes* their ideas in a way that is consistent with their orientation or belief system. They may do so by verbal, written, or nonverbal communication. The person who receives the communication, in turn, *decodes* or interprets it in terms of their orientation and then *encodes* their response within the same general framework so that the person who originated the message becomes the decoder. The process is repeated as the communication continues. This phenomenon is shown in Figure 4.1.

Thus each message is created in part by the person who encodes it and partly also by the values and belief system of the person who decodes it. In this way, not only does the belief system of the person change the meaning of the communication that is sent to them, but it is also possible for a message to influence the belief system of the person receiving it.

In an interview, communication represents the efforts of two or more people to establish a commonness concerning some area of experience. Regardless of whether the people are trying to share facts, thoughts, emotions, or opinions, their endeavors are always directed toward creating a picture in the mind of the receiver that will resemble as closely as possible the one in the mind of the sender (Erb & Hooker, 1967).

A communication skills program based on this theory focuses on developing interviewer skills that give the interviewer an added ability to decode messages from the interviewee and encode messages in a fashion that enhances the commonness of experience between the two. Simply stated, an interviewer should be highly competent in encoding and decoding messages both verbal and nonverbal.

The way that a person remembers something is supported by a similar model. Three processes support the complex phenomenon of remembering. *Encoding* concerns the process through which information is entered into memory. Once the information is encoded, it is *stored* in memory. At a later time, in an interview, an interviewee may

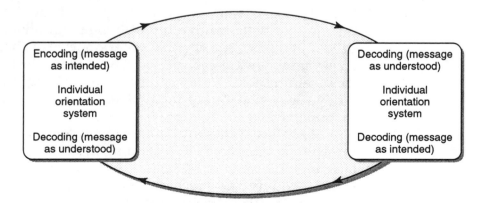

Figure 4.1   The Nature of Communication

be asked to *retrieve* this information from memory. The interviewee's memory can fail at any one of these stages. A variety of factors, such as stress, inattention, threat, level of involvement, and the influence of alcohol or drugs, can affect memory retrieval (Milne & Bull, 1999).

Confession Theory

Gudjonsson (2003) reviews five theoretical models of confession that attempt to explain the mechanisms and processes that facilitate a confession during a custodial interrogation.

- *The Reid Model.* A suspect confesses when the perceived consequences of a confession are more desirable than the anxiety generated by the deception. The perceived consequences and perceived anxiety can, therefore, be manipulated by the interrogator.
- *The Decision-Making Model.* The basic theory of this model is that when suspects are interrogated, they become engaged in a complicated and demanding decision-making process. This process is governed by what the suspect *believes* to be the consequences of telling the truth of not.
- *Psychoanalytic Model.* This model rests on the assumption that the feeling of guilt is the fundamental cause of true confessions and false confessions. The theory rests on the Freudian assumption that an unconscious sense of guilt produces false confessions, exaggeration of the crime, commission of the crimes, and a need for self-punishment.
- *Interaction Process Model.* This model looks at the importance of background characteristics, contextual characteristics, and interviewer questioning techniques. The first two factors influence the interrogator, which in turn influences the suspect's behavior.
- *Cognitive-Behavioral Model.* This model draws heavily from social learning theory. The theory looks at the relationship between the suspect, the environment, and the important other people in the environment. There are *antecedents* and *consequences* of confession. Antecedents are the events that occur prior to interrogation and consequences can be either long or short term.

Interpersonal Deception Theory (IDT)

The primary focus of IDT is the concept of strategic communication. The plans and intentions of a communicator are translated into large behavioral routines (strategies) comprised of specific actions (tactics). IDT stipulates that both strategic and nonstrategic behaviors are likely to be present during interactive deception. Even though some deceiver behaviors are likely to be deliberate, other behaviors may be inadvertent. These inadvertent behaviors are called *leakage*. The forms of leakage are:

- arousal and nervousness cues
- negative affect cues
- incompetent communication performance

IDT specifies four strategic categories:

- vagueness/uncertainty
- withdrawl/reticence/nonimmediacy
- disassociation
- image-protecting behaviors

The combination of strategic and nonstrategic behavior management entails reduced conversational involvement and impaired communication performances. Theoretically, truth tellers, compared to deceivers, display less of these behaviors (Burgoon & Buller, 1994).

Emotional Arousal and Performance in an Interview

Another theory that relates to interviewing concerns the relationship between emotional arousal, such as fear, anxiety, or stress, which can interfere with attention, memory retrieval, judgment, and decision making. Emotional arousal can have negative effects on several types of performance, but it isn't automatically the case. The *inverted-U hypothesis* predicts that performance in an interview should improve with decreased stress, for example, up to a point, after which further increases in stress become disruptive and the interviewee's performance in the interview deteriorates. The question associated with the inverted-U hypothesis then becomes: What is the optimal level of arousal for performance in an interview? According to this hypothesis, the optimal level of arousal depends on whether the task in the interview is simple or complex. For medium levels of arousal with a medium level of complexity, the inverted-U is similar to the curve in Figure 4.2.

In this figure, the optimal level of arousal is at point "A," and any stress increase past this point would decrease performance. Prior to point "A," performance is likely to increase. The inverted-U hypothesis provides, for beginning interviewers, a theoretical model of how stress or fear can be either beneficial or disruptive in an interview, particularly on complex tasks such as memory retrieval or information processing (Weiten & Lloyd, 2003).

Figure 4.2   The Inverted U

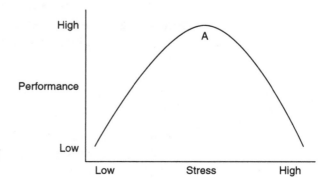

Preassessment

You may want to complete the communication pretest (Assessment 4.1), and you will probably find it helpful to complete the "First Interview" part of the *Pre-Interviewing Self-Rating* (Assessment 4.3). This rating scale has proven useful to others in helping them see how their feelings and attitudes have changed after interviewing training.

As you proceed through this presentation of interviewing skills, two major concepts are useful in skill acquisition: communication and discrimination.

Communication

The ability to act in an interview—getting your mouth open and speaking out—is communication. "A good communicator can translate his perceptions, insights, and discriminations into effective interpersonal transactions" (Egan, 1975, p. 57). Communication means acting and speaking in an interview. A communicator is an active agent rather than an observer or spectator. One way that helps one learn to be an effective communicator is to write out questions or responses as if one were in a face-to-face situation with an interviewee. Another way is to interview role players in a simulated criminal justice encounter. Finally, and this is the ultimate goal of training, the interviewer conducts interviews in actual criminal justice encounters with feedback from a supervisor.

Discrimination

Being able to accurately identify the effectiveness of an interviewer's question or response is referred to as discrimination. This means picking from an array of possible questions or responses those that are more effective than others. "Just because a person is a good discriminator or perceiver does not mean that he is automatically a good communicator. On the other hand, a good communicator must be a good discriminator, for a good communicator is one who acts on accurate discriminations" (Egan, 1975, p. 58).

In the previous communication pretest, you were instructed to discriminate which of the responses were more effective than others. Similarly, as you listen to others conduct interviews, developing a keen sense of perception as to their questions or responses helps you in your skill acquisition.

Interview Appraisal Scales

In order to provide a brief definition of the interviewing skills and a complete objective evaluation (discrimination) of each of the skills, Interview Appraisal Scales have been developed. These scales appear in Assessment 4.2. Each of the seven skills to be covered in detail later are presented on a five-point scale with capsule definitions for each of the ratings, one through five. The scales can be used by the interviewing trainer or trainees to rate each other on skill proficiency and obtain an overall numerical level of skill proficiency. Experience has shown that it is easier to rate one or two skills at a time and then build on skill proficiency by adding skills as training progresses.

For an in-depth and extensive evaluation, the *Class Interview Rating Worksheet* or the *Interviewing Training Self-Efficiency Assessment: Knowledge and Skills,* found at the end of several chapters, can be used to appraise interviewing skills. The evaluation scales may be used to complement each other, or used at the same time to provide an extensive evaluation of an interviewer's skills and attitudes.

Basic and Specialized Skills Hierarchy

In addition to a competency-based skills approach, another assumption of the model is that basic communication skills underlie all forms of communication—from less specialized to highly specialized. Figure 4.3 illustrates this assumption. In the pyramid, all of the more specialized skills draw from and use the basic skills along with the nonspecialized skills. As an interviewer becomes specialized, the range of questions and responses narrows while still drawing on basic skills. From a practical standpoint, this means that the best way to begin training as a legal or psychiatric interviewer is to begin by learning basic communication skills.

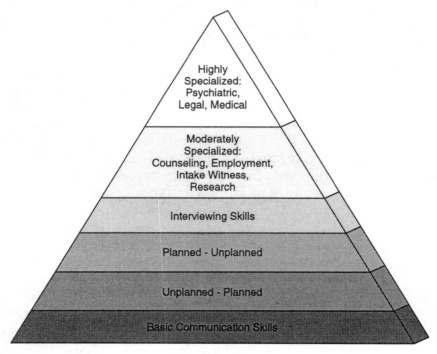

Figure 4.3   Basic and Specialized Skills Hierarchy

- **Basic Communication Skills.** These are the skills necessary for day-to-day living experiences. They are critical for effective interpersonal relations whether one is in an interview or not.
- **Unplanned–Planned Interviewing Skills.** The next level past the skills needed for living is the encounter between two people that begins not as a planned interview but becomes planned during the course of the encounter. A police officer, for example, having a cup of coffee off duty with a fellow officer, discovers the other officer has recently gone before the department promotional review board for sergeant. He says after realizing his friend's recent experience, "I think I need to talk to you. Could I ask you some questions about how it went when you were before the board?" In this case the first officer originally did not intend to interview his friend but soon realized that it would be to his advantage to do so. Most of us are also familiar with the "unplanned" business interview that is purposely set up to appear spontaneous but is actually quite formal.
- **Planned–Unplanned Interviews.** The next level of specialization involves interviews that begin planned but change to a topic or concern for which the interviewer was unprepared. An officer, for example, appears for an annual performance review by a superior officer and during the interview becomes very emotional about a personal crisis such as an impending divorce. In this case, the original plan of the interview would likely change and the necessary skills to conduct the interview would change.
- **Interviewing Skills.** The skills needed at this level incorporate the necessary basic communication skills and traditional interviewing skills. The primary focus at this level would be formulating and asking questions. These skills will be covered in a subsequent chapter.
- **Moderately Specialized Skills.** At this level we find skills that require additional training and education beyond basic communication and interviewing skills. This usually takes the form of additional academic work, for example, in counseling, or agency-specific in-service or pre-service training. Employment interviews, intake interviews, discipline interviews, witness interviews, and research interviews are included.
- **Highly Specialized Skills.** The most specific interviewing skills are found in interviews requiring advanced training and education. Examples of this would include a psychiatrist interviewing an offender to determine insanity or incompetency. Also included would be legal and medical interviews. If highly specialized interviewing skills are combined with basic interpersonal skills, the highly specialized interviewer increases his or her effectiveness in his or her particular area of expertise (see Figure 4.3).

Levels of Encounter

When there is an encounter between an interviewer and an interviewee, a range of behaviors is possible, from a positive initiative to a negative attack. The range of possibilities in this encounter is illustrated in Figure 4.4. This range of behaviors can be evaluated according to *facilitation, focus,* or *value.*

- **Facilitation.** If the behavior in the interview increases the possibility of further or increased communication, then it can be considered facilitative. Ignoring, scolding, judging, harassing, and attacking a person in an interview tends to reduce communication. The interviewee tends to withdraw—"psychological withdrawal if physical departure is not feasible" (Boshear & Albrecht, 1977). The resultant behavior is likely to be silence, daydreaming, or role playing.
- **Focus.** The range of behaviors in an interview also tends to be either interviewee or interviewer focused. Specifically, this refers to whose needs are being met in the interview. Between −1 and −5, the interviewer's needs are being met. From +1 to +5, the interviewee's needs are being met.
- **Value.** The more the interviewer's needs are being met, the less likely communication will take place. There may even be a subtraction or condition of "losing ground" in the interview. Consequently, the challenge of the interviewer is to maintain the interview in the more additive direction so that there is a gain in information.

As a note, this particular training will go as far as the 3.0 level of "responding." Training in counseling, psychotherapy, or social casework would move past the 3.0 level into "caring" and "initiating."

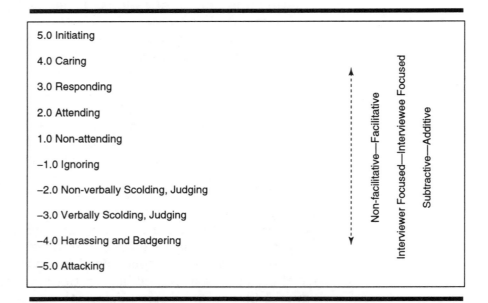

Figure 4.4   Levels of Encounter

■ **Multicontent Communication.** The encounter between two people in an interview in the previous discussion can occur through a variety of content areas. These transactions between two people take place through four distinct, but overlapping content areas:

- *Facts:* objectively verifiable aspects of experience; inferences, conjectures, or assumptions that are believed to be true; information or data having no particular emotional connotation.
- *Feelings:* emotional responses to experience; here-and-now reactions that influence the transaction.
- *Values:* ideals; behavioral standards based on one's sense of propriety; relatively permanent ideas about what should be; experiences, people, concepts, or institutions that one holds dear.
- *Opinions:* a belief of judgment that falls short of certainty and is oriented to the immediate situation; short-range ideas about what is happening, how others are behaving, what is being said or proposed; attitudes associated with a decisive stand or a position one has adopted.

Referring to an earlier point in this chapter, the focus of this training model is on behavior even though all four of the above kinds of information are exchanged to some degree in any dyadic interaction. The focus of the model in criminal justice interviewing will be on the predominant modes of facts and feelings with the recognition that others are used from time to time.

The Primary Interviewing Skills

The primary interviewing skills in this training are presented in Figure 4.5 and they will serve to initiate and support the *understanding–prediction–action* model. These skills do not include every and all possible skills a person could learn in order to conduct interviews. Rather, they serve as a foundation of basic communications skills that the criminal justice student can build on as they acquire specific agency training. The primary skills are displayed in the lefthand column in Figure 4.6.

Skill Definition

Figure 4.6 presents an abbreviated array of the seven skills and their definitions. All of the skills will be covered in subsequent chapters but this guide provides an overall perspective on the primary skills.

Preliminary Training Considerations

As the text has indicated, role playing can be an effective training technique, but a specific role-play situation may be uncomfortable for a trainee. In this case, it is expected that the role player be responsibly assertive by indicating that he or she would prefer not to

Skills

Empathy	Speed and Pacing	Summarization	Concreteness	Immediacy	Confrontation	Assertion
Inter-changeable expressions	Pauses; well timed; paced	Effective cognitive or affective summary or both	Being specific between interviewer and interviewee	Saying what's going on	Telling it like it is with empathy	Responsibly assertive
Not understanding but good intentions	Average speed and pacing	Brief summary	Not being specific; being vague	Not saying what is going on between interviewer and interviewee—avoiding	Not telling it like it is; little preparation	Irresponsibly assertive
Really not hearing and understanding; subtracting	Interview rushed	No periodic closure	Really not being specific; globalisms, trite cliches, and generalities	Really not saying what is going on—pretending, avoiding, or faking	Really not telling it like it is or being abusive without empathy	Aggressive or non-assertive

Figure 4.5 Definitions and Levels of Primary Interviewing Skills

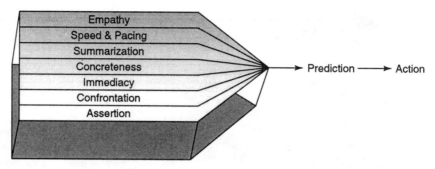

Figure 4.6

play the role. The trainee should take it upon him- or herself to suggest a different and more comfortable role.

Second, role players may be prompted by the instructor to play roles of offenders who may be quite unsavory characters. For example, trainees may be asked to role-play a prostitute, child molester, or drug dealer. The suggestion of a specific character does not, in any way, indicate that there is something about the way the trainee looks or behaves that is cued by the suggested character.

Finally, it is quite likely most offenders, in actual interviews, will use obscenities in their communication. There are two schools of thought about the use of obscenities by the interviewer. The first school takes the position that the interviewer needs to communicate with the offender in his or her level of language that the offender understands, that is forceful, and that is clear and direct. On the other hand, it can be argued that the interviewer should model appropriate language and behavior. In this case, obscenities would not be used by the interviewer. In any case, two preliminary considerations are: (1) the use of inappropriate language is a personal *choice* and not required and (2) the class or training group should discuss with the instructor, prior to training, how obscenities will be approached in training.

Beginning in the next chapter, each skill will be presented step by step.

Skills Acquisition

In all of the skills, you will acquire competency when you build on preceding skills and maintain competency in preceding skills as new skills are mastered. The ultimate objective is for you to be able to demonstrate competence in all of the seven skills.

Skills Focus

Figure 4.7 presents the focus of five of the skills in this model and the content of each of the skills. Speed and pacing and summarization are not included because they do not have separate components. The skill of empathy is broadly focused and includes thoughts, feelings, behaviors, and perceptions. Assertion is a narrowly focused skill that includes both directive and protective assertions.

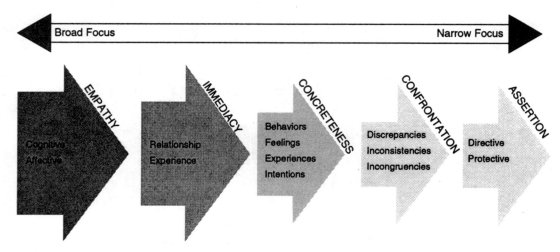

Figure 4.7   Skills Focus

Summary

Interviewing in this training/education program is based on a basic skills model: understanding, prediction, action. There is considerable research and theoretical support for the model. Seven skills are the basis for interviewing training.

Now that you have completed Chapter 4 and the pretraining assessments, you may want to look forward to the activities at the end of this chapter. Exercises 4.1, 4.2, and 4.3 and the Interview Challenge are provided for you to explore some of the ideas and concepts presented in the chapter.

Study Questions

1. Why do we need a model of communication in interviewing?
2. What do we mean by "competency-based" interviewing training?
3. Explain interviewing communication theory.
4. What is discrimination in interviewing?
5. What do we mean by a specialized skills hierarchy?
6. What are the primary channels of communication between two people in an interview?
7. What are the basic communication skills covered in the training model?
8. What are some of the nonverbal skills to look for in training?
9. What was the difference in outcomes when interviewers used humanity instead of dominance?
10. What skills were found to be most important by police officers?
11. Explain the types of confession theory.
12. Explain the inverted-U hypothesis.

Exercise 4.1

Class Interview Rating Worksheet

Directions: As each role play and response is made in class, rate the response on a 1–5 scale after writing the response exactly the way the student responded.

First Interviewer

Response: _____

_____

_____

Rating (circle)　　　1　　　2　　　3　　　4　　　5

Second Interviewer

Response: _____

_____

_____

Rating (circle)　　　1　　　2　　　3　　　4　　　5

Third Interviewer

Response: _____

_____

_____

Rating (circle)　　　1　　　2　　　3　　　4　　　5

Fourth Interviewer

Response: _____

_____

_____

Rating (circle)　　　1　　　2　　　3　　　4　　　5

Fifth Interviewer

Response: _____

_____

_____

Rating (circle)   1   2   3   4   5

Sixth Interviewer

Response: _____

_____

_____

Rating (circle)   1   2   3   4   5

Assessment 4.1

Self-Ratings and Communication Pretest

Before you proceed with the basic interviewing skills, you are asked to respond to a series of statements in order to determine your present understanding of communication. Below are five statements. You are to read each statement as if it were being said to you. In the space to the left of each response, indicate whether the response to the statement is a TURN-ON, TURN-OFF, or STAY-WITH response according to the following criteria:

TURN-ON   This means the interviewer provides more for the interviewee than was said to the interviewer. The response may be a turn-on because of greater clarification or deeper levels of understanding. It may also include areas that the interviewee is not openly talking about, but only providing hints and clues to the interviewer.

STAY-WITH   If the interviewer gives back to the interviewee a response at an *energy* level at the same level as it was given to them such that the statements are interchangeable.

TURN-OFF   If the statement takes away from what the person said, then it is a turn-off because some of the intensity or accuracy is lost.

First Statement

I get mad whenever I think about women because of my past experiences with them. They have messed me up every time and ruined my whole life.

Show Rating Here:

_____ 1. Would you listen to me if I could show you how you created this mess for yourself?

_____ 2. Who were these women?

_____ 3. It sounds like you've got some kind of hang-up with women.

_____ 4. You feel angry, disgusted, and cheated.

Second Statement

I'll never be able to get a job with a felony record. It's useless to work.

Show Rating Here:

_____   1. It sounds to me like you've really got a bad attitude.

_____   2. You're feeling very hopeless, trapped, and bewildered. You know, like you ought to give up.

_____   3. Where have you tried to get work?

_____   4. If at first you don't succeed, try again.

Third Statement

They set me off again—I don't know what I'm going to do. I can't take much more of this.

Show Rating Here:

_____   1. You feel desperate.

_____   2. Don't be so stupid. You knew you weren't going to get paroled before you went up.

_____   3. You sound very disappointed and hopeless almost to the point where you're at the end of the line on this and almost ready to panic.

_____   4. You've got to start handling this better and get your head straightened out.

Fourth Statement

I get depressed when I think about getting out and having to start all over from scratch.

Show Rating Here:

_____   1. Life's a bitch.

_____   2. There's no point in getting depressed—it won't get you anywhere.

_____   3. When do you get out?

_____   4. It won't be that bad—lots of dudes get out and make it all the time.

Fifth Statement

Sometimes I don't want to go home because my girlfriend is always bitching to me. She wants to get married and I don't. What in hell am I supposed to do?

Show Rating Here:

_____ 1. You feel really trapped. On the one hand, you want to see your girlfriend; on other hand, you don't. It's really painful to be caught in the middle.

_____ 2. Wait just a minute. You're not really a saint yourself, you know.

_____ 3. It's only normal she would want to get married.

_____ 4. That's women for you.

Exercise 4.2

Stress, Memory, and Information Processing and the *Inverted-U*

Directions: *Using the following plotted curves, identify and discuss the possible dynamics of the relationship between stress and task performance and the optimal level of arousal for each of the interviews. Assume a complex task is required in each interview.*

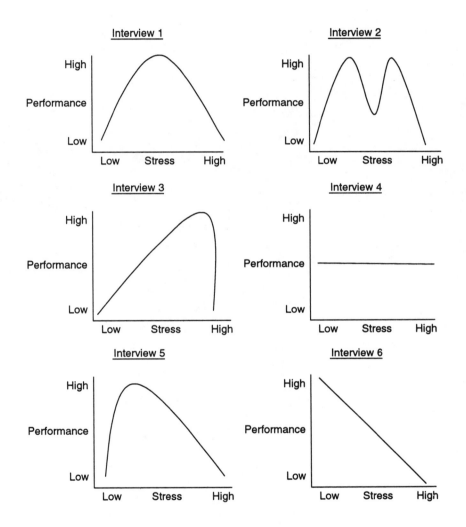

Assessment 4.2

Interview Appraisal Scales

Directions: *To obtain an appraisal score, add the total ratings and divide the total by the number of ratings to obtain an average rating.*

Person being rated _____

Interview No. _____

Average rating _____

Total rating _____

Grade _____

[ ] HANDLING OF SIGNIFICANT FEELINGS EXPRESSED BY THE INTERVIEWEE

1	2	3	4	5
Interviewer ignored them completely or interviewer went off on irrelevant tangents	Interviewer did not seem to be "with the interviewee"	Interviewer accepted feelings but was neither good nor poor at making meaningful reflections	Interviewer accepted feelings and generally was able to make meaningful reflections	Interviewer accepted feelings, was able to make meaningful reflections, and was "with interviewee" at all times

[ ] SPEED PACING

1	2	3	4	5
Questions or responses asked much too quickly; bombardment, interview rushed	Interview rather hurried, questions or responses not paced; few pauses	Average speed and pacing	Generally well-paced questions or responses at appropriate times	Excellent use of time with well-paced questions and responses

[ ] CONFRONTATION

1	2	3	4	5
Irresponsible and unfacilitative confrontation; tended to reduce communication; hostile confrontation	Confrontation was attempted but was generally ineffective	Confrontation was neither communicative nor destructive	Confrontation was generally helpful in pointing out discrepancies	Soft confrontation; very facilitating, assisted in pointing out discrepancies; communicative

(continued)

Assessment 4.2

Interview Appraisal Scales (*cont'd.*)

	1	2	3	4	5
[ ] SUMMARIZATION	Very limited use of summary; no periodic closure either cognitive or affective	Attempted to summarize but was not very effective	Summarized cognitive information effectively	Summarized affective information effectively	Interviewer summarized both cognitive and affective information effectively
[ ] ASSERTION	Interviewer was aggressive; violated rights of interviewee	Interviewer was generally non-assertive; violated personal rights	Average level of assertion; did not violate personal rights	Generally assertive; no indications of aggression or nonassertiveness	Interviewer was responsibly assertive; did not violate interviewee or interviewer rights
[ ] CONCRETENESS AND GETTING AT SPECIFICS	Vagueness, generalities, abstractness, cliches, and globalisms dominated the interview	Interview rather vague and nonspecific	Neither noticeably vague nor specific	Rather specific and concrete; avoided generalities and abstractions	Very specific; used "how" and "what" questions; concrete actions, feelings, thoughts, intentions, and information
[ ] IMMEDIACY	Avoided what was going on; allowed interviewee to stay in the past	Did not say what was going on	Recognized what was going on but did not say it	Hinted about what was going on in the interview	Really said what was going on during the interview

Exercise 4.3

Distinguishing Between Thoughts, Feelings, and Behaviors

Directions: *During a practice interview in class, observe the inter-action between the individuals in the interview and complete the following sentences. Check your responses with other individuals.*

Behaviors

1.   Now I see the interviewee

_____

_____

_____

2.   Now I see the interviewee

_____

_____

_____

3.   Now I see the interviewee

_____

_____

_____

Thoughts

1.   Now I think the interviewee thinks

_____

_____

_____

2.   Now I think the interviewee thinks

_____

_____

_____

3. Now I think the interviewee thinks

_____

_____

_____

Feelings

1. Now I think the interviewee feels

_____

_____

_____

2. Now I think the interviewee feels

_____

_____

_____

3. Now I think the interviewee feels

_____

_____

_____

Note: Avoid using the phrases "I feel that" and "I feel like."

Assessment 4.3

Preinterviewing Self-Rating

Rate yourself from 1 to 10 on each item.

1—not like you
10—much like you

FIRST INTERVIEW	LAST INTERVIEW	
_____	_____	I would hate to do the wrong thing.
_____	_____	I can't imagine myself being a successful interviewer.
_____	_____	I worry about being observed by my instructor/trainer.
_____	_____	It makes me nervous to be in front of the class/group.
_____	_____	A video recorder bothers me.
_____	_____	I talk too much in the interview.
_____	_____	I want to get the interview over as soon as possible.
_____	_____	I'm afraid I might forget what to say in the interview and almost panic.
_____	_____	I feel a lot of pressure to keep the interview going.
_____	_____	When the interviewee gets upset, I want to smooth things over.
_____	_____	It is difficult for me to confront the interviewee.
_____	_____	I'm afraid I will be too shy and not talk loud enough in the interview.
_____	_____	There are certain topics I feel uneasy about discussing in the interview.
_____	_____	If the interviewee stops talking, total silence scares me.

FIRST INTERVIEW   LAST INTERVIEW

_____   _____   I can't imagine conducting an interview without notes in my hand to look at.

_____   _____   Interviewing an offender who has committed a terrible crime makes me nervous.

_____   _____   I don't think I could interview victims of crimes.

_____   _____   I wouldn't know what to do if I suspected the interviewee of lying.

_____   _____   I don't feel comfortable interviewing in serious situations.

_____   _____   I don't think I can handle interviews with people of different cultural backgrounds than my own.

Interview Challenge

How would you complete the following encounter? Keep in mind the concerns raised by the questions following the preliminary interview narrative.

You are a female police officer interviewing a victim of sexual assault in a hospital room. You need to eventually get a complete statement from the victim. The victim is in a state of shock and, since you have been in the room, has said nothing. When she looks at you, she begins to shake uncontrollably and sob. She hangs her head, then lifts it and the sobbing begins again.

1. What skills will you need to get the interview started?

    _____

    _____

    _____

2. What will you want to get accomplished in the interview?

    _____

    _____

    _____

3. How will you divide your interview time between official objectives and personal concerns in the interview (i.e., how closely will you stay with required questions)?

    _____

    _____

    _____

4. What do you anticipate the major segments of the interview to be?

    _____

    _____

    _____

5. What would be the most appropriate interview style to use in this situation?

_____

_____

_____

6. What will be some of the barriers to communication in this interview?

_____

_____

_____

7. What would you need to minimally accomplish in this interview for you to consider the interview successful?

_____

_____

_____

5

Skillfully Communicating Accurate Empathy

Learning Objectives

Subject. Skillfully communicating accurate empathy.

Objectives. At the end of a period of instruction and training, the student (trainee) will:

1. Understand the skill and types of empathy.
2. Understand the basic model of empathy.
3. Understand intensity of words describing emotions and how to diagnose conservatively.
4. Demonstrate the use of the skill of empathy at a minimal level of competency.

Learning domains.

    a. Cognitive
    b. Affective
    c. Psychomotor

> I could explain to my imaginary jurist but never to a real one about the instinct—the stage in this business when, like an animal, you can *feel* you've got one, and it can't be explained. You *feel* the truth, and you know. Try telling *that* to the judge, I thought. Try explaining *that* sometime.
>
> Joseph Wambaugh
> *The Blue Knight* (1972)

The first and most important skill in the interviewing training model is empathy. The skillful use of empathy in an interview involves translating our understanding of the interviewee's experiences, behaviors, and feelings into a response that verifies that we understand the interviewee's point of view.

Basch (1983) identifies empathy as "coming to know." It means experiencing the other person's experience while at the same time maintaining our own integrity. "One sometimes enters into another's situation not to help but to expose and evaluate motivations and behavior" (p. 102). In criminal justice interviews, we strive to be empathic with what the interviewee is trying to communicate to us, not with the person or their conduct.

Empathy is an interpersonal skill that consists of an empathizer who understands (1) another person's situation and emotions, (2) the other person is experiencing one or more emotions, (3) the empathizer perceives a similarity between what the other person is experiencing and something the empathizer has experienced previously, and (4) the empathizer takes actions associated with concern, such as giving time, paying attention, doing something for the other person, or being concerned for the other person (Hakansson & Montgomery, 2003).

For our purposes, we will settle on a definition that has been used in a skill assessment instrument, *The Personal Skills Map:*

> Empathy: Interpersonal Sensitivity: Your empathy score is an indication of your current skill and ability to accurately understand and accept another person's thoughts, feelings, and behaviors. Accurate empathy is a well researched characteristic of skilled communicators. . . . A high score (skill strength) on empathy would indicate an ability or skill to accurately understand and feel what others are saying, feeling, and doing. A low score (skill change) may indicate personal difficulty or skill deficits in understanding and communicating with others on an emotional level. (Nelson & Low, 1981, p. 9)

Empathy is a capacity (Basch, 1983). Based on the previous definition, it is a measurable capacity. Empathy is the ability to put oneself in the place of another. Empathy leads to knowledge. What the interviewer does with the knowledge is determined by the purpose of the interview in the first place (Basch, 1983). For example, a police officer may use empathy in approaching a car that he has stopped for a violation. Approaching the car, the officer ascertains the violator's emotional condition. In this case, the officer wouldn't make a response based on this empathy. Rather, he would use his perceptions of the violator's emotional condition to predict how cautious to be in approaching the car. After the officer assesses the knowledge of the other person's condition, he then reasons, calculates, predicts, and acts on this knowledge.

In a different situation, such as interviewing a rape victim, the officer would probably make extensive use of empathy in order to understand an extremely difficult experience the victim is going through. In this case, the feelings and emotions of the interviewee are very important and precede logic and reasoning. "Where 'reason' is commonly used to indicate that a judgment is supposedly being made on the basis of logic alone, i.e. emotionally, 'empathy' should be used to indicate that a judgment is being made through a process that specifically does take one's pertinent affective responses into account" (Basch, 1983, p. 110).

By understanding the other person's thoughts and feelings, we can better predict what they are going to do or what we should do.

Without empathy we would be left with prediction from fantasy, pure logic, wishful thinking, or the interviewer's point of view. When an interviewer deliberately disregards the existence of the interviewee, it is termed *anti-empathetic,* as when used by manipulative con artists and ruthless politicians. When the interviewer is negligent in understanding the interviewee because of cultural, ethnic, economic, or social background reasons, it is termed *unempathetic.* For example, the interviewer was grossly insensitive to cultural practices in an interview because of simple lack of knowledge or cultural awareness. The oversight wasn't malicious or intentional but the outcome was still lack of understanding. In either case, the movement of the interview is in the direction of *autistic interviewing,* which means acting, behaving, or predicting as if the other person does not exist. *Empathic interviewing* means acting in relation to the interviewee. *Autistic interviewing* means conducting an interview outside the reality that the interviewee is a person with thoughts, feelings, and concerns. For example, using an interview to exploit, manipulate, or harm an interviewee would be very autistic and unethical.

If interviewing as if the other person is not there seems rather insane, it is consistent with our conceptions of insanity. Empathy is consistent with mental health or wellness and autism is consistent with insanity or mental disturbance.

Benefits of Empathy

What advantages do we gain when we use empathy in an interview? Egan (1994) has suggested that empathy can help do the following:

- It can help establish rapport with interviewees. Specifically, this means not being authoritarian, condescending, arrogant, patronizing, or judgmental. Elimination of these behaviors will certainly enhance communication.
- Checking understanding is also aided by the use of empathy. The interviewer may think they understand the interviewee but with empathy they may find they were wrong.
- Empathy helps lubricate the communication process. It keeps the conversation running smoothly and encourages dialogue.
- Empathy keeps the interviewer from asking too many questions and giving premature and inept advice. It tends to keep the focus on the interviewee, who is the primary source of information.
- Empathy paves the way for stronger actions that may have to be taken by the interviewer later in the interview. For example, the interviewer may have to say "no" to a request by an interviewee. If it is said after empathy, the answer will still be a "no" but will perhaps be a bit easier for the interviewee to accept.

Empathy is the primary and most important interviewing skill. It is not a magic cure-all for communication, but it has been established as the most important element of communication.

Types of Empathy	Function as	Consequences
no sensitivity	psychopath; cold; heartless	inhibits communication
intellectually sensitive	interviewer	facilitates communication
therapeutic sensitivity	counselor, therapist	facilitates growth and/or healing
hypersensitive	"bleeding heart" low objectivity	lost in the other person's world: mix thoughts and feelings with other's thoughts and feelings

Figure 5.1   Types of Empathy, Types of Functions, and Consequences

Intellectual versus Therapeutic Empathy

Empathy is the basis for understanding a client in a therapeutic relationship, particularly understanding emotions. Therapeutic empathy, which involves feeling the client's emotions, would not be the type of empathy used in most interviews in criminal justice. The situation where therapeutic empathy would be appropriate would be community and institutional correctional counseling or treatment programs.

For most criminal justice interviews, however, intellectual empathy would be the most appropriate of the two types. Intellectual empathy is the understanding of the interviewee's concerns without the depth of involvement in another person's frame of reference that is required in therapeutic relationships (Tryon, 2002). Consequently, in criminal justice interviews, the interviewer needs to remain sensitive to the other person's thoughts and emotions, but not at the level that empathy is used as a curative agent. Neither is being an advocate the focus of most criminal justice interviews, nor do criminal justice personnel have the time to establish in-depth relationships, which require therapeutic empathy. Figure 5.1 presents the types of empathy and their functions and consequences.

Empathy versus Sympathy

It is important at this point to make a distinction between empathy and sympathy. The two are often confused. Sympathy has to do with pity and agreement with the misery of a person's condition. In sympathy, you feel sorry for the person, as when you send them a sympathy card when they have suffered a misfortune. "Empathy is often confused with sympathy, kindness, and approval" (Book, 1988, p. 421). Most people find it difficult to be sympathetic toward offenders, but empathy denotes understanding of the offender. You could understand what the offender did or why they did it without feeling sorry for them. Offenders who have been erroneously incarcerated are likely to invoke sympathy.

In interviewing, empathy has an important role but seldom would sympathy be called on because, in most cases, the interviewer would need to maintain objectivity and refrain from taking sides with the interviewee. The interviewer's task is to obtain information from the interviewee in an objective fashion that eliminates bias and contamination of the data whether the interviewer is in agreement or disagreement with the interviewee. This sometimes is a difficult task when you are called on to interview those who have committed heinous crimes. The rule is the same for the perpetrator and the victim—objectivity.

Empathy, Experience, and Talent

Some frequently asked questions about empathy concern the role that experience and natural talent play in obtaining the skills. Two of these questions are:

Question: Are people who have had an actual experience in a certain area more empathic than those who haven't?

Answer: People such as ex-alcoholics, ex-convicts, and ex-victims certainly have an advantage when it comes to empathy. The key is whether they can communicate effectively with others their understanding gained from special experiences. "A person can be highly capable of internal empathic responses but poorly endowed with the interpersonal skills required to communicate that condition. Another person may be so skilled in communication processes as to sell you the George Washington Bridge, but at the same time, lack even the most elemental sensitivities on which empathy is built" (Hackney, 1978, p. 38).

Question: Are there some people who have natural gifts or talents in communicating empathy?

Answer: Yes, there seem to be a few rare individuals who have a natural talent in communicating empathy. Unfortunately, in the field of criminal justice we need many trained interviewers so we can't rely on those who are gifted. We need skills development programs to provide skilled interviewers for a wide variety of agencies in criminal justice. Waiting for a few gifted individuals to conduct interviews will not meet the manpower needs of criminal justice.

Cautions on the Use of Empathy

Before discussing the "how to" of empathy, several points of caution are necessary. As with any communication technique, empathy will not be effective with all people in all situations.

Panacea

The use of empathy in all interview situations is questionable. Responding to the interviewee's feelings is not very helpful for problem-solving and action-oriented interviews. In these situations, information from the interviewer is needed, so empathy alone is not sufficient (Gladstein, 1983). In addition, there are some criminals and sociopaths who are so manipulative, emotionally callused, and irresponsible that empathy has little effect on them. Consequently, in order for the interviewer to prevent being manipulated, the full complement of skills, culminated with assertion, needs to be mastered. In many cases, empathy is necessary but not sufficient.

Parroting

Empathy is not simply restating what the interviewee has said. The interviewer needs to provide more than what a tape recorder could do. Empathy means responding to expressed and unexpressed feelings. It means picking up the theme or meaning of what the interviewer is saying or inferring.

Green Apples

Frequently, beginning interviewers will eagerly respond to the first feeling presented in an interview. They will respond to it with great enthusiasm and energy. Schutz (1973) identifies this as the *green apples* phenomenon. The difficulty is that the interviewer frequently will find they responded to a shallow feeling not attached to much energy. Very quickly the energy is dissipated and the interview degenerates into shallow chit-chat. This leads to *bullshit,* a term Schutz uses to identify talk unconnected to feelings.

Response Burst

Occasionally, beginning interviewers experience an intense elevation of emotions by the interviewee when the interviewer responds with empathy. This can be quite frightening and unsettling and would appear that the interviewer has "made" the interviewee angry, for example. This phenomenon is termed a *response burst* and it frequently occurs when the interviewer has minimized their empathic response. In other words, they failed to respond to the full intensity of the interviewee's emotions. On the other hand, their response was close enough to signal to the interviewee that it is safe to fully express their feelings, hence a burst of emotions after a rather mild interviewer response.

Emotional Repression

Communication based on empathy and emotional expressiveness is counterindicated as a technique in emotionally repressive environments such as prisons and jails. The specific environmental factor that leads to this caution has been identified as "emotional feedback" (Toch, 1977; Wright, 1985). In an environment where emotional feedback is limited or nonexistent, the use of empathy could be very risky because it could lead to explosive behavior and violence, both of which are discouraged in institutions. In addition, emotions in many correctional institutions are perceived as a sign of weakness and personal inferiority. The rule is that the use of empathy should be considered in relation to the degree that emotions are taboo in a particular setting.

Normal Communication

The technique of empathy as it is presented in this interviewing training program is based on the assumption that the interviewees are functioning in a normal range of personal adjustment. This particular interviewing approach is counterindicated for interaction with seriously disturbed individuals.

Communicating Empathy

Communicating accurate empathy involves directing, identifying the mode, labeling the thought or emotion, and reflecting the emotion or thought.

Directing

Establishing to whom the response is being made involves directing. When we respond to the other person, we start with "you" as opposed to "they," "it," or "someone."

Identifying the Mode

Gladstein (1983) identifies two different modes of empathy, which have been referred to in developmental research as role-taking: "Cognitive role-taking refers to the person's ability to perceive how the other is thinking. Affective role-taking refers to the person's ability to perceive how the other is feeling" (p. 473).

Consequently, we have two forms of empathy that may be called for in responding to an interviewee: cognitive empathy and affective empathy.

As was mentioned in the first chapter, the choice that the interviewer responds to can affect the flow and outcome of the interview.

Cognitive/Affective Relationship

Even though the interviewer has a choice of whether to stay in cognitive or affective areas in the interview, the choice is not an even one. Cognitive information is a fact. Affective information is a fact. For example, it is important to record that the lady's husband returned home at 3:00 A.M. with a loaded .38 special revolver. He fired three shots at her, she left the house, and so on. These facts are vital. It is also important to record that she was frightened, desperate, and panicky. She could, at any time, do something very irrational.

Both sets of facts are important but the latter set is probably more important for prediction.

The influence of affective information over cognitive information is stated by Fenlason and colleagues (1962) as a basic behavioral operative in interviewing: *"Emotional needs take priority over reasoning."* If this concept seems rather academic, perhaps an analogy will provide clarification. If a professional baseball pitcher is going to throw a round object at you, it is important to note the size of the object before you decide how fast and how far to get out of the way. It is important whether he is going to throw a baseball, softball, ping-pong ball, or bowling ball (cognitive facts). It is even more important for your prediction, as to how fast and how far to get out of the way, to know how fast he is going to throw the round object because almost any round object traveling at ninety-five miles an hour will cause you difficulty. In this analogy there are facts about the actor's behavior—the pitcher—and facts about his energy—the speed of the ball. Most people would rather know the speed of the ball before they had specifics about its size.

This basic concept leads to several practical directives for interviewers:

- Factual, cognitive data obtained in an overriding emotional interview is suspect of being garbled and unreliable.
- Prediction is most reliable if both cognitive and affective facts are available. If both are not available, affective facts are the next most reliable.
- Pretending affective facts (emotions) are not relevant will not improve the low reliability of the information.
- The interviewer's emotions (affective facts) will lead to a poorly conducted interview if their emotions override their reasoning ability.

Neglect of the basic truism that emotion transcends reason results, at the most, in errors of prediction in criminal justice interviews. At the least, it leads to futile arguments with interviewees.

The statement made by the interviewee probably contains simultaneous thoughts and feelings, so that we only separate the two in our responses for training purposes. It makes it a little easier for the interviewer to focus on how to respond.

Often, *thought* responses are mistaken for *emotional* responses, especially if they begin with "you feel." It is important to remember this rule: If "think" or "believe" can be substituted for the word "feel" in a response and not lose the meaning, it is not an emotional response. "You feel your parents are too restrictive of you" is a thought response. This is a thought or belief, not a feeling. The appropriate phrasing is "You believe your parents are too restrictive of you." Nor is it an emotional response if the word "that" follows the word "feel." For example, "You feel that detention will be hard for you" is not an emotional response. The appropriate phrasing is "You think detention will be hard for you" (D'Augelli, D'Augelli, & Danish, 1981).

Labeling the Emotion

Discriminating the accurate emotion the interviewee is expressing from other possible emotions is the next step in communicating accurate empathy. Figure 5.1 displays most of the possible choices. Labeling the emotion is typically accomplished using adjectives that describe emotions.

Reflecting the Emotion

Finally, the identified emotion is reflected back to the interviewee to complete the communication.

The Basic Model of Empathy

The preceding components establish the basic model of empathy:

YOU FEEL (adjective).

Direct Empathy

This is the most direct form of empathy. All other forms are modifications or derivatives of this form. It is better to learn the basic form first, even if it seems mechanical, and then to modify it to fit your personal style of responding. Quite often the basic model will seem quite mechanical and the goal is for it to become natural and spontaneous with practice. Experienced interviewers who have been through empathy skills training report this transition from mechanical to natural responding. Note the following example of direct empathy:

Interviewee: My wife is really getting on my case to get out of police work. She thinks I don't make enough money and she says she doesn't enjoy being married to someone she only sees occasionally. I don't know what the hell to do.

Interviewer: You feel trapped and desperate.

Here the interviewer chooses to emphasize the interviewee's feelings because they believe the feeling of "trapped and desperate" are very important right now. With a different interviewee in a different situation, the interviewer may have made a different choice.

Indirect Forms

Other designs of this basic model that are not as direct and are consequently less effective are:

You feel _____?

Notice that in this form the empathy comes as a question. This tends to indicate that the interviewer missed the communication the interviewee made. The interviewer is playing catch-up rather than being alert to the thoughts and feelings just expressed by the interviewee.

You just feel _____.

In this form, the word "just" tends to discount the interviewee's feeling or makes it seem the feelings were not very important. What is communicated is mild denial of seriousness or importance.

You feel like _____.

This form is also indirect because it denies that the person is actually feeling the way they do. It is similar to a person who feels this way. An analogy is to say to a person who is dying, "You feel like you're dying." In the same sense, a person who is angry does not *feel* like they are angry; they *are* angry.

Superficial Forms

A couple of forms of empathy are to be avoided because they are superficial and difficult for the interviewee to believe. They are "I understand" and "I know just how you feel." The interviewee thinks "You can't possibly know how I feel." Saying "I understand" accomplishes very little except to underscore the interviewer's naiveté. If the interviewer does understand, they can prove it by describing accurately the interviewee's feelings with the basic model of empathy: YOU FEEL _____. Even with a degree of inaccuracy, they will be establishing intent to understand, which will be far superior to the trite, overworked, cold, and superficial phrase "I understand."

Rating Responses

Now that you have the basic form of empathy, let's look again at the simple rating system you used in Chapter 3 to assist you in being able to evaluate responses rapidly, thereby helping discriminate the effectiveness of your own and others' responses. As other interviewers make responses, listen carefully and discriminate their responses according to the following scale:

STAY-WITH: If the interviewer gave back to the interviewee a response at an energy level at least at the level that was given to them so that the statements are interchangeable. No intensity of emotion was lost in the interchange, as can be seen in Figure 5.2. In this case, the energy communicated to the interviewer was at a triple plus level (+++), for example, and the interviewer responded at the same level (+++).

TURN-OFF: If the interviewer makes a response that takes away from what the interviewee said, then it is a turn-off because some of the intensity or accuracy is lost. For example, in Figure 5.2, if the interviewee had expressed to the interviewer a

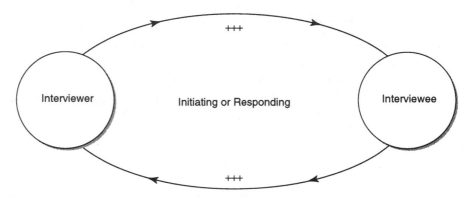

Figure 5.2 Interchangeable Responses

triple plus (+++) emotion and the interviewer responded at a single plus level (+), some of the intensity was lost. This will tend to turn off the communication.

TURN-ON: This means the interviewer provides more to the interviewee than was stated on the surface of the conversation. The response may be a turn-on because of additional clarification or deeper levels of understanding. It may include areas that the interviewee is not openly talking about, but about which they are providing hints and clues to the interviewer. In Figure 5.2, if the interviewer responds at a four plus level (++++) to a three plus (+++) interviewee stimulus, the interviewer's response is additive.

If the interviewer's responses are accurate, and they either *stay with* or *turn on* the interviewee, the interviewee will often confirm the accuracy of the response by:

- A nonverbal response such as a nod, eye contact, or a change in body posture.
- A word or phrases such as "You got it," "That's right," "Yes," or "Exactly."

The interviewee will also then go on to further explain the situation, sometimes with increased intensity or enthusiasm. The interviewer's task at this point is to allow this to occur without interrupting or jumping in too quickly.

Now let's look at examples of each of the three types of responses to see how they differ:

Stay-With

Interviewee: I don't understand why I always get passed over for sergeant. I know I can do a better job than most who have gotten it. I can't stand much longer being messed over.

Interviewer: You feel trapped and cheated.

Turn-Off

Interviewee: I don't understand why I always get passed over for sergeant. I know I can do a better job than most who have gotten it. I can't stand much longer being messed over.

Interviewer: How many times have you been passed over?

Turn-On

Interviewee: I don't understand why I always get passed over for sergeant. I know I can do a better job than most who have gotten it. I can't stand much longer being messed over.

Interviewer: You feel trapped, cheated, and desperate almost to the point of doing something drastic.

In the first example, the interviewer responded at a level that was interchangeable with what the interviewee had said. In the second example, the interviewer made a response that completely missed the message the interviewee was trying to communicate. The interviewer asked a question completely irrelevant to the emotions being expressed. This would communicate to the interviewee that the interviewer had little intent in talking about the interviewee's concerns. In the last example, the interviewer not only responded to the interviewee's feelings and concerns but also responded to what the interviewee was hinting at. The response also moves in the direction of possible drastic behavior based on strong feelings and what the interviewee is not saying but inferring.

Finally, *STAY-WITH* and *TURN-ON* responses are a signal to the interviewee to "Go on," "Continue," or "It's okay to tell me more," without the interviewer having to say these things. The interviewee then goes on to give more specifics about the situation so that the interview has movement and the interviewer is staying on track.

Modes of Interchangeable Responses

The previously discussed interaction process seen in Figure 5.2 has been identified as a fundamental concept underlying a two-person model of communication. Boshear and Albrecht (1977) refer to it as the "closed-loop" interaction process. "A's behavior is in response to B's behavior, which was in response to A's behavior, and so on, endlessly" (p. 53).

This "closed-loop" process, discussed in the previous section, includes the following parts: the *sender* of the original message; the *receiver* of the message; *encoding,* which is the translation of personal meaning into symbols; *decoding,* which is the reverse of encoding; and *channel,* which is the means by which stimuli are sent and received (Brill, 1973; Pine, 1974).

These more elaborate explanations of the process seem logical and quite thorough but difficult to apply to practical interviewing situations. Consequently, the ensuing focus of this book is on skill development with an anchoring in minimal interaction theory.

Perhaps more functional is a presentation of the modes that are possible in an interview. Figure 5.3 illustrates the eight possibilities of interaction. The interviewer can *initiate* or *respond to cognitive* or *affective* data either *verbally* or *nonverbally.* A brief explanation of each mode follows:

Mode 1: Responding verbally to cognitive data. This includes summarizing back to the interviewee facts and information. It can be as simple as "Let me see if I have the number correct. You said it was 875-2221. Is that correct?" Or it can be a rather lengthy summarization of an entire probation interview back to the probationer to make sure they know what is expected on probation.

Mode 2: Responding nonverbally to cognitive data. This includes shaking your head to indicate "yes" or "no," putting a hand up to indicate you would like the other person to stop talking, or the extreme form of putting your hands over your ears to indicate you will not listen to the other person.

Mode 3: Initiating verbally cognitive data. This mode concerns giving information in an interview. When the interviewee need facts, procedures, or statistics, this is included in this mode. For example, the

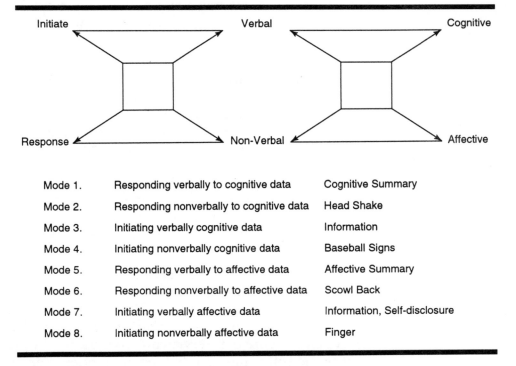

Mode 1.	Responding verbally to cognitive data	Cognitive Summary
Mode 2.	Responding nonverbally to cognitive data	Head Shake
Mode 3.	Initiating verbally cognitive data	Information
Mode 4.	Initiating nonverbally cognitive data	Baseball Signs
Mode 5.	Responding verbally to affective data	Affective Summary
Mode 6.	Responding nonverbally to affective data	Scowl Back
Mode 7.	Initiating verbally affective data	Information, Self-disclosure
Mode 8.	Initiating nonverbally affective data	Finger

Figure 5.3 Modes of Interchangeable Responses

interviewer might say "You are suspended without pay until further notice."

Mode 4:   Initiating nonverbally cognitive data. This is an interesting mode but one that isn't very useful in an interview. When a baseball third-base coach gives a "steal" sign to the runner on first, he is initiating nonverbally cognitive data. If the runner misses the sign and gets caught stealing, which results in an "out," the third-base coach may then use Mode 8.

Mode 5:   Responding verbally to affective data. This mode is the central element of empathy and a summary of feelings. When an interviewer responds to the interviewee concerning feelings or makes a summarization of the interviewee's feelings, they are using this mode.

Mode 6:   Responding nonverbally to affective data. This mode has two parts, one that is recommended in an interview and one that is not.

- It is very important and facilitative for the interviewer to use nonverbal gestures with their hands, for example, to encourage communication from the interviewee. This type of nonverbal response is not only acceptable but encouraged.
- When the interviewer "telegraphs" their approval or displeasure through nonverbal responses, it is not very effective because the interviewee will soon discover what the interviewer wants to hear or what will irritate the interviewer and then attempt to manipulate the interviewer. The result would be bias and contamination, not to mention loss of control, in the interview. This part of Mode 6 is discouraged.

Mode 7:   Initiating verbally affective data. If the interviewer discloses their feelings to the interviewee, the communication is classified in this mode. Self-disclosure, while not included in this interviewing text, is frequently covered in counselor training programs.

Mode 8:   Initiating nonverbally affective data. Any physical gesture by the interviewer that represents emotional expression is included in this mode. Some of the more commonly recognized forms are sticking out your tongue and the seemingly universal "bad finger."

In learning how to interview it is virtually impossible to implement all of the aforementioned modes. In some cases, it is frivolous because a particular mode is inappropriate for an interview. In this text, the primary modes on which we focus are Modes 1 and 5. They serve as the core of interviewing preparation but they certainly don't cover the full range of interviewing modes. For example, an agency is likely to train an employee in specific procedures in Mode 3, initiating verbally cognitive data, when they are supposed to give information to victims, witnesses, offenders, and so on as part of their job responsibilities.

Semantic Hierarchy of Emotions

In the third part of the basic empathy model (You feel   ), the requirement for the interviewer was to provide an accurate descriptive adjective. This requirement made it necessary that the interviewer have a vocabulary of descriptive adjectives to call on to do this. Most of us don't use a very wide variety of adjectives on an everyday basis to describe our or others' emotions. We tend to use overworked words or clichés that aren't very descriptive or accurate.

As a remedy for this, a semantic hierarchy of emotions has been developed and appears in Figure 5.4. Note some of the specific designs of this hierarchy.

Intensity of Words

The hierarchy of emotions in Figure 5.4 ranges from rather mild adjectives in the upper left corner to the more intense words in the lower right corner. The task of the interviewer is not only to incorporate a broader vocabulary of descriptive adjectives, but also to recognize the range of intensity of these words. In addition, it is recommended that beginning interviewers note the differences in how interviewees respond when the interviewer uses adjectives with greater intensity.

Pain–Joy Directionality

Embedded in the hierarchy of emotions is a single continuum that ranges from pure pain to pure joy, with all other words occupying a position at some place in the continuum. In other words, emotions tend to be either positive (joy) or negative (pain) and the interviewer's immediate task in formulating a response is to perceive this directionality.

Noncommittal Words

A series of words sounds as if they convey meaning, but most of the feeling is hidden. These words appear in the second column in Figure 5.4. If, for example, the interviewer responds, "You feel bad," little feeling is communicated unless "bad" is followed by more descriptive adjectives such as "humiliated," "anguished," or "hurt." Two of the noncommittal words are ineffective because they are overused: "frustrated" and "confused." They have lost much of their meaning and an effective interviewer would be well advised to avoid them in favor of more descriptive words.

Relative Intensity of Words

Relative Intensity of Words	Happiness	Noncommittal	Conflict	Anger	Fear	Sadness
Low	Amused	Curious	Blocked	Annoyed	Apprehensive	Apathetic
	Anticipating	Different	Bound	Bothered	Concerned	Bored
	Comfortable	Funny	Caught	Bugged	Tense	Disappointed
	Confident	Interested	Caught in a bind	Irked	Tight	Discontented
	Contented	Strange		Irritated	Uneasy	Mixed Up
	Glad	Surprised	Pulled	Peeved		Resigned
	Pleased	Upset		Ticked		Unsure
	Relieved					
Medium	Delighted	Frustrated	Locked	Disgusted	Afraid	Abandoned
	Eager	Confused	Pressured	Hacked	Alarmed	Burdened
	Happy	Good	Torn	Harassed	Anxious	Discouraged
	Hopeful	Bad		Mad	Fearful	Distressed
	Joyful	Awful		Provoked	Frightened	Down
	Surprised	Great		Put upon	Shook	Drained
	Up	Terrible		Resentful	Threatened	Empty
		Terrific		Set up	Worried	Hurt
				Spiteful		Lonely
				Used		Lost
						Sad
						Unhappy
						Weighted
High	Bursting		Ripped	Angry	Desperate	Anguished
	Ecstatic		Wrenched	Boiled	Overwhelmed	Crushed
	Elated			Burned	Panicky	Deadened
	Enthusiastic			Contemptuous	Petrified	Depressed
	Enthralled			Enraged	Scared	Despairing
	Excited			Fuming	Terrified	Helpless
	Free			Furious	Terror-stricken	Hopeless
	Fulfilled			Hateful		Humiliated
	Moved			Hot	Tortured	Miserable
	Proud			Infuriated		Overwhelmed
	Terrific			Pissed		Smothered
	Thrilled			Smoldering		Tortured
	Turned on			Steamed		
	(Pure Joy)	(?)	(Pain)	(Pain)	(Pain)	(Pure Pain)

Figure 5.4 Semantic Hierarchy of Emotions

Diagnosing Emotional Content Conservatively

Finally, in the "You feel _____" model, we need to look at an additional principle underlying the formulation of empathic responses. When an interviewer selects an emotion from the pain–joy continuum to complete the "You feel _____" model, two possible errors can occur.

TYPE A ERROR: This error occurs when the interviewer labels the interviewee's emotion at gradient point "y" in Figure 5.5 when the interviewee is actually at point "x." This error means the interviewer missed the depth of the emotion. Frequently, this happens when the interviewer selects a word from the "noncommittal" area (confused, frustrated, curious, etc.). When this occurs, the interviewer is not likely to be corrected by the interviewee and the interview will remain a less intense conversation. The end result will be that the error of failing to label conservatively will result in an error in predicting the interviewee's behavior. This could result in further victims of crime or a visit to the morgue. Type A errors occur frequently when interviewees are relating their concerns about family members or close working associates. *When family or close working associates are referred to in an interview, the descriptive adjectives used by the*

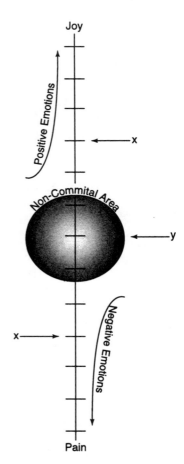

Figure 5.5 Diagnosing Emotional
Content Conservatively

interviewer should always be in the high intensity areas, as in Figure 5.5. For example, the adjectives "pain" and "hurt" should be used to refer to negative family concerns. Note the following exchange:

Interviewee: My partner, who I've worked with for four years, is drinking himself to death.

Interviewer: It's very painful to see someone, that you're so close to, destroying their life.

The interviewer's response captures the depth of the emotion when very close associates are in a crisis. Using descriptive adjectives such as "upset," "frustrated," or "confused" would miss the intensity of the feelings and constitute a Type A error.

TYPE B ERROR: This error occurs when the interviewer labels the interviewee's emotion at gradient point "x" in Figure 5.5 when the interviewee is actually at point "y." This error is harmless because it is likely to assist the interviewee in exploring and labeling the gradient of their emotions. The interviewer is more likely to be corrected by the interviewee. Note the following exchange:

Interviewee: I'm sick and tired of this graveyard shift. I'd sure like to get back on day patrol. This is for owls!

Interviewer: You feel miserable and depressed. (Type B error)

Interviewee: Naw! It's not that bad. I guess I'm just kinda tired and bored. I'll get through it like I did the last time.

In this conversation, the interviewer chose to select very strong words in the response. The words were too strong and they were corrected. The error led to a clarification by the interviewee so the interviewer now knows exactly how the interviewee feels.

If the exchange had been the other way (Type A error) and the interviewee had actually been depressed, the interviewer would likely have missed the intensity with "tired" and "bored." Most often, the interviewee will not correct a Type A error because the interviewer has communicated their inability to sense how serious the situation is or they have communicated they are not ready to discuss a serious topic.

By using the basic model of empathy, pushing for additive responses, identifying accurate words, avoiding noncommittal words, and avoiding errors in selecting adjectives, an interviewer can stay on track with an interviewee regardless of the direction the interview takes or how serious it gets.

Summary

The first and most important skill in interviewing and communication training is empathy. There are types, cautions, and benefits of empathy. Empathy requires directing, identifying the mode, labeling, and reflecting. Empathetic responses should be interchangeable, and content should be diagnosed conservatively. Interviewers should be minimally competent in the use of accurate empathy.

Now that you have completed Chapter 5, you may want to look forward to the activities at the end of the chapter. Exercise 5.1 and the Interview Challenge provide additional learning activities to reinforce some of the materials in the chapter.

Study Questions

1. When empathy is used in an interview, what kind of information is included?
2. Explain what is meant by anti-empathetic, unempathetic, and autistic interviewing.
3. What are some of the advantages of empathy?
4. Explain the difference between empathy and sympathy.
5. What is meant by *green apples*?
6. What is *response burst* and when is it likely to occur?
7. Under what conditions is the skill of empathy counterindicated?
8. What is the relationship between reason and emotion?
9. How can you discern an emotional response?
10. Explain Type A and Type B errors.
11. What is meant by an interchangeable response?
12. Distinguish between intellectual and therapeutic empathy.

Exercise 5.1

Empathy

Directions: *The following statements are measures of what you know and understand about yourself. They are descriptions of the ways that you see yourself thinking, feeling, and behaving. Give an honest response of how you describe yourself as a person. For each statement, circle:*

> M—most descriptive of me
> S—sometimes descriptive of me
> L—least descriptive of me

1. I can understand the emotions of a person who steals other people's property.

   > M—most descriptive of me
   > S—sometimes descriptive of me
   > L—least descriptive of me

2. I think a rapist would feel comfortable about talking to me about private concerns and feelings.

   > M—most descriptive of me
   > S—sometimes descriptive of me
   > L—least descriptive of me

3. I can understand the guilt that a child molester may be feeling.

   > M—most descriptive of me
   > S—sometimes descriptive of me
   > L—least descriptive of me

4. Even though some people in the criminal justice system have almost no feelings for other people, I could still understand their viewpoint.

   > M—most descriptive of me
   > S—sometimes descriptive of me
   > L—least descriptive of me

5. I have a good ability to listen and understand what a gang member is feeling.

   > M—most descriptive of me
   > S—sometimes descriptive of me
   > L—least descriptive of me

6. Other people I work with would consider me a good listener.

   > M—most descriptive of me
   > S—sometimes descriptive of me
   > L—least descriptive of me

7. I seem to be able to sense what is going on in the minds of criminals.

>   M—most descriptive of me
>   S—sometimes descriptive of me
>   L—least descriptive of me

8. I can understand some people who break the law because they have such disturbed thinking patterns.

>   M—most descriptive of me
>   S—sometimes descriptive of me
>   L—least descriptive of me

9. If I was supervising a group of offenders, they would feel comfortable talking to me about their personal problems.

>   M—most descriptive of me
>   S—sometimes descriptive of me
>   L—least descriptive of me

10. If a person who had murdered someone told me what they were thinking or feeling, I could understand and listen to them.

>   M—most descriptive of me
>   S—sometimes descriptive of me
>   L—least descriptive of me

11. I can understand and be patient with someone who is in trouble with the law.

>   M—most descriptive of me
>   S—sometimes descriptive of me
>   L—least descriptive of me

12. I seem to be able to feel the emotions that other people feel better than most people.

>   M—most descriptive of me
>   S—sometimes descriptive of me
>   L—least descriptive of me

Interview Challenge

How would you complete the following encounter? Keep in mind the concerns raised by the questions following the preliminary interview narrative.

You are a correctional officer assigned to the personnel department. One lower-level officer says to you in your office, "I was passed over for promotion. I've got a master's degree and the guy who got the promotion doesn't even have a bachelor's degree. I don't think that's very fair. What's going on here?"

1. What skills will you need to get the interview started?

   _____

   _____

   _____

2. What will you want to get accomplished in the interview?

   _____

   _____

   _____

3. How will you divide your interview time between official objectives and personal concerns in the interview (i.e., how closely will you stay with required questions)?

   _____

   _____

   _____

4. What do you anticipate the major segments of the interview to be?

   _____

   _____

   _____

5. What would be the most appropriate interview style to use in this situation?

_____

_____

_____

6. What will be some of the barriers to communication in this interview?

_____

_____

_____

7. What would you need to minimally accomplish in this interview for you to consider the interview successful?

_____

_____

_____

6

Skillful Use of Speed and Pacing

Learning Objectives

Subject. Skillful use of speed and pacing

Objectives. After a period of instruction and training, the student (trainee) will:
1. Identify the models of interview interaction.
2. Understand how to pace an interview.
3. Understand how to control the speed of an interview.
4. Understand how to use silence skillfully.
5. Understand the components of effective listening.
6. Demonstrate the use of speed, pacing, and listening at a minimal level of competency.

Learning domains.

    a. Cognitive
    b. Psychomotor

> After three months on the street, I began to realize that it's not what I expected. The big thing that hit me is I'm a social worker, that just blew my mind. I was looking for car chases and shoot-'em-ups, all the things I saw on every cop show for twenty years of my life. Now I come on the street and they expect me to fill out a bunch of forms and mediate family fights, child abuse, people OD'ing on the street.
>
> Mark Baker
> *Cops* (1985)

For most beginning interviewers, silence can be frightening. They would rather say or do anything to prevent silence. Silence seems to make interviewers very self-conscious. Most beginners can't stand the pressure. At least this is how many beginning interviewers in criminal justice relate their experience with silence.

Added to the fear of silence is the anticipation that the interviewee is likely to be angry and unhappy before the interview begins. A mother is angry because her son was brought to the juvenile detention center. An inmate is angry because he was denied parole. A probationer is angry because he has to attend AA meetings. A police officer is angry because she is being sexually harassed. The combination of the pressure to say something and the pressure of unhappy interviewees typically leads to questions or responses that are not well thought out and a hurried interview. Consequently, an important skill for effective interviewing is knowing when to remain silent. Ineffective interviewers often take too much control of the interview, ask ineffective or inappropriate questions, and interrupt too much (Yuille et al., 1999).

In this chapter we want to look at control, speed, pacing, and silence in interviews. In the end, it is hoped that the beginning interviewer will be more comfortable and controlled in interviews and will be able to use the pressure to their advantage.

Models of Interview Interaction

The interaction in an interview can be viewed and analyzed from the standpoint of the sequence of who speaks in the interview, how often they speak, and whether they speak at all. In the following models, we will let "x" represent one of the individuals in the conversation and "y" represent the other. A solid line represents silence in the interview.

Social Interaction

In a social conversation the typical design can be represented by the following sequence:

x y x y x y x y x y x y x y

In this conversation, the participants alternate speaking. When the first person (x) finishes speaking, the next person (y) immediately carries the conversation without any breaks or silence in the interchange. This is the basic form of social conversation. You speak, then I speak, then you speak, and so on. We seem to take turns talking. Silence is uncomfortable and eschewed. This is a well conditioned and deeply ingrained form of interaction that is socially reinforced and difficult for most beginning interviewers to break. The point is that if this occurs in an interview, it usually signals the interviewer is out of control and responding to the interviewee in a knee-jerk fashion.

In most cases, the person speaking will exhibit a *nonverbal signal* to indicate that they are finished speaking or about to finish. Some of the signals you may wish to note as you observe interviews are:

- Their voice level may increase with the last two or three words of the conversation or it may taper off in intensity.
- They may suddenly look directly at you with eyes slightly wider.

- They may shift their posture in a way to indicate "That's it, I'm through."
- They may gesture with their hands in a way that shifts the pressure to begin to the other person.

In any case, the signals mean that the other person is finished for the moment and you can pick up the ball and carry it for a while. They need a break. If you don't respond, only two things can happen: silence or they begin talking again. When this occurs, the interviewer approaches some degree of control in the interaction.

Lecture

In an interview where the interviewer is doing most of the talking, the interaction approaches a lecture. The interviewee says very little so that the communication is one-way, from the interviewer to the interviewee. The interviewee only listens. This can be represented by the following design:

y y y y y y y y y y y y y y

This form of social interaction in criminal justice interviews is appropriate when the following points are kept in mind:

- The attention span of many people, especially individuals involved with the criminal justice system, is quite short. Consequently, lectures should be used sparingly unless they are to be a waste of time and effort.
- Lectures can be very effective when they are used to give needed information to the interviewee.
- Lectures can easily turn to scolding and patronizing in a "parent role" interview situation. If this occurs, the interviewer is likely to be very ineffective.

Controlled Interview

In a controlled interview model, a greater variety of conditions exist between the "x's" and "y's." For example, note the following sequences:

x y _____ x x y x

x y x x _____ x x _____ x x _____ y x y x

In these sequences, for convenience we will assume that "y" is the interviewer and "x" is the interviewee. The interactions are not as constricted as there are periods of silence and periods where the interviewee said several things in succession. We could also infer that the interviewer was more in control than in a social conversation. In addition, the interviewer wasn't monopolizing the conversation. Finally, it is apparent from this model that the interviewer was comfortable with silence because they did not respond after a period of silence. In each case, "x" picked up the conversation after a period of silence. In interviewing training the goal is to have the interviewer conduct an interview designed similarly to the controlled interview. Obviously, all interviews will not fit this model, but obtaining the skill of controlling the interview will mean the interviewer can maintain control when the interview situation is appropriate for this skill.

Speed and Pacing

Skillful use of speed and pacing involves pacing and controlling the interview to avoid each of the participants taking turns in the interview.

Response Set

When each of the participants in an interview begins to anticipate the pattern of how the interaction is going to proceed, it is termed a *response set* (D. W. Johnson, 1981). Once the pattern is established, it becomes quite difficult to break or change. For example, if the interviewer starts at a slower pace, this is conducive to a more thoughtful set in the interview. On the other hand, a quick pace communicates lack of attention to thought and anxiety. In addition, the previously discussed "x y x y x y" sequence communicates to the interviewee that we will be taking turns in this interview and this is what he or she is likely to expect. Consequently, the following sequence would be very difficult to establish:

y y y y y x y y y ———————————— y y x

Why? The answer is because in this interview, the interviewer has established early that they are going to do most of the talking. In addition, the interviewee has perceived the response set correspondingly and will probably assume that the interviewer will break any silences in the interview. So they will simply wait on the interviewer.

Matching the Pace

Skopec (1986) defines *pace* as the "speed at which people present and digest information" (p. 161). The interviewer's task is to *pace* the interview to match the interviewee's communicative style. You have probably encountered difficulties in pace when you were talking to someone who talked very fast or very slow. How did you feel when they talked too fast or too slow? Most people are annoyed or bored.

These problems are magnified when the interviewee is scared, threatened, or nervous as in many criminal justice interviews. If you go too fast, they will have trouble keeping up with you. If you interview too slowly, they will likely become bored and disgusted. Beginning interviewers in criminal justice have a tendency to talk too fast for most interviewing situations in the field. Specifically, they *pace* the interview too quickly.

The key for the interviewer is to match your speed with the interviewee's speed so that you don't lose him or her. Very little is known about how this is accomplished other than that experienced interviewers seem to have gained the intuition to recognize the interviewee's communication style.

Slowing the Pace

The situation in some interviews is the opposite and the interview begins to be uncontrolled "x's." The interviewee is doing *too much* talking. The interviewer may need to interrupt the interviewee when:

- The interviewee is talking too much.
- The interviewee's conversation is irrelevant, rambling, nonsense, or alien to the purpose of the interview.

When these conditions are met, the interviewer needs to get the interviewee to stop talking or at least break the uncontrolled digression. The interviewer is not obliged to listen to any and everything the interviewee says. When they need to get the interviewee to stop talking, the interviewer has two options:

- *Inattention.* The interviewer can indirectly make a gesture that the interviewee may perceive as an indication they need to stop. The interviewer might break eye contact, look at their watch, pick up a piece of paper, or put down their pencil. Hopefully, one of these gestures will signal to the interviewee that they need to stop talking. If one of these gestures doesn't work, the interviewer may have to resort to more direct measures.
- *Interruption.* If the interviewer decides to interrupt the interviewee, the most effective way is to use both verbal and nonverbal initiatives. The interviewer can say "hold on" or "wait" while simultaneously holding an open hand in front of them, similar to the way a traffic cop stops traffic. Then the interviewer might follow with: "You've lost me. Let me stop you and see where we are" or "We've gotten off track. Let's stop a minute and see where we're going." In most situations, this interruption will effectively keep the interviewee from talking too much so that the interview can be paced and on track once again.

By using one of these techniques, the interviewer can slow down the interview and bring it back under control. When the interview is under control, several advantages are realized by the interviewer.

Outcomes of Controlled Interviews

Skillfully pacing an interview may provide the following outcomes in an interview:

- The traditional social interaction will be avoided or minimized so that the interviewer is more in control.

- The interview will be slowed so that the interviewer has more time to concentrate, think, and plan during the interview. The primary disadvantage of an uncontrolled interview is that topics are covered quickly so that the interviewer misses important concerns or subjects.

- The interviewer will communicate less stress and anxiety in the interview. "In interviewing, silence not only acts as punctuation but also communicates a mood. The lack of any pauses in the interview often indicates that the interviewer is anxious and insecure. This tends to make the respondent feel the same" (Gordon, 1975).

- The stress and anxiety brought by the interviewee to the interview either leads to more talking, which produces more information for the interviewer, or it can lead to shyness and withdrawal. The hope is that (1) the interviewer's anxiety is lower than the interviewee's and (2) if the interviewee is experiencing stress and anxiety, it will lead to the exchange of information rather than withdrawal. "An interviewer may be unwilling to leave the safety of small talk, and spend an unusual amount of time in irrelevant discussion. It goes without saying that prolonging small talk makes less time available for the actual work of the interview. The prolongation of small talk may be an indication of nervousness on the part of either or both interview participants" (Molyneaux & Lane, 1982, p. 93).

- Slowing the pace in an interview may be counterproductive. If the time allotted for an interview is very limited, slowing the pace will eat up valuable time.

Effective Use of Silence

One of the paradoxes of interviewing is that when the interviewer seems to be doing nothing, they may be invoking one of the more meaningful and powerful techniques in interviewing. In a world where conversation consumes the airwaves and "talk shows" are extremely popular, it is extremely difficult to remain silent when others stop talking.

Kinds of Silence

Beginning interviewers can anticipate some of the situations where silence might occur and, in time, learn to differentiate among silences. Eventually, they will be able to perceive the different kinds of silences and react to them differently. Some of the most common forms of silence have been identified for beginning interviewers.

Benjamin (1981) identifies five kinds of silence. They are:

- *Thinking silence.* The interviewee may be exploring their thoughts and when they get ready, will continue. The interviewer should wait until the interviewee has time to sort out their thoughts. If the silence persists to the point that it becomes extremely uncomfortable, the interviewer might use one of the following responses:

"I can see it's very important for you to think through this."
"There is no hurry, take time to think this over carefully."
"Right now you're deeply absorbed in important thought."

The interviewer can facilitate the interviewing process by being patient and letting the interviewee speak when they are ready.

■ *Respite.* Occasionally, the emotional intensity of the interview reaches a level where both participants need a break. The intensity level has led to a pause that will usually be broken by the interviewee. Responding with empathy will also help move the interview along. For example:

"Right now, you're exhausted and drained."
"You feel shocked and frightened beyond words."

■ *Confusion.* The interviewer may say something that confuses the interviewee or the interviewee may say something that confuses them. In any case, the confusion results in silence. The interviewer may want to rephrase or restate a response or question so that the confusion doesn't persist (Chapter 8). The interviewer's initiative will usually move the interview along after a silence caused by confusion.

■ *Bewilderment.* The interviewee may not know what to do next. They may be bewildered as to what to say or do. This can also lead to silence. The interviewer may want to help the movement of the interview with one of the following statements:

"Let's back up a little and start over."
"You're at a loss to know what to do next."
"What I've said has left you completely shaken and stunned."

■ *Resistance.* Perhaps the most frequent form of silence in criminal justice interviews is caused by interviewee resistance and opposition. Milne and Bull (1999) have identified four origins of resistance:

   • The interviewee is willing to talk and has the ability to tell. This results in a cooperative and accurate interviewee.
   • The interviewee is unwilling to talk and has the ability to tell. The interviewee has knowledge but will not reveal it.
   • The interviewee is willing to talk and is unable to tell. The interviewee either cannot remember or doesn't know.
   • The interviewee is unwilling to talk and unable to tell. The interviewee seems resistant, but actually does not have any information.

The resistance can be precipitated by threat, fear, disgust, or anger. Interviewers usually find this kind of silence the most difficult to handle because of its confrontational nature. It approaches a struggle between the interviewer and interviewee. The interviewer may feel threatened or rejected. An angry and hostile silence can best be processed with the skill of direct, mutual talk (called immediacy, to be discussed later). As we will see, this skill is vital in handling resistance. For now, the interviewer can best deal with this kind of resistance by (1) expecting resistance when interviewing offenders in quasi-adversarial interviews and (2) avoiding making defensive responses as if under personal attack. Some of the various responses that can be used when the interview is silent because of resistance are:

"You don't have to say anything. In fact, I don't want you to if you don't want to."

"Talking to me is a real hassle. You're pretty fed up and disgusted."

"It's really painful to be in this situation."

"Your silence is so firm, it almost appears as if you had it planned."

Overcoming resistance in criminal justice interviews is difficult at best and unavoidable at worst. Since many interviews with offenders are quasi-adversarial, the interviewee should expect some level of resistance and lack of cooperation. By establishing a solid base of empathy, resistance encounters can be reduced so that the interview can progress.

On the other hand, you may have to break the silence in an interview. An interview should not develop into a "staring contest" or a struggle to see who is going to be the first to give in and break the silence. The silence should not reach the point of being ridiculous. In this case, prolonging the interview can only lead to further anger and confusion.

The central point of this discussion is that silence can facilitate movement in an interview if it is used skillfully. This skill can be developed by experience, practice, and focused listening techniques.

Skillful Use of Silence

The skillful use of silence involves active listening. When the interviewer is carefully noting what the interviewee is saying verbally and nonverbally as well as simultaneously monitoring their own reactions to information, they are listening actively (Wicks & Josephs, 1977).

Even though the interviewer is not asking questions or making responses, he or she is very active in processing information cues. Several suggestions about active listening techniques are offered at this point.

■ *Give yourself time to think.* Beginning interviewers ask too many questions. They don't give themselves enough time to reflect on what the interviewee has just said. They pass over critical statements by the interviewee, especially at the beginning and end of the interview.

■ *Don't intellectualize or give speeches.* Use short responses and single questions. Beginning interviewers tend to be long-winded so that they monopolize the interview.

■ *Strive for pauses and periods of silence.* You will communicate a mood of confidence, listening intensity, and relaxation when the interview is spaced with a few pauses. "The interviewer can pause for two to twenty seconds before asking the next question and yet be interrupting. Ordinarily, if the respondent has completed a sentence with a tone of finality and then looks at the interviewer expectantly, a two-second pause assures that he has finished the comment; but if the respondent stops obviously in the middle of a sentence or is gazing thoughtfully into space, a silence of ten seconds before asking the next question is no guarantee against interruption" (Gordon, 1975, p. 377). This mood will likely be contagious for the interviewee. This mood shows the respondent that the interviewer expects him to take time to give thoughtful answers, and it allows time for the respondent to retrace his own paths of association to revive faded images and feelings" (Gordon, 1975, p. 378).

■ *Don't interrupt.* Let the interviewee finish what he or she is saying. Don't finish sentences for him or her when he or she stumbles or hesitates.

■ *Use minimal encouragers.* The flow of information can be encouraged by using the verbal expressions of "Uh huh," "Hmm," "I see," "What else," and "Tell me more." These encouragers tend to slow the interview and create an interview climate where it is expected that the interviewee is to take time to give thoughtful answers.

■ *Maintain personal wellness.* If the interviewer maintains a lifestyle characterized by pervasive anxiety, his or her interviews are likely to be driven by anxiety. Maintaining a lifestyle characterized by low stress and anxiety will assist interviewers in conducting interviews that are also not characterized by stress and anxiety. Active listening demands low interviewer anxiety because it's very difficult to focus on another person when you are focusing on your own lack of control.

Controlling the interview, pacing the interview, and using silence effectively are critical skills in interviewer training. They are difficult skills but their mastery can pave the way for effective use of further skills in this training.

Listening

Good interviewers must be accurate and effective listeners. "A common error of inexperienced interviewers is to talk too much and listen too little" (Kadushin, 1990, p. 243). If an interviewer spends most of the time in the interview talking, then they won't hear much in the interview. Most experts in interviewing recommend that if an interviewer spends more than a third of the interview talking, they are talking more than they should.

Effective listening consists of several essential elements in order to reach the goals of an interview. These elements are:

Active Silence

Accurate and effective listening requires active silence. Active silence means the interviewer is focusing on what the interviewee is saying, how it is said, and perceiving the meanings of what is said. So, listening is a very active process with a great deal of internal cognitive processing taking place.

Covert Meanings

Good listening includes following what is overtly said as well as the covert or hidden messages in an interview. In other words, this means listening for the "story behind the story" or the underlying theme of the story the interviewer is communicating, which may be different from the overt theme in the interview. In Chapter 8 this is referred to as "hidden agendas." In order to pick up these covert meanings, the interviewer must be actively silent.

Attending Skills

Listening requires deliberate and effective attending skills. Attending skills communicate an intent to listen and pay attention to what the interviewee is saying. Deliberate attending skills communicate the interviewer is trying to listen and is focused on the task. Attending skills include:

- Direct and continuous eye contact
- Directly facing the interviewee
- A slight forward lean toward the interviewee
- Clear articulation of speech that is strong enough in volume to be easily heard by the interviewee
- Hand gestures that complement what the interviewer is saying

Good listeners should be careful to avoid the nonverbal behaviors that indicate inattention in an interview. Some of these behaviors are occasionally looking at the clock on the wall or your watch, doodling on your notepad, looking at your computer screen, glancing around the room, acknowledging someone outside the room, or daydreaming.

Some of the verbal behaviors to avoid are finishing the interviewee's sentences for them or anxiously using "Yes, yes, I know" or "Okay, okay, I see." Hurrying the interviewee along not only communicates inattention but also an impatient interviewer.

"The average rate of spoken speech is about 125 words per minute. We can read, and understand an average of about 300–500 words per minute. There is, then, a considerable amount of dead time in spoken communication, during which the listener's mind can easily become distracted" (Kadushin, 1990, p. 247). During this dead time, the listener can easily become impatient, distracted, or consumed with daydreaming. Active listeners use this time to focus on nonverbal behavior or make connections to what was said earlier in the interview.

Kinesics

Active listening involves paying attention to nonverbal messages such as facial expressions, body posture, eye contact, and nervous fidgeting. This means that good listeners pay attention to silence messages as well as verbal messages.

Filtering

In interviews we may receive a lot of information that is irrelevant, superficial, or trivial. Active listening requires that the interviewer filter the overwhelming flow of sights, sounds, feelings, and thoughts that are communicated simultaneously by selectively editing this flow of information. It's almost impossible to pay attention to assimilate everything, so we tend to filter some of the information, which is either irrelevant or superficial chatter. Active listening requires this process of filtering so that only the information that is essential to the goals and purposes of the interview is the focus of the interviewer's attention.

Summary

Interviewing requires a controlled social interaction, skillful use of pacing, and effective use of silence. In addition, interviewing requires active listening and attending skills. Interviewers should be minimally competent in the use of speed and pacing.

You have now completed Chapter 6, and you may want to move forward to the activities at the end of the chapter. Exercise 6.1 and the Interview Challenge are provided as additional learning experiences, based on some of the concepts presented in the chapter.

Study Questions

1. What is meant by *response set?*
2. What is *pace* in an interview?
3. What are some of the advantages in skillfully pacing an interview?
4. Why would you expect resistance in criminal justice interviews?
5. What are some of the types of silence?
6. What are the elements of good listening?

Exercise 6.1

Speed and Pacing

Directions: In the series of diagrams below, indicate what you can infer from the interview by writing your comments on the line below each diagram. In the diagrams:

x = interviewee question or response
y = interviewer question or response
s = interviewer summary
_____ = pause or silence

1. x y x x y x y x y x y x y x y x y x y

    _____

2. x y y y y y y y x y y y y y y y y x

    _____

3. x x x x x y x x x x x x x x y x x x s

    _____

4. x y _____ y _____ y _____ y

    _____

5. x y x x x x x y x x x s x x x x x x s

    _____

6. x x x x x x x x x x x x x x x s

    _____

7. y y y y y y y s y y y y y y y s

    _____

8. x y _____ x x _____ x _____ x s x _____ x x x _____ x s

    _____

9. x _____ s

    _____

10. x y x y x y x y _____

    _____

Interview Challenge

How would you complete the following encounter? Keep in mind the concerns raised by the questions following the preliminary interview narrative.

You are a female police officer and an officer in the union. Another female officer reports to you and says, "The Assistant Chief won't leave me alone. He keeps trying to put his hands on me. He always refers to me as 'baby.' Yesterday he told me if I didn't date him—and you know he's married—I wouldn't ever get anywhere in this department. What am I gonna do? I'm sick of this mess."

1. What skills will you need to get the interview started?

   _____

   _____

   _____

2. What will you want to get accomplished in the interview?

   _____

   _____

   _____

3. How will you divide your interview time between official objectives and personal concerns in the interview (i.e., how closely will you stay with required questions)?

   _____

   _____

   _____

4. What do you anticipate the major segments of the interview to be?

   _____

   _____

   _____

5. What would be the most appropriate interview style to use in this situation?

_____

_____

_____

6. What will be some of the barriers to communication in this interview?

_____

_____

_____

7. What would you need to minimally accomplish in this interview for you to consider the interview successful?

_____

_____

_____

7

Summarization Skills

Learning Objectives

Subject. Summarization Skills

Objectives. After a period of instruction, the student (trainee) will:
1. Understand the purpose of summaries in an interview.
2. Understand when to summarize in an interview.
3. Understand how to summarize in an interview.
4. Identify the various models of summarization.
5. Demonstrate the use of a summary in an interview at a minimum level of competency.

Learning domains.

    a. Cognitive
    b. Affective
    c. Psychomotor

> The judges and probation officers and social workers and everybody else think mainly about the suspect and how they can help him stop whatever he specializes in doing to his victims, but you and me are the only ones who see what he does to his victims—right after it's done.
>
> Joseph Wambaugh
> *The New Centurions* (1970)

Once an interviewer has learned to make empathetic responses and control the interaction in the interview, it is important to be able to summarize in an interview. Making a summary in an interview will reinforce both empathy skills and pacing skills.

Empathy skills will be complemented and strengthened because in many cases the summary will contain critical affective points made in the interview. Speed and pacing skills will be reinforced by summarization skills because pausing to make a summary will slow the interview and separate it into manageable units.

However, as an interviewer, you don't want to waste valuable time in an interview by repeating or parroting the preceding discussion. This can be frustrating and time-consuming and accomplishes very little. There are times and reasons when a summary can be very effective. So, the important considerations in learning to summarize in an interview focus on *what* a summary is used for, *when* it should be used, and *how* it is made.

The Purpose

A summary in an interview provides several advantages for the interviewer. When the decision is made to use a summary, one or several of the following can be accomplished or facilitated:

- The pace of the interview will be controlled so that the conversation doesn't move too quickly from one topic to another without some degree of closure on each topic.
- The interview can be formed or structured into manageable units for the interviewee and interviewer. These units frequently make it easier for the interviewer to remember the critical parts of the interview if they so desire or are required to make a written summary at the conclusion of the interview. The importance of legal documentation and record-keeping in criminal justice interviews makes this one of the central purposes of a summary because very few individuals are interviewed in law enforcement, corrections, or the courts without a subsequent written report documenting the interview.
- Critical points in the interview can be emphasized and reemphasized in the interview by using a summary. For example, a probation officer may decide that the reporting procedures and requirements established by the court need to be emphasized several times to a probationer who has a past record of unconscientious behavior on probation. A summary will serve this purpose.
- The listening ability of the interviewer is further established because they have to actively focus on and follow what the interviewee is saying in order to make a summary.
- By choosing what to summarize in an interview, the interviewer can set the tone of the interview. Consistent with the discussion of "influencing" in Chapter 1, this choice of summarizing facts or emotions can affect the direction and outcome of an interview.
- By requesting that the interviewee summarize in an interview, the interviewer can gain hunches or clues to the comprehension and retention level of the interviewee. These clues may then lead to a complete reevaluation of how to proceed in the interview.

Now that we have looked at a few of the purposes of an interview summary, we need to know when to use a summary.

When to Summarize

There are certain times when summaries prove particularly useful. Usually the importance of the information being communicated in the interview dictates when and how often to summarize. Molyneaux and Lane (1982) point out that "if the accuracy of the information obtained is so important that errors could prove disastrous—or even fatal—the interviewer might very well wish to repeat certain information in detail" (p. 145). Some criminal justice interviews certainly fit this description. Others are not this critical.

Miller, Wackman, Nunnally, and Miller (1988, pp. 196–197) have presented the most complete list of situations where summarizing is most important. They say you should think of summarizing when you want to:

- guarantee that an important message is heard
- minimize guesswork
- demonstrate respect for others by showing an interest in understanding them
- help yourself to hear others accurately
- track a difficult or mixed message
- send a positive, intimate message and minimize its being discounted
- confirm a contract
- set priorities on issues
- clarify perspectives
- take a positive step toward resolving a conflict
- confirm action plans

From the above list, it can easily be seen how summaries are needed in criminal justice interviews where misunderstanding would be costly. Because of the importance of accurate and precise information and understanding in criminal justice interviews, summaries should be used to a greater extent than in other, less formal interviews.

How to Summarize

When the interviewer has been actively listening to the interviewee or has covered a block of related information, a summary is appropriate. Also, a summary should be made after several interchangeable or additive empathetic responses.

Summaries involve three components:

- A *lead* such as:

    "What I hear you saying is . . ."
    "You appear to be saying . . ."
    "Putting this all together . . ."
    "What this adds up to is . . ."
    "Let me see if I have what you've been saying . . ."
    "Okay, let's stop and try to put this together . . ."

- The *content* of what the interviewee has been saying in a simpler and clearer form. The content of the summary may focus on the facts, feelings, or both depending on what the interviewer chooses to summarize.

■ A *check* for accuracy. The interviewer checks to see if the summary is accurate by getting an acknowledgment from the interviewee. This *check* could be:

"Is that correct?"
"Am I on the right track?"
"Are we on the same page?"
"Am I hearing what you've said?"

The *check* may provide the interviewer with surprising new information and a clue to the overall accuracy of the information in the interview. In addition, the interviewer can avoid making incorrect decisions based on faulty information given to or received from an offender or witness.

Summary Models

At various times within an interview, the interviewer summarizes several facts, thoughts, or emotions stated by the interviewee. As we have seen, there are several reasons why the interviewer would want to summarize, specific times to summarize, and certain techniques for summarizing.

In addition to the "what," "when," and "how" of summaries, they can be viewed and understood according to several models that fall under two main types: selection models and content models.

Selection Models

When a summary is made in an interview, the interviewer has the choice of selecting how many of the points in the interview are to be summarized and which points are to be included, deleted, or emphasized.

■ *Perfect rehash summary.* Figure 7.1 presents a graphic display of a summary where the interviewer restated all of the main

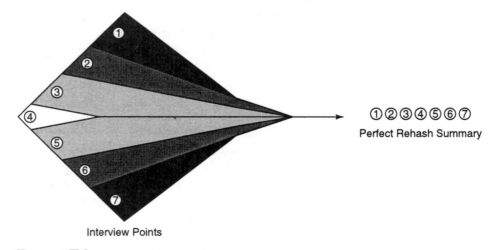

Interview Points

Figure 7.1   Perfect Rehash Summary

points in the interview with minimal alteration, modification, addition, or deletion. An example of this type is the case of a parole officer going over the entire meeting in summary fashion before the interview was ended. This is obviously very time-consuming and fails to emphasize critical points the parolee needs to remember.

- *Incomplete summary.* If the parole officer only summarized part of the interview, it would look like Figure 7.2. In this case, some of the interview was omitted in the summary and the omitted points could appear to the parolee as unimportant. On the other hand, the points could have been omitted by the parole officer because they were unimportant or were less important and were omitted because of time limitations.

- *Incomplete summary with critical point omitted.* If the interviewer only summarized part of the interview and omitted a critical point (2) in the interview, it would appear like Figure 7.3. For example, a probation officer failed to summarize one of the critical rules of probation stipulated by the court. If this omission occurs, it is quite easy for the interviewee (probationer) to get the message that this particular rule was not very important. Consequently, this model of a summary is usually one to be avoided.

- *Summary with emphasis on critical points.* A more effective summary model than the previous one appears in Figure 7.4. In this model, the interviewer included the critical point (2) in the summary with mention of the point more than one time. In this case, the probation officer referred to a critical rule of probation twice in the summary so that the probationer understood the importance of the rule.

Content Models

When a summary is made in an interview, the interviewer has the choice of also selecting the content to be summarized. Ivey and Gluckstern (1974) indicate that interviewer summaries usually focus on two major areas of the interviewee's comments: emotion and content.

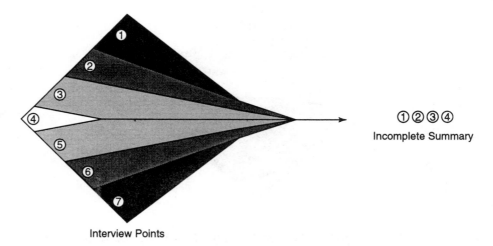

Interview Points

Figure 7.2 Incomplete Summary

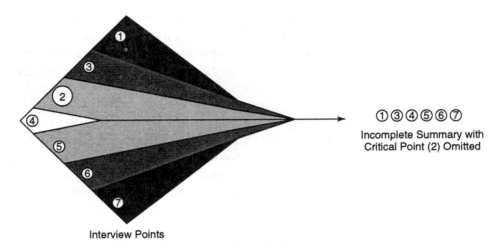

Interview Points

Figure 7.3   Incomplete Summary with Critical Point Omitted

- *Summarization of emotion.* Affective summaries are a means of picking up all of the feelings that have been communicated in the interview after several responses have been made. Affective summaries tie together what the interviewee has been saying emotionally. Usually an affective summary is made when the interviewee is exhausted or the complete depth of emotions has been reached. A model of summarization of emotion appears in Figure 7.5. In this model the interviewer summarized the primary emotions (2,4,5) from an interview consisting of cognitive and affective information. When this discrimination is made, it is likely to set an affective tone in the interview as the interview progresses.
- *Cognitive summary.* In Figure 7.6, the interviewer chose to summarize cognitive content (facts, behavior, ideas, procedures) instead of emotions. In the summary, cognitive points (1,3,6,7)

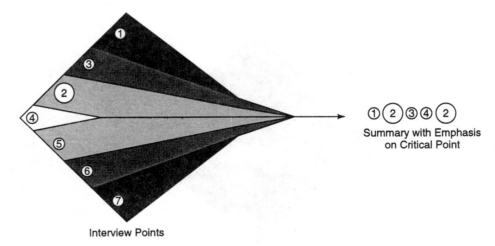

Interview Points

Figure 7.4   Summary with Emphasis on Critical Points

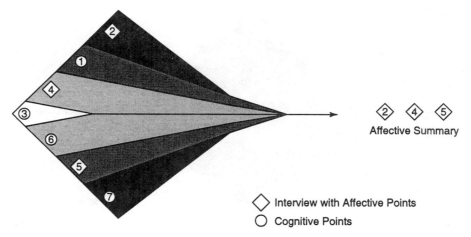

Figure 7.5 Affective Summary

were included while the affective points (2,4,5) were excluded. This discrimination will also likely set the tone of the interview so that the interviewee will expect the interview to consist of fact, information, procedures, and so on.

■ *Mixed summary.* If the interviewer summarizes both the cognitive and affective points in the interview, as can be seen in Figure 7.7, all points will be included and the summary is not likely to direct or influence the subsequent tone of the interview. On the other hand, summarizing both cognitive and affective content can communicate to the interviewee that you are attending to the total person.

In conclusion, summaries are a skill that the interviewer can *choose* to use. What the interviewer selects to include in a summary and the content of the summary can influence the understanding in the interview and the subsequent tone of the interview. Summaries of either emotional or factual information should not be overused and if summaries are used they should not omit critical points of the interview.

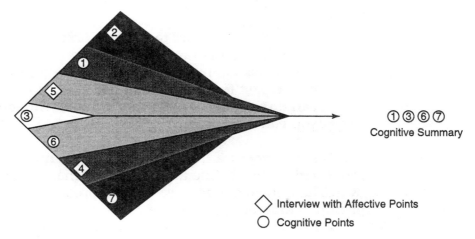

Figure 7.6 Cognitive Summary

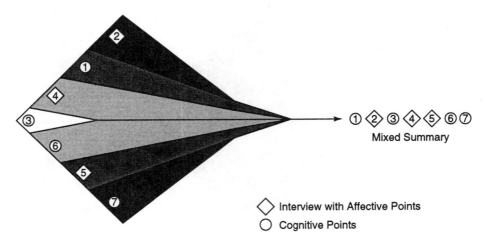

Figure 7.7   Mixed Summary

Interviewee Summaries

Frequently, interviewers need to assess how well an interviewee is retaining information, understanding main points, or letting go of misconceptions in an interview. An interviewee summarization will also provide feedback to the interviewer if they have been covering material too quickly or using overly technical language.

The interviewer requests that the interviewee summarize a unit of the conversation so that the interview doesn't continue with the assumption that the interviewee is understanding what is being said. Requests may need to be made several times during the interview. On the other hand, it is important that this request be made in a *courteous*, *diplomatic*, and *smooth* manner that is not offensive to the interviewee, whether they can or can't summarize after the request is made. The primary goal of interviewee summaries is not to find out *whether* the interviewee understands but *what* they understand.

The following stimulus statements will help initiate the request for an interviewee summary:

> "Why don't you go back over this so I can be sure I've told you everything."
> "Why don't you explain to me your probation rules so I can make sure I haven't left one out."
> "Let's run back through this so we can be sure we've got it correct."
> "For the past few minutes we have talked about the things you can do to stay out of further trouble. Would you tell me what you can do?"

What happens if the interviewee can't summarize after they are requested to do so? The answer is that the interviewer has to start over. The critical points have to be approached in a simpler fashion or from a different perspective.

So we can now see that interviewer summaries help the interviewee understand information in the interview in a more focused and concrete way. Conversely, interviewee summaries help the interviewer communicate information in the interview in a more focused and concrete way. In either case, acquisition of the skill of summarization will reinforce empathy and pacing skills and allow training to move to the next level of skill acquisition.

Summary

Interviewers need to know what, when, and how to summarize in an interview. Interviewee summaries can also be used in interviews. The skill of summarization should be used at a minimal level of competency.

Now that you have completed Chapter 7 and three skills, you may want to complete Assessment 7.1, which includes the skills of attending, empathy, speed and pacing, and summarization. Finally, you may also want to complete Exercises 7.1 and 7.2 and finish your learning experiences over this chapter with the Interview Challenge.

Study Questions

1. What are some of the advantages of using a summary in an interview?
2. When should a summary be made in an interview?
3. What are the components of a summary?
4. What kinds of summaries can an interviewer choose in an interview and how are they different?
5. What is the goal of an interviewee summary?

Assessment 7.1

Interviewing Training Self-Efficacy Assessment: Knowledge and Skills

Directions: *After completing the initial training, rate your estimation of your knowledge and skill acquisition on the following scale:*

1 = Unskilled/Unaware
2 = Awkward
3 = Average
4 = Skilled/Knowledgeable

_____ a. Knowledge of attending skills

_____ b. The effective use of attending skills

_____ c. Knowledge of empathy skills

_____ d. The effective use of empathy skills

_____ e. Knowledge of speed and pacing skills

_____ f. The effective use of speed and pacing skills

_____ g. Knowledge of summarization skills

_____ h. The effective use of summarization skills

Exercise 7.1

Summarization

Directions: *In groups of two, list the emotions that you are most comfortable and most uncomfortable with. After the list is complete, explain them to the other person. The other person summarizes what has been said when the first person concludes the explanation of the feelings. At the conclusion, the partners switch roles and repeat the exercise.*

Emotions

Very comfortable

1.
2.
3.

No experience with or neutral

1.
2.
3.

Very uncomfortable

1.
2.
3.

Repeat the exercise using the facts about your life.

Facts

Very important

1.
2.
3.

Minor importance

1.
2.
3.

Meaningless

1.
2.
3.

At the conclusion of the exercise summarizing facts, the partners switch roles and the other partner summarizes the facts.

Process the exercise by discussing the various difficulties encountered when an interviewer summarizes facts and feelings. Identify the environmental, multicultural, and temporal variables that affect an interviewer's ability to summarize effectively.

Exercise 7.2

Critical Summarization Points Inventory (CSPI)

Directions: *For each of the groups of summarization points, identify the most critical point to be emphasized in the summary. Each of the items has been mentioned in the interview. Check (√) the most important point.*

Interview 1: Probationer

_____   a. The probationer's wife got laid off from her job.

_____   b. The probationer has agreed to attend an outpatient drug and alcohol treatment program once a week.

_____   c. The probationer is angry and disgusted in most interviews.

_____   d. The probationer missed his last scheduled meeting with the probabation officer.

Interview 2: Witness

_____   a. The witness thinks the suspect was tall.

_____   b. The witness thinks the suspect was wearing jeans.

_____   c. The witness is sure the suspect had a dragon tattoo on his left forearm.

_____   d. The witness is sure the suspect was wearing a cap.

Interview 3: Parolee (Prospective)

_____   a. The parolee thinks he has been rehabilitated.

_____   b. The parolee has changed his life.

_____   c. The parolee has become more religious.

_____   d. The parolee has a job at the meat-packing plant when he gets out.

Interview 4: Juvenile on Probation

_____ a. The juvenile thinks her grandmother is too strict.

_____ b. The juvenile is disrespectful toward the grandmother.

_____ c. The juvenile has agreed to sign a contract to stop swearing at the grandmother if she can stay out thirty minutes longer on weekends.

_____ d. The grandmother is angry, resentful, and hurt by the juvenile's mother who left the child with the grandmother.

Interview 5: Police Officer–Partner

_____ a. The partner said he and his wife had a big fight last night.

_____ b. The partner said his wife was arrested for shoplifting yesterday.

_____ c. The partner said he and his wife haven't been getting along recently.

_____ d. The partner is grouchy and doesn't want to talk about his "worthless" wife.

Interview 6: Prisoner/Inmate

_____ a. The prisoner said a carton of contraband cigarettes appeared on his wing last week.

_____ b. The prisoner just completed his GED test.

_____ c. The prisoner is agitated.

_____ d. The prisoner said his wife is coming to visit next weekend.

Interview Challenge

How would you complete the following encounter? Keep in mind the concerns raised by the questions following the preliminary interview narrative.

You have been sent to interview a prominent community leader to gain their support both publicly and financially for a major crime prevention effort in the community. To begin the interview, he says, "You know, I don't think women should be police officers. It's one of the biggest mistakes we've ever made."

1. What skills will you need to get the interview started?

   _____

   _____

   _____

2. What will you want to get accomplished in the interview?

   _____

   _____

   _____

3. How will you divide your interview time between official objectives and personal concerns in the interview (i.e., how closely will you stay with required questions)?

   _____

   _____

   _____

4. What do you anticipate the major segments of the interview to be?

   _____

   _____

   _____

5. What would be the most appropriate interview style to use in this situation?

_____

_____

_____

6. What will be some of the barriers to communication in this interview?

_____

_____

_____

7. What would you need to minimally accomplish in this interview for you to consider the interview successful?

_____

_____

_____

8

Immediacy Skills

Learning Objectives

Subject. Immediacy Skills

Objectives. After a period of instruction, the student (trainee) will:

1. Understand the concept of immediacy.
2. Understand the use of immediacy in an interview.
3. Identify the types of immediacy.
4. Use immediacy of experiencing in an interview at a minimal level of competency.
5. Use immediacy of relationship in an interview at a minimal level of competency.

Learning domains.

    a. Cognitive
    b. Affective
    c. Psychomotor

> Police see a hundred percent of criminality.
>
> Joseph Wambaugh
> *The New Centurions* (1970)

When we leave the skills of empathy, speed and pacing, and summarization, we move to skills with greater levels of action and difficulty. These more advanced skills often demand competence in all of the above skills. In addition, these new skills demand a greater level of *awareness* in the interview so that the interviewer doesn't become absorbed with the process and fail to recognize when to be more or less active in the interview.

The Concept of Immediacy

When two people are interacting with one another, in an interview, a "third factor is introduced—the *relationship* itself" (Boshear & Albrecht, 1977). The relationship can modify, have little effect on, or seriously subvert the interview process. For the interviewer, immediacy involves being aware of what he/she is doing as the interviewer while at the same time being aware of the relationship between themselves and the interviewee. Doing this is sometimes difficult and demanding.

In an interview, the interviewer is faced with three options when immediacy is a factor:

- *Respond to relationship issues and then continue the business of the interview.* In this case, the business of the interview may be minimized at the expense of the relationship. In highly structured information giving or getting interviews, this could be very costly to the results of the interview. Valuable time could also be wasted.
- *Ignore relationship issues and hope or pretend they will go away or not seriously affect the interview.* The risk of this option is that the information obtained in the interview is contaminated by the relationship to the point that it is invalid. Also, pretending that relationship issues will disappear is usually unrealistic.
- *Use relationship issues to facilitate the process of the interview.* This final option fully embraces immediacy to the point that the interview moves in the direction of counseling and therapy, which can be the goal of some criminal justice interviews. If, on the other hand, the interview has a goal and purpose different from counseling, then the original purpose of the interview would be subverted.

Each of these options has assets and liabilities and the interviewer's choice will affect the outcome of the interview. In each case something will be gained and lost in the interview.

Use of Immediacy Skills

Immediacy skills are used when interview situations need to stay in the here-and-now, or present-moment experiencing. Immediacy is particularly necessary when an interviewee persists in talking about past or future feelings or experiences. Specifically, he/she dwells on what he/she has accomplished or is going to accomplish with few references to the present. Immediacy is also called for when the interviewer sees that he/she or the interviewee has *nonverbalized* thoughts and feelings about what is taking place in the interview that are getting in the way.

Prediction

Predictions about future behavior based on an interview are more reliable and accurate if they incorporate present moment experiences. Rehashed past experiences (war stories) and anticipated future experiences (dreams) tend to be quite unreliable in determining future behavior because the "present" is very real while the past and future are unreal. In criminal justice we rely heavily on past behavior such as "criminal histories" to predict an offender's likelihood of recidivism. In the absence of immediate behavioral information, an offender's past behavior is the best that we have. If we had both, our predictions about their future performance would be more accurate but perhaps still below public expectations.

Staying in the Here-and-Now

Here-and-now immediacy refers to the interviewer's ability to discuss with an interviewee what is happening between the two of you in the present moment. It is also referred to as "us" discussions. It is not about the entire relationship but only about what is occurring at the moment. As a word of caution, staying in the here-and-now is not a search for blame when there are relationship difficulties, but rather a bringing up to a level of awareness and labeling what is *really* going on in an interview.

Hidden Agendas

When the interaction in an interview is not what it seems to be, there may be a hidden agenda. When the interviewee's wants are unknown or are known but left unstated, they can affect interaction adversely. The interviewer has to guess at the intentions of the interviewee.

If, for example, the interviewee's behavior is strange, irrational, uncooperative, or manipulative, it may be generated by a "hidden agenda." Miller and colleagues (1988, p. 101) indicate that "hidden agendas" can happen if the interviewer or interviewee:

- Are *unaware* of what they really want.
- Are aware of what they want, but fail to be clear with each other about what they want. They may genuinely forget or think their wants are not important enough to disclose.
- *Choose* to keep their wants unstated for one reason or another.

"Hidden agenda occur most often when we think other people would not like our wants or 'buy into' them. So, rather than disclose them directly, we try to work around others to get what we want. We also usually try to hide our intentions when they are ornery, mean, or embarrassing" (Miller et al., 1988, p. 101).

Notice the hidden agenda in the following criminal justice interviews:

Surface—"I want to interview you for a job as a police officer."
Hidden—*"I want to impress you with how 'macho' I am."*

Surface—"I would like to have a job as a probation officer."

Hidden—*"I want you to find me physically attractive."*

Surface—"I am here for my parole meeting."

Hidden—*"I am angry at you and the system for giving me orders."*

Surface—"I want to get my probation meeting over as soon as possible."

Hidden—*"I resent being supervised by someone younger than myself."*

Surface—"I want to get the facts from you as to exactly what you saw when the crime occurred."

Hidden—*"I get off in thirty minutes and I'm tired, impatient, and fed up. Let's get this over quickly."*

Surface—"I'll do whatever it takes to stay out of any more trouble."

Hidden—*"I don't trust you or anybody else in this place."*

When communication in an interview becomes confusing, hidden agendas and unstated resentments are often at work. The use of immediacy skills is central for clearing the air and understanding what is *really* going on in the interview. The goal is direct, "telling it like it is" information rather than information that is contaminated by hidden wants, desires, or resentments. These skills are used whenever the interviewee is indirect with their experiences or relationships.

When the interviewer has a hidden agenda, the purposes of the interview are usually confused, corrupted, or compromised, because the interviewer is no longer objective, authentic, and honest. The interviewer is saying one thing but meaning another. These phony interviews sometimes occur in criminal justice agencies. For example, all the sergeants in a police department are required to be interviewed for a promotion to lieutenant, even though it is widely known who will receive the promotion. Phony interviews are conducted so that the department appears to consist of enthusiastic and interested candidates. Hidden agendas on the part of the interviewer usually lead to invalid and unreliable information at best and anger and hostility at worst.

Immediacy of Experiencing

Using the skill of immediacy of experiencing refers to getting the interviewee to communicate in the here-and-now as opposed to the there-and-then and to directly "own" their experiences. Interviewees typically avoid direct experiencing in two areas.

Staying in the Past/Future

If an interviewee says, "When I got home from work last night and found my husband drunk and the house torn up, I was very upset," the person is vaguely in contact with the concept of anger, but not the actual anger. They were upset—no doubt very angry—last night, but how are they feeling at the time of the interview? The interviewer, in order to bring the person into the here-and-now, might reply:

"Even now you're angry at your husband for being so inconsiderate."

Another example is an offender who says:

"When I get out there's no way I'm coming back."

The interviewer, in using immediacy of experiencing, might reply:

"Right now, you're very scared about getting out and even more frightened at the thought of returning."

Impersonal Pronouns

Another way interviewees reduce their awareness is through the use of impersonal pronouns—"It," "you," "a person," "we," and so on. Notice the following statements made by a probationer:

"This probation makes me sick of all the rules and regulations. It is getting to be too much."
"You can't get a fair deal in this county."
"A person is in for big trouble if they get probation in this state."
"We really don't give ex-convicts much of a chance, do we."

All of these statements will be more directly "owned" by the interviewee by the following immediacy of experiencing response:

"You're fed up and disgusted with probation and angry with the whole mess."

Here the interviewer focuses on the interviewee—"you"—and specific emotions—disgusted and angry—so that the communication is direct and owned.

Immediacy of Experiencing Techniques

Several techniques may be used to bring an interview into the here-and-now:

- Use present-tense feelings, words, and verbs. The interviewer should grasp how the person feels now—not how they felt yesterday, last week, last month, or last year.
- Use responses with stems like "and you still feel . . . ," "and even now . . . ," or "At this moment . . ."
- Listen for "cold potatoes" (Schutz, 1973). Listen for the interviewee saying something about themselves that they have said many times before so that the account is "warmed over." In these cases, the feeling behind the account is hollow and without much present-moment energy. The conversation is a repetition,

recounted tale, or "war story" that may be hiding information of greater importance.

■ Ignore references to the past or future and respond to only here-and-now statements.

■ Encourage the interviewee to use the first-person, singular pronoun "I" in speaking about themselves.

In using these techniques, the interviewer will be able to more accurately assess the need for action based on what has transpired in the interview because he/she has based the decision on direct, immediate information.

Immediacy of Relationship

Immediacy of relationship deals with overt and covert interviewee relationship issues between the interviewer and interviewee. It is called for when these issues are of a magnitude that they interfere with the business of the interview or contaminate the results of the interview. A skillful interviewer is one who can "tell it like it is" and label obvious relationship issues as well as hidden agendas when the need arises.

When the Skill Is Needed

The need to use the skill of immediacy of relationship is frequently cued by the interviewee's use of the following stems:

"This place . . ."
"You people . . ."
"The system . . ."
"Y'all . . ."
"They . . ."

The interviewee is trying to tell you something indirectly with these leads—namely, that they have a problem with you as the interviewer. In addition, the interviewee's nonverbal behavior will frequently cue their relationship concerns. The interviewer's task is to try to find out what the interviewee is trying to tell you verbally and nonverbally that he/she can't tell you directly.

Relationship Issues

Even though there are probably countless relationship issues that can arise between the interviewer and interviewee, there are several major issues that the interviewing trainee can master. In the following discussion, these major issues will be identified along with a response that illustrates the use of the immediacy of relationship skill.

Since each response could be cued by either a verbal or nonverbal stimulus, a stimulus will not be provided. In addition, each of the responses are taken out of context and therefore it is difficult to judge their appropriateness. The goal is to observe *what* can be said in an interview in response to one of the major relationship issues.

- *Embarrassment.* When embarrassment is making it difficult to continue the interview:

  "What I have said (or asked you) makes you very embarrassed."
  "What we are discussing here is very embarrassing to you."
  "It's very difficult to talk about this in front of me."

- *Anger.* When anger seems to be disrupting the interview:

  "You feel very angry at me right now."
  "You're furious at me."
  "When you think about what I did, it makes you mad at me right now."

- *Dependency.* When dependency seems to be interfering with communication, the interviewer needs to discriminate between neurotic dependency that could quickly lead to a dependency relationship and realistic demands for assistance. In the first case, "any factor which promotes dependency and interferes with the attainment of independent security is a factor which interferes with full communication" (Jourard, 1974, p. 224). Since the criminal justice interviewer is frequently in a parent role, it is very easy for a dependency relationship to develop. Typical responses using the skill of immediacy are:

  "You feel dependent on me right now to take you out of your drug program."
  "You seem to be very dependent on me to keep you out of trouble."
  "You're very dependent on me right now to give you a simple answer."

- *Distance.* When there is perceived or assumed distance between the interviewer and the interviewee:

  "You feel that because I'm black and you're white this probation relationship will never work out."
  "There are some hints that the fact that I'm young and you're old is going to make it very difficult for us to work together."
  "Because I'm not from the ghetto, you feel I could never work with you or understand you."
  "Because you own a large company and make a lot of money, you resent me being your probation officer."

  As can be seen in these illustrations, *immediacy of distance* can be in terms of social class, age, race, cultural background, or socioeconomic status.

An exercise in interviewing various types of offenders appears at the end of this chapter.

■ *Similarities.* When there is perceived or assumed similarities between the interviewer and interviewee:

> "Because I'm Mexican American and you are also, you feel that you will receive special favors on parole."
>
> "Because we're both from the west side of the city, you feel that you will have it easier on parole."
>
> "You feel that both of us being black will somehow make it easier for us to get along."
>
> "Since both of us are ex-convicts, you feel that I will not be too demanding of you."

■ *Distrust.* When not trusting the interviewer seems to be an issue:

> "You're really not sure whether you can trust me right now."
>
> "Right now you don't trust me the slightest bit."
>
> "You find trusting me very difficult."

■ *Trust.* When trust seems to be very strong in the interview:

> "I can see you really trust me right now because of the difficult things you're telling me."
>
> "When you tell me such intimate things about your life, I can tell you really trust me."
>
> "You feel very comfortable with my trust right now."

■ *Tension.* When there is tension between the interviewer and interviewee:

> "We seem to be getting on each other's nerves. Let's stop a moment and clear the air."
>
> "This discussion is getting very stressful. Perhaps we should take time to cool down."
>
> "You seem to be getting pretty nervous about what we have been discussing."

■ *Directionless.* When an interview seems to not be going anywhere:

> "I feel we're bogged down right now. Let's stop for a moment and see where we're going."
>
> "You seem to be lost, so let's back up and start over."
>
> "We've kinda lost track of where we're going, so let's talk about that. It might help."

■ *Attraction.* When the interviewee is attracted to the interviewer so that the interview is threatened:

> "I sense you like me. It could be that this might get in the way of what we're trying to get accomplished on your probation."
>
> "We've worked together as officers for quite some time and we seem to get along quite well, but if you and your wife (husband) aren't getting along, I wouldn't want our friendship to

get in the way. Instead of talking to me, why don't you see a professional."

"I think we've liked each other from the beginning of your parole. We can talk to each other quite easily, but I want to be sure that our relationship doesn't complicate or interfere with the successful completion of your parole."

Immediacy of attraction is a particularly difficult skill because the interviewer may have to set limits in the interview without communicating rejection. In situations where strangers are attracted to you, you can tell them to "buzz off" either verbally or nonverbally. On the other hand, in criminal justice interviews, you probably are going to be contacting the interviewee over a period of subsequent weeks, months, or years.

In this case, overt rejection will only make your job more difficult. Consequently, using immediacy of attraction skills will help maintain the delicate balance of attraction and rejection.

This is, obviously, not a complete list. In other situations you will have to question what unresolved issues exist in the interview and bring them up to level of awareness—an immediacy issue to be discussed in the interview.

You may find that as you bring interview relationship issues up to awareness, you will become more powerful and perceptive in future interviews. You may also find interviewees in criminal justice avoiding immediacy issues, which can give you further clues as to the interviewee's "real" agenda.

Summary

Immediacy is a skill that helps the interviewer to keep the interview from drifting away from the present moment. It helps the interviewer detect hidden agendas and ambiguity of relationships. Relationship issues are various and complex. Interviewers should be minimally competent in the use of immediacy skills.

Before leaving the skill of immediacy, you may want to complete Exercises 8.1 and 8.2 and then finish with the Interview Challenge. These activities may provide an increased opportunity for understanding the skill of immediacy.

Study Questions

1. What is the third factor in interviewing?
2. What is a hidden agenda in an interview?
3. How do interviewees avoid direct experiencing?
4. What is meant by "cold potatoes?"
5. What are the major relationship issues?

Exercise 8.1

Immediacy

Directions: *For each of the stimulus statements below, indicate the relationship issue(s) evident in the interview based on the stimulus. Indicate whether the interviewee is showing:*

1. Anger
2. Dependency
3. Distance
4. Distrust
5. Attraction

1. **Interview stimulus statement**

"You can't fool me. You may call yourself a probation officer, but you're really a cop and you're all alike. The first time I do the smallest thing you're going to try to put me in jail."

Issue: _____

_____

_____

_____

2. **Interview stimulus statement**

"We're going to have an office party at the bank Thursday evening and I'd like for you to be there. Nobody at the bank knows I'm on probation and they won't know who you are either."

Issue: _____

_____

_____

_____

3. **Interview stimulus statement**

"What in hell were you doing coming to the bank to see me? I'm a vice president and now people are wanting to know what's going on. I'm probably going to lose my job and it will be your fault. Why do you have to come snooping around?"

Issue: _____

_____

_____

_____

4. **Interview stimulus statement**

"Look lady, I don't have anything against you personally, but if it's all the same, I'd rather have a man as my parole officer."

Issue: _____

_____

_____

_____

5. **Interview stimulus statement**

"You gotta get me out of that program or something bad is gonna happen."

Issue: _____

_____

_____

_____

6. **Interview stimulus statement**

"You are just doing your job. You don't care about me. If I come back to prison, it won't mean a thing to you."

Issue: _____

_____

_____

_____

7. **Interview stimulus statement**

"I wanna know why I wasn't considered for promotion to sergeant. I didn't even make the first round and I'm more qualified than any of the male officers you considered."

Issue: _____

_____

_____

_____

8. **Interview stimulus statement**

"I need to tell somebody, but I could—if things didn't work out just right—get in bad trouble."

Issue: _____

_____

_____

_____

9. **Interview stimulus statement**

"I know I've been kinda messed up lately, but you are the only other cop I can trust. You gotta hang in there until I get through this divorce."

Issue: _____

_____

_____

_____

10. **Interview stimulus statement**

"Y'all must be perverts to want to watch people pee in a bottle."

Issue: _____

_____

_____

_____

Exercise 8.2

Social Distance Scale—Interviewing

Directions: *Read down the list of potential interviewees in criminal justice and indicate your comfort level in interviewing this particular person. Indicate your initial comfort level prior to the encounter, not after extensive interaction, by placing a check (√) in the appropriate space.*

VC-Very Comfortable
C-Comfortable
NS-Not Sure
UC-Uncomfortable
VUC-Very Uncomfortable

		VC	C	NS	UC	VUC
1	Armed Robber					
2	Pedophile					
3	Serial Murderer					
4	Rapist					
5	Wife Batterer					
6	International Drug Dealer					
7	Street Drug Dealer					
8	Incest Victim					
9	Incest Offender					
10	Kidnapper					
11	Terrorist					
12	Pornography Peddler					
13	Prostitute, Male					
14	Prostitute, Female					
15	Prostitute, Child					
16	Organizer of Child Prostitution					
17	Drug Addict					
18	Multiple DWI Offender					
19	Necrophiliac					
20	Pyromaniac					

Interview Challenge

How would you complete the following encounter? Keep in mind the concerns raised by the questions following the preliminary interview narrative.

You are riding in a squad car with your partner of several years. He has appeared upset all morning and finally says, "My wife and I got into it last night . . . we had a helluva fight . . . she's in the hospital now. What am I gonna do?"

1. What skills will you need to get the interview started?

   _____

   _____

   _____

2. What will you want to ideally get accomplished in the interview?

   _____

   _____

   _____

3. How will you divide your interview time between official objectives and personal concerns in the interview (i.e., how closely will you stay with required questions)?

   _____

   _____

   _____

4. What do you anticipate the major segments of the interview to be?

   _____

   _____

   _____

5. What would be the most appropriate interview style to use in this situation?

   _____

   _____

   _____

6. What will become the barriers to communication in this interview?

_____

_____

_____

7. What would you need to minimally accomplish in this interview for you to consider the interview successful?

_____

_____

_____

9

Concreteness Skills

Learning Objectives

Subject.   Concreteness Skills

Objectives.   After a period of instruction, the student (trainee) will:

1. Identify the types of questions that are most effective in interviewing.
2. Identify the types of questions that are least effective in interviewing.
3. Explain the cognitive interview.
4. Explain brief motivational interviewing.
5. Identify the forms of concreteness.
6. Use the skill of concreteness in an interview at a minimum level of competency.

Learning domains.

    a. Cognitive
    b. Psychomotor

> If he is fortunate enough to arrive soon after the crime has been committed, the detective will try to interview the victim or other witnesses to the crime. He must sort through the confusion of hysteria, panic, and fear for the hard facts that might help him.
>
> Mark Baker
> *Cops* (1985)

Because of strict legal and procedural concerns, criminal justice interviews usually have to stress specifics rather than vague generalities. As criminal justice interviewers we are most often interested in specific actions, specific feelings, or specific thoughts.

The skill of concreteness will help the interviewer conduct an interview in which the conversation is precise, exact, and specific. It serves little purpose, for example, to determine that your probationer is "doing fairly well" on probation. Or, it doesn't help to solve a case by concluding that the witness observed the suspect and victim "having a fight." We want to know specifics and in this chapter we want to attack the social conversation tendency to speak vaguely and in generalities. The chapter includes *when* to be concrete, *how* to ask questions, *what* techniques work best, and *what* kinds of concreteness can be used by an interviewer.

Use of Concreteness

Concreteness means that communication from the interviewer needs to be highly specific. The interviewer may, for example, give the interviewee instructions, directives, or information. These need to be specific and concrete. In addition, concreteness means encouraging the interviewee to speak concretely. This usually involves repeated clarification or direct questions so that the interviewee provides more specific information in the interview. Consequently, concreteness skills involve moving into modes 3 and 7, discussed in Chapter 4. Therefore, we have moved from responding skills discussed in previous chapters to initiating skills beginning in this chapter.

Asking Questions

Most people who are unfamiliar with interviewing probably assume that asking questions is primarily what interviewers do. Many interviewers assume that questioning is the primary technique of interviewing. As we have seen in previous chapters, several other techniques are used in interviewing; however, asking questions is an important part of getting concrete, specific information in an interview.

Open and Closed Questions

Most interview situations call for the use of questions that are open-ended, which tend to lead to answers that are more than brief, factual, yes–no responses. Open-ended questions direct the interviewee to tell the interviewer more about a subject. Closed-ended questions, in contrast, ask questions that can be answered with "yes," "no," one word, or a short phrase. An open-ended question might ask, "How did you decide to go to a halfway house?" A closed-ended question might ask, "Did you decide to go to a halfway house?" In the above example, the open-ended question will probably elicit a relatively lengthy response as opposed to the closed-ended question, which will probably elicit a "yes" or "no" response.

Benjamin (1981) differentiates the two forms of questions:

> The open question is broad and the closed question is narrow. The open question allows the interviewee full scope; the closed question limits him to a specific answer. The open question invites him to widen his perceptual field; the closed question curtails it. The open question solicits his views, opinions, thoughts, and feelings; the closed question usually demands cold facts only. (p. 73)

Depending on time limitations and the purpose of the interview, the choice of either type of question may be appropriate. Both types of questions have their places in the interview. Some interviewees may feel more at ease answering a series of closed-ended questions at the beginning of the interview and become more comfortable with open-ended questions as the interview progresses. The interviewer may have very little time to conduct an interview, which would rule out a lot of open-ended questions. For example, a police officer interviewing witnesses to a crime would probably want to rely heavily on closed-ended questions because another call for the officer could be made at any time. The officer in this case doesn't have the luxury of unlimited time to ask open-ended questions. In addition, open-ended questions are almost impossible to score in an interview where quantification or ranking is required (E. S. Johnson, 1981). On the other hand, when time or measurement is not a critical factor, the interviewer should guard against overreliance on closed-ended questions (Ryals, 1991).

Being concrete and specific in an interview means the interviewer needs to ask open-ended questions that start with *what, when, how, how much, where,* or *how often.* Some examples of open-ended questions using these leads include:

"What happened when your husband came home drunk?"
"When do you think you will have kicked this habit?"
"How are you going to get off days?"
"What were you doing while the robber was in the store?"

Some typical closed-ended questions include the following examples:

"Were you intoxicated?"
"Did you find a job?"
"Do you like your drug program?"
"Did the robber get in a car and drive away?"

The two types are easy to differentiate and the interviewer, after weighing external considerations, such as time and place, needs to decide whether to leave the door to further information open or to keep it shut.

Specific Intent Questions

Beyond open and closed questions, an interviewer's use of questions can become more sophisticated than simple *what, when,* and *how* questions. Tomm (1987a, 1987b) has proposed a general model that classifies questions that can be useful for criminal justice interviewers, as cited by Young (1992). Drawing on Young's condensation of Tomm's original discussion of specific intent questions, the four dimensions of interviewer intent are: investigative, exploratory, corrective, and facilitative.

Investigative Intent. Questions with an investigative intent are *linear questions* that ask who, what, where, and when. A typical question that is investigative would be, "How did you feel when you were arrested?" These questions are consistent with the previous discussion of open-ended questions and ask for specific behaviors. Investigative questions can elicit information quickly but they may threaten the interviewee by being too invasive or prying.

Exploratory Intent. The intent of *circular questions* is to explore. Like linear questions, they seek information about complex interpersonal relations. Circular questions assume a circular model of causality, meaning that events reciprocally influence and cause each other. For example, many alcoholic individuals alienate others with their excessive drinking and this in turn leads to more rejection and further drinking. Using our example from above, a circular question might be, "When you looked frightened at the time of your arrest, what effect do you think this had on your family?" Circular questions may also ask about differences between events to further clarify connections. For example, "What is the difference between your relationship with this fiancée and the last one?" or, "How is this AA group different from the last one you attended?"

Corrective Intent. A *strategic question* is a question with corrective intent. Strategic questions are attempts to stop the interviewee's behavior and persuade them to change in a particular way. For example, a probationer says, "I want to quit drinking." The probation officer says, "What stops you from quitting?" The officer is trying to influence the probationer toward a particular course of action. Such questions tend to be confrontational, judgmental, and accusatory.

Facilitative Intent. Finally, Tomm identifies questions that he calls *reflexive questions*. These questions assume a circular model of causality and yet are attempts to influence the interviewee. It is hoped that these questions will trigger the interviewee to find his or her own solutions. The intent is to get the interviewee to dig deeper. For example, an interviewer might say, "If you continue to drink and get arrested for DWI, what do you expect will be the effect on your relationship with your family?"

In summary, the four question types are:

Linear Question	What goes through your mind when you feel a need for drugs?
Circular Question	How does your family react when you start doing drugs?
Strategic Question	Probationer: I can't stay away from drugs. Probation Officer: Don't you mean, 'I won't stay away from drugs?'
Reflexive Question	Do you think your relationship with your stepmother would be different if you thought she really liked you?

Questions used in interviews overlap categories, but the value of Tomm's model is that it recognizes that questions have underlying assumptions and biases. They can reflect the interviewer's belief or value system about the interviewee's problems and perceptions. The various questions can produce different results in the interview, such as gathering information or influencing the interviewee.

Asking "Why" Questions

It is obvious that in the previous discussion no mention was made of the open-ended question form that begins with "why." The reason is that "why" questions present a special case of open-ended leads. As Benjamin (1981) points out, "A legitimate basis for the use of this word in our language undoubtedly exists; but I maintain that 'why' has so often been misused, its original meaning has become distorted. It was once a word employed in the search for information. It signified the investigation of cause or reason. When employed in this manner today, it is appropriate, and I know of no other to take its place. Unfortunately, this is generally not the way it is used at present" (p. 86).

Generally, "why" questions should be avoided for the following reasons:

- It is very difficult to use the word without being judgmental and indicating the interviewee has behaved "wrong." "Why" implies blame, condemnation, and disapproval.
- The use of "why" will frequently cause the interviewee to withdraw, rationalize, defend, or attack because of threat regardless of the interviewer's intent.
- The use of "why" asks for complex motivations for behavior that may not be readily understood by the interviewee. The interviewer is likely to get an answer to a "why" question of "I don't know," "because," or a blank stare.
- The use of "why" questions frequently communicate gross naiveté and insensitivity. An example of this is "Why did you get a divorce?" Most divorcees will spend the rest of their lives sorting through the reasons for the separation. To ask for a short and brief answer indicates a gross lack of sensitivity to complex human conflicts.
- Questions using "why" also may be probing or prying into embarrassing or sensitive areas that may be too difficult for the interviewee to explore, consequently leading to defensiveness and evasion.

In conclusion, "why" questions should be used as sparingly as possible because of the many liabilities associated with their use. According to Benjamin (1981), the two conditions that make the use of "why" questions safer are:

- When you are looking for simple facts. For example: "Why did you sell your car?"

■ When an atmosphere has been established in an interview that is nonthreatening, where trust and respect are present.

Direct and Indirect Questions

All of the questions discussed so far are direct questions. On the other hand, there are questions that don't seem like questions. These are called indirect questions and are questions nonetheless. For example, notice the difference between the two types of questions:

DIRECT:	"Have you paid your probation fees?"
INDIRECT:	"I'm wondering how you're coming along with the payment of your probation fees."
DIRECT:	"Are you still fighting with your husband?"
INDIRECT:	"I'm wondering how you and your husband are getting along."

Notice that the indirect question has no question mark at the end. Even so, a question is being asked and the interviewee is looking for an answer.

Indirect questions are recommended for interviews because they are questions without the threat associated with direct probes. In addition, they give the interviewee a way to act on subtle cues and hunches without making an outright suggestion or conclusion. For example, the following indirect question suits this frequent interviewer's need:

"I'm wondering if your desperation is to the point that you're going to do something very drastic."

In this response, the interviewer is focusing on the interviewee's desperation (empathy) and the hunch that the desperation is going to lead to possible violence. All of this is accomplished without a direct question that may be too suggestive or strong at the time.

Antecedent Questions

Now that we have explored what types of questions can be used in interviews, we want to look at how they can be asked. One way that questions can be asked is through antecedents.

Antecedent questions do not ask about the specific behavior in question, but rather pinpoint specific antecedent events that occur *right before* the event you are investigating (Cormier & Cormier, 1979). Antecedent questions might concern the interviewee's thoughts, attitudes, feelings, or behavior immediately preceding an event. For example, a police officer may wish to establish what a witness saw, heard, and felt prior to witnessing a specific crime. In another setting, the officer may want to ask antecedent questions concerning what was said or done immediately preceding a domestic disturbance.

There are two important reasons why an interviewer might want to identify antecedents in an interview. First, the information about what immediately preceded a crisis can give the interviewer knowledge about the times and situations when the crisis is likely to occur. Second, often an alteration or elimination of an antecedent event can prevent the ultimate event. For example, a probation officer may, through antecedent questions, determine that a probationer drinks heavily before committing a crime (a very frequent and strong antecedent to criminal behavior). By requiring the probationer to successfully complete an alcoholism treatment program, the ultimate behavior can be reduced by eliminating the antecedent.

Chaining

Another way that questions can be asked when investigating behavior is by asking questions that establish the sequence that begins with antecedent cues and ends with the undesirable behavior. This sequence of events is referred to as a *chain* (Cormier & Cormier, 1979). Much criminal behavior is the result of a long chain of events. For example, a variety of behaviors make up the sequence of robbing a drive-in grocery. Each is a critical link in the chain that connects to the act of armed robbery.

Link:	The offender is bored, depressed, and broke
Link:	Which leads to a need for alcohol or drugs
Link:	Which leads to a search for money
Link:	Which leads to anger and frustration when there's no money
Link:	Which leads to theft of a case of beer
Link:	Which leads to intoxication and disinhibition of getting caught for a serious offense
Link:	Which leads to looking for a gun
Link:	Which leads to taking a gun from a relative's house
Link:	Which leads to a rush of confidence and determination
Link:	Which leads to armed robbery of a drive-in grocery

In this example, a variety of behaviors makes up the sequence of armed robbery. By establishing the chain of events, the interviewer can get a complete picture of the resultant behavior.

Funnel Sequence

Another way that an interviewer can sequence questions is by focusing on whether the question moves from general to specific or from specific to general. The funnel sequence starts with the most general or broad questions at the top of the funnel, and each succeeding question narrows the focus and becomes more specific (Downs, et al., 1980). Since general questions come first, they are likely to be open questions. Closed questions are correspondingly likely to come at the bottom of the funnel. For example:

Top of the Funnel—"How do you see your five years on probation changing your life?"

Bottom of the Funnel—"Have you paid your probation fees this month?"

The funnel sequence has certain advantages and there are situations when it might be most useful.

- It lets the interviewer discover the interviewee's frame of reference.
- It avoids leading the interviewee or shaping the interviewee's responses.
- It satisfies a need for the interviewee to communicate opinions.
- It maximizes the interviewer's options about what can be probed.
- It can be used by supervisors in order to get their subordinates to bring up specific problems (Downs et al., 1980, p. 63).

Inverted Funnel Sequence

This method of sequencing questions in an interview is the exact reverse of the funnel sequence just described. The inverted funnel sequence "starts with specific questions, proceeds to more general questions, and concludes with the most general question" (Downs et al., 1980). For example:

Top of the Funnel—"Are you taking any kind of drugs now?"
Bottom of the Funnel—"How do you plan to stay free of drugs in the future?"

As an interviewer, you may want to note the advantages of using the inverted funnel sequence in determining whether to use it.

- It forces the interviewee to think through specific attitudes or facts before articulating a general reaction or conclusion.
- It motivates the reluctant interviewee to communicate. Shyness or the reluctance to relive a bad experience makes a person reluctant to talk. However, answering some specific questions often opens a person to greater expression later.
- It primes the interviewee's memory. When a person has forgotten an event, specific questions can help reconstruct the event and perhaps "jog the memory."
- An initial commitment (yes or no) can be invaluable in interpreting the more general responses that come later (Downs et al., 1980).

Base Rates of Behavior

A sequence of questioning that attempts to obtain a concrete picture of a person's current behaviors or feelings can be accomplished by determining rates of occurrence. This is typically referred to as a *base rate of behavior* (Craig, 2003). This base rate can be used as a benchmark for determining progress or severity of current problems. A base rate of behavior involves asking questions about *quantity* and *frequency* of behavior. Quantity of behavior involves asking questions about behavioral or affective severity. Frequency of behavior is determined by asking questions about the number of times an event occurs. For example:

Quantity (Q)

How much heroin do you use?
How hard did you hit your girlfriend?
How intense are your cravings for alcohol?
How detailed are your thoughts about molesting again?
When you drink beer, how much do you usually consume?
How much money do you usually write a hot check for?
How depressed do you usually get?

Frequency (F)

How many times a week do you use heroin?
How often, in a month, do you hit your girlfriend?
How many cravings for alcohol did you have last week?
How many deviant sexual fantasies did you have last week?
How many times a week do you drink beer?
How many hot checks did you write last month?
How many times a month do you get depressed?

A combination of the Q–F relationship can provide estimations of current functioning and behavioral severity levels. In addition, it gives the interviewer a point of comparison in the event of further contact with the individual.

Questions to Avoid

Several types of questions or question sequences have limited utility for an interviewer. These would include:

- *Double Questions.* "Do you like the night shift or the day shift?"
- *Bombarding.* Probing in rapid-fire fashion to the point that the interviewee doesn't have time to fully explain or catch a breath. This is mutually unproductive in interviews.
- *High social desirability questions.* In interviewing, these are sometimes referred to as "Do you love your mother" questions. They are the form of question that virtually everyone would answer yes or no because it is highly socially desirable to do so. Other examples of this type question are:

"Are you an honest person?"
"Do you like being around people?"
"Are you dependable?"
"Are you a friendly person?"

Getting a "no" answer to any of these questions would be highly unlikely and if it did occur, it would probably indicate the interviewee was having serious difficulty with social awareness and expectations.

Early Negating Questions

Sometimes interviewers construct an interview with a question at the beginning of the interview that, if answered with a "yes" or "no," eliminates the need for the rest of the interview. For example, in interviewing citizens about their beliefs about capital punishment, the interviewer will ask if they believe in capital punishment in the first question. If the interviewee says no, then the interview is over. By using the funnel sequence mentioned earlier, this problem can be avoided.

Rhetorical Questions

This is a form of question that doesn't require an answer and, in many cases, has no answer. Rhetorical questions are a way for the interviewer to state a given belief or fact in the form of a question. For example:

> "What is wrong with kids today that they could do something so violent?"
> "How can a person work in this field and still maintain their sanity?"

Rhetorical questions have a tendency to retard communication in an interview because they are loaded with value judgments that can alienate the interviewee. "They also have a tendency to elevate the discussion to a high level of abstractness by talking in vague generalities rather than specifics and thus are of little value to facilitating self-understanding" (Long, Paradise, & Long, 1981, p. 26). For these reasons, rhetorical questions should be avoided.

Accusative Questions

"The purpose of accusative questions is to accuse the speaker of specific acts rather than seek information or facilitate self-exploration" (Long et al., 1981, p. 26). For example:

> "What were you doing in a bar in the first place?"
> "How can you say that when you know I know differently?"
> "Do you think I'm stupid or something?"

Accusative questions will do little to increase communication because of their highly threatening nature and have no useful function in an interview. They have no place in interviewing.

Explanatory Questions

In this type of question, the interviewer describes their position on an issue rather than obtaining information from the interviewee. This type of question is also not very useful in an interview because of its negative affect on communication. For example:

"Are you aware that I'm one of those people who believes strongly in capital punishment?"

"Do you have any idea how many times I've heard that story from parolees?"

"Do you have any idea as to how little they pay us to put up with you people?"

Questions of this type are not facilitative and should be eliminated or changed to positive responses. Specifically, explanatory questions shift the focus away from the interviewee and his/her concerns and redirect the interview toward the interviewer's special concerns (Long et al., 1981).

Cat and Mouse Questions

This form of question toys with the interviewee so that the interviewer is playing a game in the interview. Cat and mouse questions can take either the direct or indirect question form. For example:

"I bet you can't guess why I called you in today?"

"You'll never guess what the judge is going to do with you."

"Why do you think I am going to write a report on you?"

"What do you think the reasons are for being demoted in rank?"

These questions border on sadism and certainly do not facilitate communication in the interview. They tend to communicate interviewer hostility, which puts the interviewee on the defensive. They should be avoided in favor of more direct and straightforward approaches.

Leading Questions

A question that is not neutral and leads the interviewee to the correct answer is a leading question. By the way it is constructed, it implies the answer that should be given. For example:

"Was the bank robber wearing a mask?"

"Did the purse snatcher have a tattoo on his forearm?"

"When you saw the robber leave the convenience store, did he ride away on a bicycle?"

All of these questions reveal information the interviewee may not have known and lead to a desired response. Rewritten, they would be worded differently:

"What was the bank robber wearing?"

"Did you notice anything about the purse snatcher?"

"When you saw the man leave the store, how did he leave?"

By not using leading questions, a witness will be less likely to provide information that is erroneous. The most effective technique is to use the most neutral terms possible in questioning sequences (Milne & Bull, 1999; Sandoval, 2003).

Misleading Questions

A question that leads the interviewee to an incorrect response is a misleading question. For example:

> "Did the inmate stab the other inmate with a screwdriver?" (A stabbing had not been revealed by the inmate and it was with a knife)
> "Did you see the inmate hide the tobacco under the mattress in the cell?" (The cell and tobacco had not been mentioned by the inmate and it was money hidden in the inmate kitchen)
> "Was the juvenile wearing gang colors?" (Age had not been mentioned and gang affiliation had not been mentioned)

All of these questions can also be reworded to reflect neutral information. For example, it is better to ask "Did you see a . . . ?" than "Did you see the . . . ?" Using the word "the" leads the interviewee to believing the item exists (Milne & Bull, 1999).

The Cognitive Interview

Interviewing training—both at the recruiting and in-service level—generally has focused on the simple and traditional aspects of eyewitness interviews. For example, most police interviewers are taught to rely on the traditional "who, what, where, when, and why" questions discussed earlier in this chapter. Such training may equip them as report takers, but it does not give them the foundation they need to gather information in interviews. Interviewers need concreteness skills that will significantly increase the amount of useful and correct information obtained from a victim or witness.

The Need

Whether or not a case is solved depends often on the information obtained from eyewitnesses in investigative interviews. Eyewitness reports of crimes, however, are known to be incomplete, sometimes unreliable, and often at least partially incorrect.

Even though the accuracy of a report is important in solving a case, police interviewers often have minimal training and direction in interviewing skills that will help obtain facts about a criminal event. Most police and corrections investigators have learned interviewing in pre-service academies, in on-the-job training, and from popularized media examples. Very little of their training involves techniques that enhance the completeness and accuracy of reports developed from interviews. This lack of training exists even though many police officers stress the importance of eyewitness reports.

Rationale

The cognitive interview technique was developed by Geiselman and Fisher (1985) in response to the need to improve police interview techniques. The techniques are based on two generally accepted principles of memory. First, a memory is composed of a collection of several elements. The more elements a memory retrieval aid has in common with the memory of the event, the more effective the aid is. Second, a memory has several access routes, so information that is not accessible with one retrieval may be accessible with a different one (Geiselman & Fisher, 1985).

The Technique

In standard police interviews, victims and witnesses are asked first to give a narrative report of what happened in their own words. The interviewer then follows up on the narrative report with questions intended to enhance the completeness of the report.

The cognitive interview consists of four general methods for jogging memory plus several specific techniques. The four techniques are explained to the witness before the narrative report. The first two methods attempt to increase the overlap of elements between the stored memory and retrieval cues. The last two methods encourage using many retrieval paths.

- *Reconstruct the circumstances.* In this method the interviewer instructs the witness to reconstruct the incident in general: "Try to reconstruct in your mind the circumstances that surrounded the incident. Think about what the surrounding environment looked like at the scene, such as rooms, location of furniture, vehicles, the weather, lighting, any nearby people or objects. Also, think about how you were feeling at the time and think about your reactions to the incident."
- *Report everything.* The investigator explains that some people hold back information because they are not quite sure that the information is important. The witness is asked not to edit anything, even things that may not seem important.
- *Recall the events in different order.* The instructions may be: "It is natural to go through the incident from beginning to end. However, you also should try to go through the events in reverse order. Or try starting with the thing that impressed you the most in the incident and then go from there, going both forward and backward in time."
- *Change perspectives.* In this method witnesses try to recall the incident from different perspectives that they may have had at the time or adopt the perspectives of others who were present during the incident and think about what he or she must have seen (Geiselman & Fisher, 1985).

There aren't any studies available to determine if police and corrections interviewers have already been using these techniques. It is possible some of the techniques may be used at present in police departments, prisons, and probation departments. However, the cognitive interview technique has been subjected to research and field testing with promising results in enhancing eyewitness memory.

The Research

The cognitive interview was first evaluated positively in experiments conducted with college students serving as the witnesses to live events and films, and in an experiment with noncollege volunteers serving as the witnesses. In each case, the cognitive interview elicited up to 35% more details than standard police interview procedures, and at no cost (Geiselman & Fisher, 1985).

In addition, the technique was field tested in the Metro-Dade Police Department using seven experienced detectives who were trained to use the technique and were compared with nine untrained detectives. The trained detectives elicited 47% more information after having been trained, and 63% more information than did the untrained detectives. Overall, research results indicate that the technique should be useful for a variety of investigative interviews (Fisher, Geiselman, & Amador, 1989). Finally, research evidence has continued to accumulate supporting the effectiveness of the cognitive interview technique (Bennett & Hess, 1991; Colwell, Hiscock, & Memon, 2002; Fisher & Geiselman, 1992; Geiselman, 1999; Milne & Bull, 1999).

Limitations

Although the cognitive interview technique is an effective investigative instrument, a few of the following limitations are noted:

- It is less useful in crimes where the bulk of the evidence is physical rather than eyewitness.
- It can only be used with cooperative witnesses.
- It may take longer to conduct than traditional investigative techniques.
- It requires considerable mental concentration on the part of the interviewer (Fisher et al., 1989).

As with other skills presented earlier, cognitive interview techniques can become part of the interviewer's repertoire through practice and renewal.

Brief Motivational Interviewing (BMI)

In recent years some very interesting questioning approaches have been developed that are designed specifically for interviewing relatively unmotivated interviewees, particularly substance abusers (Miller & Rollnick, 1991). With the increase in the frequency of drug and alcohol abusers appearing in the criminal justice system, these brief intervention techniques seem to hold a lot of promise for probation, parole, and correctional officers in both the adult and juvenile systems.

These questioning procedures are worth mentioning in this chapter for several reasons:

- They recognize that many interviewees in criminal justice do not want to talk about their substance abuse or offense, let alone admit they have a problem or a need to change their behavior. The therapeutic concept of *resistance* is an everyday occurrence in interviews with offenders.
- They recognize that offenders with serious needs for behavior change are more likely to initially encounter criminal justice workers with basic interviewing skills, a "nonspecialist," than a highly specialized counselor. This recognition is very consistent with the primary purposes of this text in interviewing, which is to provide interviewing skills for the nonspecialist in criminal justice.
- The specific skills of brief motivational interviewing overlap the interviewing skills presented in this text. Specifically, the skills of empathy, open-ended questioning, confrontations (discrepancies), and concreteness of intentions are common to both approaches.

In interviewing offenders with substance abuse problems, Miller and Rollnick (1991) have suggested a series of "strategies" to use in your questioning when you are not sure about the offender's readiness to change his or her behavior once the subject of substance abuse enters the conversation. The following questions are suggested:

- Ask about substance use in detail.

   Examples:

   What kind of drinker are you?
   How does alcohol affect your mood or emotions?
   What effect does cocaine have on you?

- Ask about a typical day or extended period of use.

   Examples:

   How long do you usually continue drinking?
   When you started drinking, what effect did the first drink have on
      you?
   The last drink?
   How long does a typical crack session last?

- Ask about lifestyle and stresses.

   Examples:

   What kind of pressures are you under?
   What do you do when you're stressed out?
   What are the ways you like to relax?

- Ask about health, then substance abuse.

  Examples:

  How does your use of cocaine affect your sleeplessness?
  How is your problem with high blood pressure?
  How long have you been diabetic?

- Ask about the good things, then the less good things.

  Examples:

  What are the good things about having a drink?
  What are the less good things about having a drink?
  How much do the less good things bother you?

- Ask about substance use in the past and now.

  Examples:

  What's the difference between your use of marijuana compared to 10 years ago?
  How has your drinking changed over the years?
  Over the last year, when did your cocaine use increase or decrease compared to now?

- Provide information and ask, "What do you think?"

  Examples:

  I wonder, how does this apply to you?
  What do you make of that?
  What do you think is a safe level of assumption?

- Ask about concerns directly.

  Examples:

  What are your concerns about your drinking?
  What other concerns do you have?
  What exactly are you worried about?

- Ask about the next step.

  Examples:

  I wonder where this leaves you now?
  What's the next step?
  Where do you go from here?

Contrary to many behavior change techniques, according to BMI, the interview doesn't have to end with the interviewee agreeing to do something. "Success can be gauged by the extent to which the person has moved along the 'reading-to-change' continuum." The interviewer should end the interview by summarizing the expressed concerns and be available to make a referral, explain options, or provide support for constructive choices.

Brief motivational interviewing is a questioning technique that has been utilized in effecting therapeutic change with resistant substance abusers. It was specifically designed to prepare people to change addictive behavior. In this sense it does seem to offer both the specialist and nonspecialist a brief intervention technique to use with these clients. The evidence supporting the effectiveness of BMI continues to be positive (Burke, Arkowitz, & Menchola, 2003).

Beyond these uses, BMI would also seem to have considerable utility in interviewing offenders on probation or parole. In the previously outlined nine steps, the words "crime" or "offense" could be easily substituted for substance use and the same procedures used to prepare offenders to change their behavior. Whether the probation officer sees themselves as a case worker or police officer, changing the offender's behavior is still a major concern of the court.

Forms of Concreteness

Interviewees frequently communicate information that is vague and nonspecific. In response to this tendency, the interviewer needs to question the vague and nonspecific information by striving for concreteness in several areas—behavior, experience, emotions, and intentions.

Concreteness of Behavior

Concrete questions about behavior means determining specifically what the interviewee did, does, is doing, or failed to do. Notice the following examples:

> *Vague statement of behavior.* "We weren't doing anything—just messin' around."
> *Question by interviewer.* "What specifically were you doing?"
> *Vague statement of behavior.* "My wife and I aren't getting along too well."
> *Question by interviewer.* "Could you be more specific when you say 'getting along'?"

In these examples, key words and phrases accentuate the vague conversation. In the first example, the key words are "messin' around." These words cover a wide range of possibilities and the interviewer would not want to assume what the terms mean so they would need to follow up with an attempt to get more specifics. In the second example, the key words are "getting along." These words leave the interviewer with unspecified information as to what the interviewee is doing in the relationship with his wife. Consequently, in the example, the interviewer asks for clarification.

It should be noted at this point that the interviewee may not provide the specifics requested by the interviewer, at which point the interviewer can conclude that the original vague language was a subtle way for the interviewee to say, "It's none of your business." If this is the case, the interviewer would probably need to return to the skills of empathy and immediacy.

Concreteness of Experience

Concreteness of experience means determining what has happened to the interviewee or what others did to them. It concerns past experiences. Note the following examples:

> *Vague statement of experience.* "My husband slapped me around the other night."
> *Question by interviewer.* "What exactly happened?"
> *Vague statement of experience.* "My mother was turned against me."
> *Question by interviewer.* "What exactly happened?"

Again, the interviewer is asking concrete questions that will hopefully lead to specifics about past events. The interviewer would not want to assume that he or she knows exactly what "slapped around" and "turned against" means.

Concreteness of Emotion

Questions that attempt to elicit specific information about feelings are considered concreteness of emotion. These questions press for specificity when the interviewee communicates vague feelings that relate to their behavior and experiences. Note the following illustrations:

> *Vague statement of emotions.* "It really bothers me to have to report to you."
> *Question by interviewer.* "What exactly do you mean by bothered?"
> *Vague statement of emotions.* "That drug program is giving me a hard time."
> *Question by interviewer.* "You seem to have some very strong feelings about the program. I'm wondering what they are" (indirect question).

The key words in the two statements by the interviewee are "bothered" and "hard time," respectively. Both of these words were vague and the interviewer responded to the vagueness with an attempt to gain specific feelings.

Another technique for getting specific information about emotions is to quantify the emotional intensity. This can be done by creating a hierarchy of emotional intensity for the interviewee when a particular emotion is in question, and the resulting behavior that could be a manifestation of the emotion, is serious or critical. This can be done by scaling the emotion and identifying *subjective units of discomfort*, frequently referred to as SUDs.

First, an imaginary hierarchy is created, with the emotion in question, ranging from the most intense experience to the least intense. A hierarchy with a ten-point range (0–10) would be appropriate with interviewees with limited levels of abstract visualization. For other interviewees, a scale between 0 and 100 is appropriate. In either case, 0 represents the lowest level of emotional intensity, and 10 or 100 represents the highest level. Second, the interviewee is asked to choose a number that represents the current emotional state on the scale. Be sure to tell the interviewee that 10 or 100 represents high intensity. Third, once the number has been selected, the interviewer can then have the interviewee speculate on what the emotional intensity is likely to lead to or use the number to compare different parts of the interview or compare this interview with forthcoming contacts with the interviewee. Finally, the emotional states that can be scaled using SUDs have typically been:

> Cravings for alcohol or drugs
> Anxiety
> Depression
> Anger
> Desperation
> Fear

The use of SUDs levels can assist the interviewer and interviewee in quantifying subjective emotional states that may lead to drastic, desperate, or irrational behavior. This gives the interviewer an advantage in being able to predict the interviewee's behavior.

Note the following conversation between a probationer (PR) and his probation officer (PO) at a regularly scheduled meeting:

PR: Well, Mrs. Martinez, I've been staying clean and not doing any cocaine.

PO: I can see that you are excited and relieved to be free of drugs, and your UAs have been clean. So, your rehab program must be working for you.

PR: Oh yeah, they help us learn ways to not want the drugs anymore.

PO: You really are pleased with your progress, but you still have cravings, don't you? That's pretty frightening, isn't it?

PR: Oh yeah! I have them, but not as bad as I used to.

PO: Okay, I want you to imagine a ladder with ten rungs and each rung us a level of craving. The highest run on the ladder is cravings that lead to using again or relapse. Okay?

PR: Yeah, I see.

PO: The lowest rung on the ladder stands for only the slightest most amount of craving for cocaine. Remember 10 is high and 1 is low cravings. Have you got that in mind?

PR: Yeah, and the rungs in between are the other levels of craving.

PO: What I want to know is where on the ladder is your craving right now?

PR: Hum, I guess . . . that's kinda hard to say . . . I'd say I was on about the fourth rung.

PO: How high on the ladder would your cravings have to get before you started using drugs again?

PR: Well, I'm not too strong in staying away from them this soon after getting clean, so I would probably get messed up at an 8 level.

PO: What's gonna happen if you get to the 8 level?

PR: I'd have to go back to jail and my probation would probably be revoked.

PO: So, you're feeling scared and frightened of that possibility?

PR: Yeah, you're right.

In the preceding conversation, the interviewer used the skills of empathy, confrontation, concreteness of intentions, and concreteness of emotions. There are several directions the interviewer could take at the conclusion of the conversation:

- Notify the treatment program director when cravings went over a SUDs level of 6.
- Suggest the interviewee notify the probation officer when the cravings went over 6.
- Explore how to get the level of cravings lower.
- Explore the triggers that lead to increased cravings.
- Identify the additional consequences that could occur if the probationer relapses.

In summary, cravings for alcohol or drugs are difficult to measure and the levels must be self-reported. A SUDs level helps quantify and compare this and other subjective experiences.

Concreteness of Intentions

Concreteness of intentions means attempting to get the interviewee to be specific about future occurrences that will affect themselves or others. It also means obtaining information about when events will occur or how soon they may occur. In many cases, this skill deals with specific and concrete information about the urgency and seriousness of the situation.

Concreteness of intentions is the central skill in the *prediction* phase of the UNDERSTANDING–PREDICTION–ACTION model that serves as the foundation for this approach to learning interviewing. Concreteness of intentions is used to predict and prioritize future events before the interviewer decides to move to the *action* phase of the model.

Typical questions that make the interview more specific and focus on speculation about future events are as follows:

"What will happen next?"
"What are you going to do next?"
"What is he likely to do next?"
"How much longer can you go on in the situation?"
"What will happen if I do approve your furlough?"
"What will happen if I don't recommend that you get your children back?"
"What will happen if your daughter is required to stay in the juvenile detention center?"
"How much time do I have to work on this before something drastic happens?"
"If you do return to your husband, what is likely to happen?"

In the preceding examples, it can be seen that the interviewer wants to set the stage and peer into a crystal ball to determine exactly what is likely to occur next and what options are available. When the information in an interview concerns a threat to self, others, or others' property, the information leading up to prediction becomes critical.

When the interviewer is in a position to make a prediction, two options are available with regard to action:

- The interviewer is aware of and can predict what is likely to happen to (or because of) the interviewee, but they will not take action because of legal, ethical, procedural, or jurisdictional reasons. The worst case of this option is when their awareness is high but they are helpless to act.
- The interviewer is aware of and can predict what is likely to happen to (or because of) the interviewee and they can take either minimum or maximum action to intervene in the situation. The worst case of this option is when their awareness is low and they must take action.

Concreteness skills will give the interviewer the tools to obtain information that will lead to more appropriate actions. Successful prediction can be maximized by bringing a full range of concreteness skills to the criminal justice interview. This is the professional advantage of the interviewer in criminal justice.

Summary

Concreteness skills assist the interviewer in being specific by asking questions in forms and sequences that provide reliable and valid facts, feelings, and predictions for effective decision making and planning. Concreteness involves quantifying feelings, experiences, and thoughts for making predictions. The interviewer should be minimally competent in the use of concreteness skills.

Before leaving Chapter 9, you may want to complete Exercises 9.1, 9.2, and 9.3, which will give you additional understanding about the skill of concreteness. In addition, you are also ready to complete a self-efficacy assessment over concreteness and immediacy skills in Assessment 9.1. Finally, the Interview Challenge may be helpful in applying some of the skills and knowledge attained up to this point.

Study Questions

1. What are the differences between open and closed questions?
2. What are some considerations to use in deciding to use open or closed questions?
3. What are the forms of specific intent questions?

4. Why is "why" discouraged?
5. What are the advantages of indirect questions?
6. Why would an interviewer want to identify antecedents in an interview?
7. What is chaining?
8. What is a funnel sequence? Inverted funnel sequence?
9. What are the techniques of the cognitive interview?
10. What are some of the strategies of BMI?
11. How does BMI gauge success in an interview?
12. What are the forms of concreteness?
13. What is the central skill of the prediction phase of the interviewing model?
14. What is a SUDs level?

Exercise 9.1

Concreteness: Open-Ended Questions

Directions: *Read each interviewer question and decide whether it is an open-ended or a closed-ended question and then make an "X" in the column to the right when appropriate. Remember, open-ended questions are those that require a relatively lengthy response and closed-ended questions are those that tend to elicit a one-word or short interviewee response.*

INTERVIEWER QUESTIONS	OPEN-ENDED	CLOSED-ENDED
Are you still drinking heavily?		
Tell me about your drug treatment program.		
Does your wife visit you often?		
What are some of the reasons you want to be a detective?		
Tell me what you saw during the crime.		
Did the suspect have a weapon?		
How long was he in the store?		
What is the AA program like?		
How did you get involved with the suspect?		
When did the trouble start?		
Did you agree to go with them each time?		
What were some of your thoughts right before the argument and subsequent fight?		

Exercise 9.2

Concreteness: Leading Questions

Directions: In the following exercise, you are to read each of the interviewer questions and then rewrite the question so that it is no longer leading.

1. How tall was the person?

   _____

   _____

2. How short was the person?

   _____

   _____

3. Was the man who was doing the shooting Hispanic?

   _____

   _____

4. Did the gang members drive away in a Ford van?

   _____

   _____

5. Was your cellmate dealing tobacco in the television room?

   _____

   _____

6. Did you see the two juveniles steal the beer?

   _____

   _____

7. Did you see the black and Hispanic juveniles fighting in the detention center?

   _____

   _____

8. What color was the ski mask that the suspect was wearing?

   _____

   _____

9. How much cocaine did you see the other officer take from the suspect?

_____

_____

10. Was the suspect driving a blue Ford Mustang convertible?

_____

_____

11. How large was the revolver the suspect used in the hold-up?

_____

_____

12. Which of the three men had the rifle?

_____

_____

Assessment 9.1

Interview Training Self-Efficacy Assessment: Knowledge and Skills

Directions: *After completing further training, rate your estimation of your knowledge and skill acquisition on the following scale:*

1 = unskilled/unaware
2 = awkward
3 = average
4 = skilled/knowledgeable

_____   a. Knowledge of concreteness skills

_____   b. The effective use of concreteness skills

_____   c. Knowledge of immediacy skills

_____   d. The effective use of immediacy skills

Exercise 9.3

Subjective Units of Discomfort: Affective Change and Severity Survey (ACSS)

Directions: *People experience a variety of emotions and sometimes these emotions change. Indicate on the ladders that follow your present emotional level in several emotional areas. Please indicate your feelings at the present time, not those in the past. Complete the exercise right before a major exam and then again after the exam.*

Example:

5	Very surprised
4	Surprised
3	Not sure
2	Slightly surprised
1	Not surprised at all

In the example, if you checked the box with the 4, this would indicate you felt surprised, but not at the highest level. If you had checked the 3 box, it would indicate you are not sure how you feel.

Remember: Indicate your feelings at the present time. Be sure to check all of the ladders.

After you have completed the ACSS, plot the scores on the graph below for the first and second set of responses. Connect the points for a visual representation of a change in subjective units of discomfort.

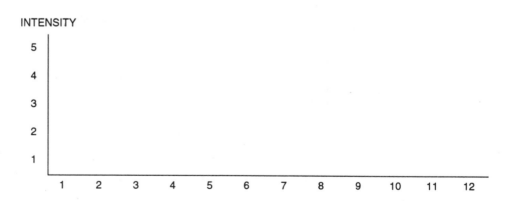

1) Depressed

5	Very depressed
4	Depressed
3	Not sure
2	Happy
1	Very happy

2) Anger

5	Very angry
4	Angry
3	Not sure
2	Calm
1	Very calm

3) Stress

5	Very stressed
4	Stressed
3	Not sure
2	Relaxed
1	Very relaxed

4) Agitation

5	Very agitated
4	Agitated
3	Not sure
2	Calm
1	Very calm

5) Hopeful

5	Very hopeful
4	Hopeful
3	Not sure
2	Discouraged
1	Very discouraged

6) Energy

5	Very energetic
4	Energetic
3	Not sure
2	Drained
1	Very drained

7) Helpless

5	Very helpless
4	Helpless
3	Not sure
2	Eager
1	Very eager

8) Confusion

5	Very confused
4	Confused
3	Not sure
2	Focused
1	Very focused

9) Boredom

5	Very bored
4	Bored
3	Not sure
2	Busy
1	Very busy

10) Worry

5	Very worried
4	Worried
3	Not sure
2	Confident
1	Very confident

11) Desperation

5	Very desperate
4	Desperate
3	Not sure
2	Contented
1	Very contented

12) Discouraged

5	Very discouraged
4	Discouraged
3	Not sure
2	Encouraged
1	Very encouraged

Interview Challenge

How would you complete the following encounter? Keep in mind the concerns raised by the questions following the preliminary interview narrative.

You are an adult probation officer who has called a female probationer into your office because her urine test indicated that she had been using drugs recently. She sits down and says, "I can explain everything. My boyfriend and I went to a party last Saturday night. There was this woman at the party who has been trying to steal my boyfriend away from me. Well, she put something in my drink because she wants me to have to go to jail so she can get my boyfriend. She's a bitch and she would stop at nothing to get him."

1. What skills will you need to get the interview started?

    _____

    _____

    _____

2. What will you want to ideally get accomplished in the interview?

    _____

    _____

    _____

3. How will you divide your interview time between official objectives and personal concerns in the interview (i.e. how closely will you stay with required questions)?

    _____

    _____

    _____

4. What do you anticipate the major segments of the interview to be?

    _____

    _____

    _____

5. What would be the most appropriate interview style to use in this situation?

_____

_____

_____

6. What will be some of the barriers to communication in the interview?

_____

_____

_____

7. What would you need to minimally accomplish in this interview for you to consider the interview successful?

_____

_____

_____

10

Confrontation Skills

Learning Objectives

Subject.   Confirmation Skills

Objectives.   After a period of instruction, the student (trainee) will:
1. Explain why confrontation skills are used in Criminal Justice interviews.
2. Explain the guidelines, techniques, and procedures for using confrontation skills.
3. Identify interviewing situations where use of confrontation would be counter-indicated.
4. Use confrontational skills in an interview at a minimum level of competency.

Learning domains.

   a. Cognitive
   b. Affective
   c. Psychomotor

> He thought of the papers he'd just signed with some fifty rules of parole, rules which would be harder to follow than the Ten Commandments.
>
> Joseph Wambaugh
> *The Onion Field* (1973)

Listening to and understanding an interviewee is not enough. Interviewers need action skills in an interview. Action skills include giving the interviewee information, making a referral, and problem solving. These skills tend to be interview- and agency-specific so the focus of this approach is to discuss the action skills of confrontation and assertion that are very basic, necessary, and not agency-specific. Action skills move the interviewer toward control, direction, and initiative in the interview. We will assume that the interviewer has become skilled in the first two parts of the model before moving to the *action* phase.

UNDERSTANDING–PREDICTION–ACTION

Confrontation in Criminal Justice

Frequently in criminal justice interviews, discrepancies arise that cloud the air in an interview. On occasion, these discrepancies cloud the air to the point that the interviewer needs to bring them up in order to reduce or eliminate distortions and confusion. "Indeed, confrontation is inherent to all human interactions other than those between two or more fully functioning persons" (Berenson & Mitchell, 1974, p. ii).

Confrontation skills are used to point out discrepancies in an interview. The need for confrontation skills arises because interviewees in criminal justice are not always consistent, straightforward, congruent, honest, and open. Consider the following possibilities that can necessitate the use of confrontation:

- **Denial.** The interviewee may deny that an incongruity exists, such as the denial of reality, consequences, or responsibility.
- **Distortions.** The interviewee may be consciously or unconsciously distorting information.
- **Lying.** The interviewee may be consciously fabricating a story with the hope that the interviewer will not suspect lying.
- **Low awareness.** The interviewee may not be aware of inconsistencies in their thoughts, feelings, or behavior.
- **Baiting.** The interviewee may be deliberately inconsistent to bait the interviewer into taking a parent role in the interview, which is a comfortable conflict position for the interviewee.
- **Games, tricks, and smoke screens.** The interviewee may be somewhat of a con-artist who enjoys manipulating, seducing or tricking others in interpersonal relations. "The number of games people play in order to avoid intimacy and other forms of effective living is seemingly endless" (Egan, 1975).
- **Evasions.** Many offenders typically blame others for everything that has gone wrong in their life. By doing this, they evade introspection, which is, of course, painful.

Confrontation, as it is presented in this chapter, means a responsible unmasking of the discrepancies, distortions, games, lies, denials, and smoke screens the interviewee uses to hide from both themselves and the interviewer.

Confrontation is often seen as hostile, aggressive, and punitive. In criminal justice interviews it is doubly dangerous because many criminal justice interviews are conducted in a hostile and punitive atmosphere. Consequently, criminal justice interviews are likely to call for confrontation skills, even though they perhaps require the most caution in the use of confrontation.

Confrontation and Substance Abuse

Confronting substance abusers has been a traditional, and somewhat controversial, technique in substance abuse treatment. This procedure is not the same as the skill of confrontation in this chapter. Confrontation in substance abuse treatment consists of:

■ Pointing out the discrepancies in the abuser's behavior or what they are saying.

■ Challenging them to take responsibility to change some aspect of the behavior or thinking.

■ Presenting them with the serious consequences that will occur if they do not change (Polcin, 2003).

The skill of confrontation in this communication skills model only includes the first of the three procedures used in substance abuse treatment. If community or institutional treatment or supervision officers choose to use the more involved procedure, the communication skill of confrontation can certainly stage this intervention.

Invitation

Confrontation is an invitation to the interviewee by the interviewer to recognize inconsistencies or discrepancies of which the interviewer is aware. Confrontation involves the following steps:

■ Identify discrepancies in the interviewee's communication.
■ Decide whether confrontation is appropriate in a situation.
■ Confront the interviewee with discrepancies that have been identified.

Discrepancies

Several discrepancies can arise in an interview that may lead the interviewer to make the decision to confront the interviewee. For example, there can be a discrepancy between:

■ What the interviewee says and his or her behavior. The interviewee says he/she is doing fine on parole but looks nervous and worried.

■ What the interviewee says and his or her past record of behavior. The interviewee says he/she is not a "criminal" but has multiple felony convictions on their record.

■ What the interviewee says and his or her acceptance of personal responsibility for their behavior. The interviewee maintains that his/her drug use is acceptable because everybody else uses drugs.

■ What the interviewee says and his or her unrealistic goals. The interviewee indicates he/she wants to be a physician even though he/she has an extensive criminal record with an eighth-grade education.

■ What the interviewee says and information the interviewer received prior to the interview. The interviewee insists that he or she has stopped drinking, but the interviewer has an offense report that indicates the interviewee received a DWI charge the night before.

Acceptance

If the confrontation is accepted, the interviewer should encourage the interviewee's consideration by positively reinforcing the interviewee.

For example, the interviewer might say, "It's good that you can work on this issue" or "It takes a lot of courage to face this and you've done very well."

Rejection

When an invitation is made, it is not customary to keep sending invitations or keep badgering the party to accept the invitation. If the invitation is rejected, the interviewer should return to empathy by saying something like, "My even suggesting that irritates you" or "Thinking that you may be doing something like that threatens you." *Do not persist in the confrontation.*

Confusion

If the expression or response of the interviewee indicates confusion or ambivalence, then catch this by saying, "You feel confused by this" or "You're just not sure you can buy that. It may be true, and then again it may not be."

Guidelines for Confrontation

Confrontation is a much-abused type of interaction in both interpersonal and interviewing situations. Confrontation is aggressive and in the hands of an inept interviewer, often destructive. To guard against the misuse of confrontation, several guidelines are suggested.

Necessary or Sufficient

Confrontation is never necessary or sufficient to effectively interview a person. Confrontation will likely only be successful when used with empathy. *Confrontation must be preceded and followed by empathy.* The greater the rapport between the interviewer and interviewee, the greater the likelihood that confrontation will be successful. Confrontation is never used as an isolated skill, but must be employed within the entire interviewing skills framework in order to be effective.

Purpose

The purpose of confrontation is to clarify communication and increase the amount of accurate information in an interview. Confrontation is not:

arguing	advising
preaching	lecturing
threatening	guilt-tripping
judging	moralizing
interrogating	badgering
blaming	patronizing

These are self-serving misuses of confrontation that fit a parental role, which typically leads to decreased communication and information in the interview. "Confrontations are most effective when non-evaluative and non-judgmental" (Ivey & Gluckstern, 1984, p. 33).

Misusers

Interviewers who specialize in, focus on, or misuse confrontation have been charged by Berenson and Mitchell (1974) as being:

Stupid.	He is committed to living without learning anything more than he already knows.
Incompetent.	He is attempting to prove that he can get along without substantive specialty skills.
Psychopathic.	He assumes life is a game and the winner is the person who has learned the most gimmicks.

They go on to point out that confrontations can be useful and helpful in interviews, but use strong language in confronting the use of confrontation.

> In the typical instance, however, the confrontation is a simple (and simple-minded) vehicle for irresponsible venting of infantile, neurotic impulses. It is designed either to humiliate, to embarrass, or to take the focus off the inadequacies of the confronter. (Berenson & Mitchell, 1974 p. 2)

The confronters have been confronted.

Techniques

Now that we have noted the cautions to observe in the use of confrontation, we need to look at several techniques for employing confrontation in an interview. The following are some techniques and "do's and don'ts" for using confrontation:

Precede and follow the confrontation with empathy. Notice the following conversation.

Interviewee: Hey! I'm doin' great. Been going to work and staying out of trouble. Like I told you before, everything's cool. Why, my old lady isn't even getting on my back about drinking anymore.

Interviewer: You feel really confident and relieved that your life is on a positive course now. (first empathy)

Interviewee: Yeah. That's right. That other stuff is all in the past.

Interviewer: (pause) I guess I'm kinda confused about what you're saying. (tentative) On one hand, you say you're doing well at work and staying out of trouble, and, on the other hand, I received a report from your supervisor at the plant that you've missed several days of work and, in fact, were reprimanded two days ago for having alcohol on your breath at work. Could you clear this up for me? (confrontation)

Interviewee: You cops are all alike . . . I miss one lousy day of work and you want to send me back to prison. You're always snooping around so you can cause me trouble. Besides, that old croak down at the plant sleeps on the job half the time and doesn't know what the hell he's doin'. He knows I'm an ex-con and he's looking for an excuse to get me in trouble.

Interviewer: It makes you angry and disgusted that I brought this up. Maybe even a little defeated. (second empathy)

In this conversation, the interviewer responded with empathy before entering the confrontation and after the confrontation. Consequently, the invitation was made but the interviewer didn't dwell on it or continue to badger the interviewee.

Never make two consecutive confrontations. Repeated confrontations typically lead to arguments, a defense of the source of the confrontation by the interviewer, and a cycle of deterioration in the communication. For example:

Interviewee: "Your sources are crazy."

Interviewer: "Well, I talked to them and they said it was true."

Interviewee: "Well, I'm here to tell you it isn't."

Interviewer: "Yes it is."

Interviewee: "No it isn't."

If the interviewer confronts once and moves to empathy, this disaster can usually be avoided.

Be tentative. Speculate on what the discrepancy might or could be. Leave the possibility of an alternative explanation. Perceptions of discrepancies may be different for the interviewer and the interviewee. For example:

What is *realistic* for one persona may be *unrealistic* for another.
What is *rational* or logical for one person may be *irrational* or illogical for another.
What *makes sense* for one person may be *nonsense* for another.
What is *common sense* or practical for one person may be *idealistic* and impractical for another.

Confront inconsistencies. Use the response, "On one hand, you say . . . but on the other hand, . . ." Notice this technique in the previous conversation. This response can be shortened to, "You say . . . , but . . ." as in, "You say you are fine but you look very nervous."

Confront distortions of reality. A good technique for confronting distortions is, "You say . . . , but what's the evidence?" An example is, "You say that they don't like you because you're an ex-con, but what's the evidence?"

Such a response reflects the speaker's internal viewpoint and then invites him or her to provide evidence to support it (Nelson-Jones, 1990).

Assume nothing. In other words, distinguish between what a person says about what they do (what has happened) and what the person does (what really happened). It is not being suggested that you distrust the individual, but that you be aware that discrepancies may exist between perceptions of reality and reality itself. The interviewer should focus on reality. The range of discrepancy is important to be aware of. For example, if a parolee tells you they are happy and confident, you should observe their behavior to see if it coincides with what he/she says and how the person acts (Danish & Hauer, 1973).

Avoid reprisals. The interviewer should not confront interviewees with outside information in situations where the interviewee can make reprisals against the outside source. This typically includes sources from work and family situations. For example, the interviewer might say, "On one hand, your wife told me . . . , but on the other hand, . . ." or "Your daughter told me . . . ," or "The man you work with told me. . . ." Confrontation in these situations is treacherous and likely to create more difficulties than previously existed. Sources that you can use include official records, reports, and information, such as arrest reports and agency records. For example, the interviewer might say "On one hand, the director of the program told me . . . , but on the other hand, . . ." Also included would be "Arrest records show . . . ," "Your case worker has indicated . . . ," or "A vice division report shows. . . ." Even when using official sources it is advisable to check with the official before mentioning a specific source. It will help you maintain your contacts in the criminal justice system.

Competency and Effectiveness

Effective interviewers should keep confrontation to a minimum, but when they do confront, the quality should be maximum. When carried out skillfully, it places many demands on the interviewer. The skillful interviewer does not focus on confrontation as a single or separate technique. Unskilled interviewers persist in confrontation, even though the confrontation is doing no good. The skillful interviewer, on the other hand, can discriminate when to confront. Confrontation involves risk, but it can increase communication in an interview if it is done skillfully.

Reverse Confrontation

Interviewers in criminal justice must be prepared to be confronted in interviews, especially when interviewing offenders (Masters, 2004). Many offenders have:

- Had experience with a broader range of components of the criminal justice system (police, courts, corrections) than a particular interviewer may have had.

- Been in the system for years and exposed to some of the injustices of the system firsthand. Consequently, they know the system quite well.
- Been through numerous treatment programs, for better or worse.
- Developed a keen sense of observation of threatening individuals in the system with little hesitance to confront threats to their well-being.
- Learned the language of the system and can use the language to avoid focusing on their transgressions, failures, guilt, and pain.

The assertion skills in the next chapter can be very helpful in an interviewing situation where reverse confrontation becomes an issue. Possessing a complete repertoire of interviewing skills, with the ability to effectively use a skill, can prepare interviewers for inevitable and challenging situations.

Summary

Frequently in interviews, discrepancies arise that prohibit clarity. Confrontation skills may be needed to clear up these discrepancies. The skill of confrontation can be misused and is only likely to be effective under certain guidelines. Interviewers should be minimally competent in the use of confrontation skills.

Now that you have completed Chapter 10, you may want to use the activities found on the next few pages for additional assistance and understanding. Exercise 10.1 can be helpful in formulating confrontations. The confrontation vignettes can be helpful in constructing role plays that require confrontation skills. Finally, the Interview Challenge can provide a stimulus to plan for interviewing skills.

Study Questions

1. When is confrontation needed?
2. Why is confrontation doubly dangerous in criminal justice interviews?
3. What are the steps of confrontation?
4. When is confrontation most effective?
5. What are some techniques for using confrontation?
6. In what situations should confrontation not be used?

Exercise 10.1

Confrontation

Before confronting others, it is best to practice on oneself. Hermans, Fiddelaers, de Groot, and Nauta (1990) have reported on the effectiveness of using self-confrontation in investigating and clarifying a person's valuation system. Think of a few areas in your life where you could benefit from some kind of challenge or confrontation, where you could examine your behavior more carefully. Then complete the following "On one hand, but on the other hand" sentences.

Example

On one hand, *I need my friends and their help a great deal,* but on the other hand, *when they help me, they seem to treat me like a child and that makes me angry.*

1. On one hand, I _____

   _____

   _____

   _____ but on the other hand,

   _____

   _____

2. On one hand, I _____

   _____

   _____

   _____ but on the other hand,

   _____

   _____

3. On one hand, I _____

   _____

   _____

   _____ but on the other hand,

   _____

   _____

4. On one hand, I _____

_____

_____

_____ but on the other hand,

_____

_____

Confrontation Vignettes

Directions: *The following vignettes are provided for practicing confrontation skills. The vignettes may be enriched by adding or altering the characteristics of the individuals in the vignettes. This would involve adding different cultural, gender, age, and handicap characteristics of the individuals.*

The Car Wash

One of the parolees under your supervision has indicated that he is no longer working in his original parole placement job. Instead, he is now working with a cousin at a car wash. The parolee likes the new job very much and is making quite a bit more money at the new unapproved job. He is hoping you will approve the new job so he can continue working there.

You need to confront this parolee about this job change because you are aware that this particular cousin is a convicted felon and ex-convict and associating with known felons is a violation of parole supervision guidelines.

The Girlfriend

One of the probationers under your supervision has asked you, during a routine office visit, to be transferred from the halfway house she is currently in to a halfway house across the city. She indicates she is not doing well in the present program and insists that the other program would be more helpful to her.

You need to confront this probationer about this transfer request because you are aware that:

a. She has been doing very well in the current program according to the chief counselor in the program.
b. Her boyfriend was recently transferred to the program that is being requested by your probationer.

The Party

One of your probationers, in explaining why her recent urine analysis test for drugs resulted in confirming she had recently been using drugs, indicates the reason why the test was positive is because someone put something in her drink at a party. She thinks it was a rival for her boyfriend's attention because she thinks that the rival thought that if the probationer got into more trouble, the rival would have the boyfriend to herself.

You need to confront this probationer about this recent urine analysis because your records show that her tests have been positive on several previous occasions.

Religious Conversion

One of the probationers under your supervision, during a routine visit, expresses his joy and excitement over a recent religious conversion that he feels strongly will keep him out of trouble with the law in the future. He indicates that part of this religious conversion involves a job working with children and youth at his church in the church's youth program.

You need to confront this probationer that having been convicted of sexual abuse of a child, he is expressly forbidden to have any contact with children as stipulated by the court and probation restrictions.

Family Reunion

One of the parolees on your caseload requests to leave the state to attend a family reunion. She is required to have permission to leave the state. She particularly wants to go to the reunion to see an elderly mother who she has not seen in several years.

You need to confront this parolee that you have information from Federal Drug authorities that her family is involved in illegal drug transactions and there are signs that a major transaction will occur on the weekend the parolee is requesting a leave of absence.

Fashion Model

In the course of a conversation during a routine visit, a probationer indicates she has a new job working as a fashion model and dance instructor. The new job pays very well and the probationer can now pay her bills and buy a car.

You need to confront this probationer that you have information from the vice section of the local police department that the probationer is actually working in a topless bar. This is a violation of probation rules, which prohibits her from working in an establishment that serves alcoholic beverages.

DWI

A probationer requests that he be allowed to discontinue his required DWI classes because he doesn't drink anymore, and therefore the classes are a waste of time.

You need to confront the probationer that you have a police report that indicates the probationer was arrested for public intoxication two nights ago.

Juvenile

A mother of a child in the Juvenile Detention Center has been asked by you to come get her child from the detention center so the child can go home. You are not going to hold the child any longer. The mother comes to your office. She is angry and insistent that the child stay in the detention center because the child is "mentally retarded" and she can't handle the child. She thinks you are more qualified to handle the child and her other three children are driving her crazy.

You need to confront the mother of the child, that during the child's stay in the detention center a psychological evaluation of the child was conducted and the evaluation indicated the child is in the normal range of ability. Therefore, the mother must still take the child home.

The Visit

During a routine office visit, a parolee indicates that he is angry because you humiliated and embarrassed him by visiting him at work. The other employees are now asking questions about who it was that visited him and why he is required to have a "social worker" coming around the workplace. The parolee is insisting that you never come back to the work site.

You need to confront the parolee that visiting him at his workplace is a condition of his parole.

Irate Parent

A very angry parent has entered your office insisting that her child be released from the detention center immediately. She indicates her child never gets into any trouble and that the police are picking on the child. She says the child is a good kid who wouldn't do anything wrong and the police have made a mistake by bringing the child to the detention center.

You need to confront the parent that the child has been in the detention center several times before because of a record of a dozen burglaries and break-ins.

Interview Challenge

How would you complete the following encounter? Keep in mind the concerns raised by the questions following the preliminary interview narrative.

You are a juvenile probation officer interviewing a runaway sixteen-year-old girl who has been referred by the police for possession of a controlled substance. Your reports indicate extensive drug use including "mainlining" cocaine, which is evident by the needle marks on her arms. She says, "I don't care what the fuck you do. It doesn't make any difference to me."

1. What skills will you need to get the interview started?

   _____

   _____

   _____

2. What will you want to ideally get accomplished in the interview?

   _____

   _____

   _____

3. How will you divide your interview time between official objectives and personal concerns in the interview (i.e., how closely will you stay with required questions)?

   _____

   _____

   _____

4. What do you anticipate the major segments of the interview to be?

   _____

   _____

   _____

5. What would be the most appropriate interview style to use in this situation?

_____

_____

_____

6. What will be some of the barriers to communication in the interview?

_____

_____

_____

7. What would you need to minimally accomplish in this interview for you to consider the interview successful?

_____

_____

_____

11

Assertion Skills

Learning Objectives

Subject. Assertion Skills

Objectives. After a period of instruction, the student (trainee) will:

1. Explain why assertion skills are needed in interviewing.
2. Distinguish between nonassertive, assertive, and aggressive responses.
3. Identify the types of assertion.
4. Identify the techniques for making assertive statements.
5. Use asssertion skills in an interview at a minimum level of competency.

Learning domains.

   a. Cognitive
   b. Psychomotor

> The physical dangers of police work are grossly overrated but the emotional dangers make it the most hazardous job on earth.
>
> Joseph Wambaugh
> *The Choirboys* (1975)

The final skill to be presented in the sequence of interviewing training is the use of responsible assertion. Assertion skills represent the final skills in the

UNDERSTANDING–PREDICTION–ACTION

model that has served as the foundation for this interviewing approach. Assertion skills are the strongest form of verbal intervention or initiation in an interview, finalizing the *action* phase of the model. The interviewer's goal is to have one of the previous skills set up communication to the extent that the interviewer will not have to employ assertion skills. Assertion skills are a last resort in an interview because they are not as facilitative as previous skills. Consequently, when assertion skills are used, we want them to be used as effectively and responsibly as possible.

Assertion Skills

Nelson and Pierce (1988) and Manis (1998) define personal assertion skills as the ability to clearly and forcefully communicate thoughts and feelings to others, specifically:

- Communicating honestly and straightforwardly.
- Directly communicating and expressing thoughts and feelings while respecting those of others.
- Giving compliments to others easily and appropriately.
- Providing objective and accurate feedback to others.
- Meeting your personal needs without experiencing excessive guilt or anxiety.

The three steps of assertion are: (1) describe the objective situation, (2) describe your feelings, and (3) request a specific behavioral change. When these steps are learned in training, interviewers become more proficient at assertion skills and less reliant on aggression in an interview, so decreased aggression is an added benefit of learning assertion skills (Brenner, Head, Helms, Williams, & Williams, 2003).

Assertion Skills in Criminal Justice

Because of the quasi law enforcement role of many criminal justice workers and the adversarial nature of the relationship in criminal justice interviews, interviewers are likely to need to be skilled in the use of assertion. The interviewee typically is not representative of "polite," middle-class society. In addition, they are more likely to be angry, disgusted, and frustrated because of their own shortcomings and the insensitivity of the justice system. There is some evidence to indicate that they are more likely to be manipulative and deceitful in their interpersonal relations. This is obviously true to a lesser extent with witnesses to and victims of crime. The rationale for the need to employ assertive skills certainly cannot be generalized to all offenders in institutions, on probation, or on parole, but the select characteristics of the offender population create a need for the interviewer to be firm, confident, direct, and responsible in working with people in the criminal justice system.

Interviewers in criminal justice frequently need to assert and define themselves with regard to personal and professional goals, responsibilities, and limitations. In this training the emphasis is on preserving the interviewer's rights, meeting the interviewee's needs, and giving responsible directives. This individualistic form of assertion takes place in many situations other than in an interview—for instance, on the job with coworkers. Consequently, the assertion skills mastered in this training (like the previous skills) can be used in other day-to-day encounters with family, friends, and coworkers. The assumption for these kinds of assertion skills is, "I possess sufficient confidence and self-esteem to assert myself on the job." A by-product of a knowledge of assertion is that it helps a person fulfill their potential in other parts of their life.

Consider the following situations in criminal justice interviews:

Situation 1: John is a parolee on your caseload who, as you are seeing him for the first time, refers to you as "honey," as in "Honey, I'm not going back this time."

Situation 2: James is a parolee on your caseload who you have interviewed several times. He has indicated that he is looking for a job but you seriously doubt that he is. You want to tell him he needs to look for a job, and you want to be taken seriously.

Situation 3: Betty is on your probation caseload and, in an interview with her, she has just said, "I'm going to kill that son-of-a-bitch if he comes around again."

Situation 4: Clarence is the perfect model of a probationer and he has just asked you to co-sign a bank note so that he can go into the car wash business with his cousin.

Situation 5: In an institutional parole interview, Alex exposes himself to you during the interview.

Situation 6: An inmate gives you a slip of paper with a telephone number on it and asks you to contact his mother in the free world to tell her he will not be able to see her during visitation hours next Sunday. She has to drive a long distance and he doesn't have any way to contact her.

The preceding situations call for the interviewer to express his or her thoughts directly and responsibly toward the interviewee. The interviewer has a right in these situations to give directions and make demands without feeling guilty. The interviewee has a right to not be abused, put down, or humiliated.

Assertive Responses

When dealing with perceived negative behavior on the part of the interviewee or when the interview calls for directions to be given, the interviewer has three options available: a nonassertive response, an aggressive response, or an assertive response. Alberti and Emmons (1986) make useful distinctions among nonassertion, aggression, and assertion.

Nonassertion

When dealing with negative behavior or giving directions to an interviewee, nonassertion implies being inhibited, submissive, and apologetic. You hear what the interviewee has said but you do not respond to it. Inside you are stewing, but you swallow your emotions. After the interview is over, you tell a fellow worker or close friend how angry you are with the interviewee. After the interview you feel empty, impotent, and anxious.

The interviewer can diagnose his or her lack of assertiveness when he or she thinks or says:

"I started to say . . ."
"I almost said . . ."
"What I really wanted to say was . . ."

It's a pretty good bet that in these situations the interviewer has sacrificed his or her own feelings and rights for those of the interviewee.

People tend to be nonassertive for several reasons:

- They tend to exhibit anxiety upon being confronted with an assertive situation.
- They may not want to risk being angry and aggressive.
- They may feel that being assertive is impolite to others.
- They may feel endlessly obligated to others.
- They may believe it is a mortal sin to refuse to help someone who needs help.
- They may never have learned that they have rights.
- They feel it would be immodest to assert themselves.
- They lack assertion skills (Allen, 1990).

The end result is that nonassertive behavior by the interviewer typically communicates self-denial, lack of responsibility, and inability to stand up for his or her own rights.

Aggression

Another option the interviewer has when dealing with negative behavior or giving directions is aggression. The interviewer listens briefly to what the interviewee has to say, and then lashes out at them angrily. Aggression implies putting the interviewee down unnecessarily, often by means of "you" statements. Aggressive responses accomplish the interviewer's goals, but at the expense of the interviewee and further communication. The result is likely to be hostility, decreased communication, and defensiveness. Afterward, the interviewer feels some guilt and a sense of isolation.

People tend to choose aggression for several reasons:

- Aggression is a primitive, easy, readily available response that is guaranteed to get attention and make one feel good about avenging a violation of personal rights.
- They resort to aggression because, feeling powerless, it seems a powerful thing to do.
- Having tried to be nice, they feel they have no choice but to fall back on nastiness.
- Old wounds have festered to the point that they erupt. If they have failed to successfully defend their rights in the past when attacked, they may not be able to now.

■ Some people believe aggression is the only way to get through to some people. When the targets of their aggression respond with aggression, it tends to prove that they only understand aggression.

■ Some people come from oppressive environments where aggression is the only method available to protect their rights (Allen, 1990).

The end result of aggression is decreased communication, guilt, or counteraggression that leads the interviewer into a deeper aggression trap. The aggression trap can be avoided by converting aggressive responses into assertive responses.

Assertion

Now that the pitfalls of aggression and nonassertion have been examined, it is time to consider assertion, the most effective way to deal with threats to the interviewer's rights and the need to give directions in an interview. Before assertion techniques are discussed, it is important to know what constitutes an assertive response.

Assertive statements are "I" statements that are direct, straightforward, and clear. Assertive statements account for the rights of the interviewer without assuming that the interviewee's rights are unimportant. Consequently, there is a dual respect for the rights of self and others. In addition, there is an understanding that the interviewee has a right to reject any assertion that interferes with his or her rights and vice versa.

Assertive interviewers choose for themselves, feel good about themselves, are expressive, and are self-enhancing (Alberti & Emmons, 1986). There is also a good chance the interviewer will achieve the desired goal in the interview. Interviewers are likely to have positive feelings about themselves because they act in a confident, responsible, and professional manner in interviews even though they don't always get exactly what they want. Figure 11.1 displays the differences in the three types of communication.

Types of Assertion

Two main types of assertion are appropriate for criminal justice interviews. Both types involve requesting a change in the interviewee's behavior. The interviewer wants the interviewee to (1) do something that they are not already doing and (2) do something better or with a greater frequency than they are already doing or (3) decrease or stop an unwanted behavior.

Protective Assertion

Frequently, interviewers in criminal justice are confronted with a situation in an interview where they need to protect their personal and professional rights and in extreme situations, their dignity. Some of the more critical situations are:

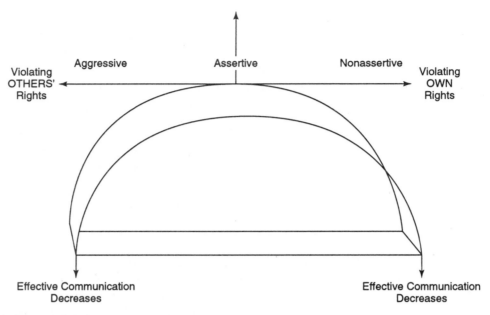

Figure 11.1 Aggressive, Nonassertive, and Assertive Communication

- *Derogatory names.* The interviewee may maliciously or unconsciously use a derogatory name when referring to the interviewer. For example, they may refer to the interviewer as "sweetie," "honey," or "baby" as in "Honey, I've really turned my life around." Other examples include, "dude," "man," "sonny," or "bubba." The interviewer needs to make a protective assertion the *instant* he/she hears a derogatory name, even if it means interrupting the business of the interview. An assertive statement is, "I would like to request that you refer to me as Mrs. Johnson." If the derogatory name is used again, then the interviewer needs to escalate the assertion to, "I insist you refer to me as Mrs. Johnson." Immediate timing is important because the interviewer has a personal right to be referred to in a professional manner.

- *Disclosure of law violations.* When an interviewee appears to be on the verge of revealing or has revealed a violation of the law or behavior that is a threat to self and others, the interviewer needs to make an *assertion of nonconfidentiality.* For example, the interviewer might say, "I will report any incident of child abuse or neglect that you reveal to me" or, "I will not keep the fact that you recently attempted suicide confidential."

- *Inappropriate behavior.* On rare occasions, interviewees in criminal justice will display inappropriate behavior. The inappropriate behavior may be slight or very gross, but in either case the behavior calls for an assertive response by the interviewer. Some of the types of inappropriate behavior the interviewer may want to be on guard for are:

- Flirting
- Malingering or deliberately acting disturbed or insane
- Exposing themselves or masturbating
- Humming or whistling

In the above situations, the interviewer needs to make a protective assertion, such as "I insist that you stop humming during this interview" or "I insist that you stop rubbing yourself immediately." To fail to make such assertions is to erode the dignity and respect the interviewer has a right to command. Most inappropriate behaviors cannot be ignored, with the hope that they will stop or go away. The interviewer must make a protective assertion the *instant they begin.*

■ *Handling requests for favors.* Frequently, interviewers are faced with a request for a simple favor from the interviewee. Some of the typical requests might be:

- a request to borrow money or a car
- a request by a prison inmate to mail a letter
- a request by a prison inmate for contraband (prohibited items)
- a request to make a contact in the free world
- a request by a probationer or a parolee for the interviewer to overlook a transgression

In the above situations, the interviewer needs to make a protective assertion for ethical and professional reasons. To not do so limits the interviewer's job effectiveness. The interviewer needs to say, for example, "I will not loan you ten dollars" or, "I will not contact your cousin for you." In addition to compromising the interviewer, failure to be firm and direct in handling requests can lead to *escalation* of the requests next time, which can lead the interviewer into legal difficulties. An assertive response is an effective means of avoiding any future difficulties.

■ *Threats.* Another type of situation that demands an immediate protective assertion is when the interviewee makes threats to others during the interview. For example, the interviewee says "I'm gonna kill that judge when I get outta here," "I'm gonna get the head of the parole board when I leave here," or "I'm going to kill my old lady next time." These statements represent terroristic threats that cannot be tolerated in an interview. The interviewer needs to make an immediate protective assertion: "I insist that you not make threats toward anyone in this interview." When interviewee threats move from idle to serious, the interviewer needs to make an *assertion of nonconfidentiality.* With or without this assertion, the interviewer is legally bound to notify authorities when a serious threat has been made.

■ *Standing.* Finally, interviewers need to make immediate protective assertions when the interviewee will not sit down for the interview or begins standing during an interview. This is particularly true when the interviewee stands up as a sign of heightened anger or emotionality. The interviewer needs to immediately insist that the interviewee sit down in order for the interview to continue.

Directive Assertion

In addition to protecting their personal and professional rights, interviewers in criminal justice regularly need to give directions to interviewees. A directive assertion means stating *what you want to happen* or *not happen* in a fashion that is clear and understandable to the interviewee.

Ivey and Gluckstern (1984) have identified three dimensions of giving effective direction.

- *Appropriate verbal and nonverbal behavior to support the directive.* This includes eye contact, strong vocal tone, and body language indicating confidence and firmness.
- *Concrete, clear directives.* The clearer and more direct the statement, the likelier it is to be heard.
- *Confirming with the interviewee that the directive was heard.* Ask the interviewee to restate the directive or ask them whether the directive was clear.

Notice the difference in the following pairs of directive assertions:

Vague Directive: "Bill, you need to change your attitude about that drug program or you're going to get yourself in real trouble."

Clear Directive: "Bill, you've missed three of your drug meetings. If you miss another I will notify the judge and recommend that your probation be revoked."

Vague Directive: "Mrs. Jones, hang around for a while because I may need to talk to you some more about what you saw."

Clear Directive: "Mrs. Jones, I want you to stay at home by a telephone for the next twelve hours or until I contact you. We will be talking to you to get more information on what you saw."

Vague Directive: "Let me know if you find a job."

Clear Directive: "As a condition of your parole, I will require that you bring me a signed statement from each of the employers that you interview with for a job. I will require that you have at least three job interviews a week."

Vague Directive: "We've got a bit of a problem with your son that hopefully you can solve for us."

Clear Directive: "We will not keep your son in the detention center. He is severely handicapped and I insist that you keep him with you at this time."

After reading and selecting the clear directives in the preceding pairs, two important points emerge about giving directive assertions in criminal justice interviews. First, giving directive assertions is an integral part of interviews conducted by police, probation, parole, juvenile, and correctional officers. As legal authorities, directive assertions are often required and are usually expected. Second, the way that directive assertions are given is very important. "Law enforcement and correctional officers sometimes fall into the trap of believing they have to present a 'macho' image. In their concern for not being seen as soft, they sometimes go to the other extreme" (Neil, 1980, p. 176). Consequently, directives are more effective if they are both assertive and not aggressive.

Techniques

A number of techniques are available to interviewers to help them make protective and directive assertions. Some of these techniques involve thinking assertively and some involve behaving assertively in an interview. The interviewer can use these techniques in conducting criminal justice interviews in order to increase their skill level and overall competency.

"I" Statements

Avoid using the pronoun "we," such as, "We don't allow you to do that on probation." "I" statements communicate more directly and responsibly. If you as the interviewer made the decision to protect yourself or give a directive, then take the responsibility for the decision by leading with "I."

External Control

Avoid using "can't" or "have to," such as, "I can't let you do that because I'm going to have to write you up." Use "I've decided to," "I will," or "I intend to." The latter leads indicate that you are in control rather than that external controls direct your behavior. Instead of communicating that you are reluctantly being forced to act, you have decided to act and you will take responsibility for your actions.

Apologies

Avoid making apologies, such as "I'm sorry, but you have to go to AA" or "I'm sorry, that's the way the system works." If the interviewer makes a decision and is responsible for the decision, he/she doesn't need to apologize for being firm, clear, and responsible.

Clichés

Avoid clichés that communicate that the interviewer is not responsible for their behavior. For example:

"It's out of my hands—I can't do a thing about it."
"My hands are tied."
"I really don't like to make exceptions."
"I just work here, don't blame me."
"I'm just doing my job."

The responsibly assertive interviewer "owns" their decision instead of giving the impression he/she is an important pawn of some great mystical bureaucratic force.

Escalation

Start with the amount of verbal force necessary when making protective and directive assertions. This minimal force is termed *minimum effective response (MER).* The MER is the accomplishment of the desired goal with a minimum effort with very little negative emotion or negative consequences (Rakos, 2003). Escalate to a more firm assertion if the interviewee persists or refuses. For example, use the escalation of:

SUGGESTING–REQUESTING–INSISTING–DEMANDING

There are two main reasons for using the minimum force necessary. "First, the more muscle you use, the more likely you will elicit resistance from the other person. Second, even if you get what you want, the more muscle you use, the more likely you will leave a residue of resentment. This unfinished business may later hinder your relationship" (Nelson-Jones, 1990, p. 192). If a minimum response doesn't work, then move the response to the next level. For example: "Go into the restroom with the assistant and provide a urine specimen now."

Behavioral

Describe the other person's behavior objectively rather than describing your reaction to it or why they did something. In addition, focus on a specific behavior rather than the whole character of the person. For example, notice the difference between the two statements:

General: "You're a good-for-nothing druggie who keeps trying to fool me. You can't pull anything on me and I'm fed up with you, your drugs, and your games."
Behavior: "I insist that you continue to provide urine specimens, and if you are dirty one more time, I will recommend that your probation be revoked."

Discriminate

Make a decision as to whether the assertion is worth the effort. Assertion can be "overkill." Some behaviors are not worth intense concern. The interviewer should decide which behaviors are likely to be changed and weigh this against the effort of the assertion. Just because the interviewer is assertive does not mean he or she is always likely to get what he or she wants. *Also, the interviewer should not make foolish assertions in potentially violent or explosive situations.*

Fogging

When the interviewer is confronted with manipulative criticism from the interviewee, he/she can employ the technique of fogging (Smith, 1975). This technique involves agreeing with the truth or principle of the criticism and not getting defensive or counterattacking. The interviewer simply does not deny the criticism and responds with assertive fogging.

Interviewee: "You may be a parole officer but you're not so hot. I bet you've done just as bad things as I have. Your daddy probably had money so you got off easy."

Interviewer: "You're right, I have done some things in my life I regret." (Fogging by agreeing in principle)

The technique of fogging gives the interviewer the confidence to know how to respond to occasional criticism without increasing their anxiety or decreasing their control in the interview.

Fogging is a protective device that allows the interviewer time to decide how to respond. It can also be used for people who:

- Will not listen
- Argue for the sake of arguing
- The interviewer has tried to be assertive, but has failed
- Are not interested in hearing what the interviewer has to say
- Only want to wear down the interviewer

Criticism is difficult to handle and in some interview situations, the interviewer needs to use the technique of fogging to reduce the interviewee's attacks (Manis, 1998).

Broken Record

Whenever the interviewee does not accept your assertion and resorts to high-pressure tactics, you can use the "broken record" technique (Phelps & Austin, 1975, p. 85): "What you do is simply become a 'broken record' and repeat your original assertive refusal each time the person tries another manipulation to persuade you to change your mind. If you remain firm with your original statement, and resist the temptation to answer 'Why?' or respond to possible insults, the person will soon run out of new materials and give up." Note the following conversation:

Interviewee: My grandmother's gonna be there and the rest of the family. It's gonna be a great family reunion. I haven't seen many of the people in years. All I need is your permission to leave the county and go to Chicago for this family reunion.

Interviewer: I've thought this over very carefully and I've decided not to give you permission to go.

Interviewee: What! You can't be serious. Why? Just why not?

Interviewer: I've decided not to give you permission to go.

Interviewee: I just wanna know why.

Interviewer: I've decided not to give you permission to go.

Interviewee: Come on and cut me some slack. All I want to do is see my family. You're not that cold-blooded.

Interviewer: I've decided not to give you permission to go.

Interviewee: You must be some kind of creep!

Interviewer: I've decided not to give you permission to go.

In the previous conversation, the interviewer simply repeats themselves and avoids answering the question "why" or getting defensive. It appears that it takes some people longer to hear what the interviewer is saying. If the interviewer is assertive, it is not as likely to take as long.

Self-Talk

In order to think yourself through a particularly challenging assertion, the interviewer can use self-talk. The following is an example of self-talk before, during, and after an interview. Joan asserts herself by insisting that a male prison inmate refrain from inappropriate behavior in an interview:

Before: Calm down. What are my goals? Just think through what skills I need to use to attain my goals.

During: I feel scared and anxious. But I know I'm in charge here. I need to keep cool and say what I have to say.

After: I feel good that I said what was on my mind in a way that he could hear. I don't need to feel so anxious, intimidated, and scared next time.

Self-talk can help you control your anxiety and achieve your goals in a way that is firm, confident, and professional.

Assertion skills are critical in conducting criminal justice interviews. The interviewer will need to make protective and directive assertions if they are going to be firm and tactful in interviews. Assertion skills involve action and taking initiative, and they can, if accompanied by the entire sequence of skills presented in this training, provide the interviewer with a comprehensive repertoire of skills to be an effective interviewer.

Summary

Assertion skills provide a repertoire of techniques for protective and directive communication in interviews. A variety of techniques of assertion help build this repertoire. Assertive statements made by an interviewer need to be grounded in personal responsibility. An interviewer needs to be minimally competent in the use of assertion skills so that nonassertive and aggressive responses can be minimized.

In the remaining sections of this chapter, several additional learning aids appear for increased understanding of the use of the skill of assertion. These aids are: Assertion Scenarios, Exercise 11.1, and the Interview Challenge. Also appearing is Assessment 11.1, which provides an opportunity for determining the level of self-efficacy on the skills of confrontation and assertion. The use of these learning aids has been found to be beneficial to individuals completing this book.

Study Questions

1. What is included in assertion skills?
2. Why are assertion skills needed in criminal justice interviews?
3. Distinguish between assertive, nonassertive, and aggressive responses.
4. Why do people tend to choose aggressive responses?
5. What are the two main types of assertion?
6. What is an assertion of nonconfidentiality?
7. What are the dimensions of effective direction giving?
8. Explain the concept of "minimum muscle"?
9. What is "fogging"?
10. What is the "broken record" technique?

Assertion Scenarios

Directions: *The following scenarios are provided for practicing assertion skills. The scenarios may be enriched by adding or altering the characteristics of the individuals in the scenario. This would involve adding different cultural, gender, age, and handicap characteristics of the individuals.*

Intake

You have worked the late shift in the detention center for a fellow detention worker several times. He has not made up the time for you. You are exhausted, fed up, and overworked. Tonight, he came by the intake desk and asked you to pull his shift again. What do you say?

Late Arrival

For the third time, one of the men on your probation caseload has made an appointment time for 4:45 P.M., right before the time for you to leave the office. You have waited until 5:30 P.M. and the probationer walks into your office. The probationer has transportation but doesn't have a job, so he doesn't have a valid excuse for arriving late for the required meeting. What do you say?

Too Much Information

One of your parolees persists in explaining in detail their sexual escapades. He has just begun to do it again. You have asked him not to do it again. He does it again. What do you say?

Grammatically Correct

You have a police officer partner who has the annoying habit of correcting your English while the two of you ride in the squad car on your assigned shift. You have asked her on several occasions not to do this in public, but your partner has just corrected you in front of citizens while the two of you were eating dinner. What do you say?

The Deer Hunt

Your spouse recently gave you a very expensive rifle. Your partner asked to try it out on the range. You let him borrow it and you haven't gotten it back in some time. A fellow officer told you that the officer that borrowed it took it on a deer hunt. You didn't give him permission to do this. You ask your partner to return it, and he says that he can't get it to you right now. What do you say?

Off Limits

You have told a correctional officer you work with every day that you do not want to discuss your interracial family at work. You do not want it brought up at work, in front of inmates. You have told him to stop bringing up your family business. He continues to mention it. He does it again. What do you say?

Assessment 11.1

Interviewing Training Self-Efficacy Assessment: Knowledge and Skills

Directions: *After completing further training, rate your estimation of your knowledge and skill acquisition on the following scale:*

1—unskilled/unaware
2—awkward
3—average
4—skilled/knowledgeable

_____ a. Knowledge of confrontation skills.

_____ b. The effective use of confrontation skills.

_____ c. Knowledge of assertion skills.

_____ d. The effective use of assertion skills.

Exercise 11.1

Assertion Skills

Directions.   *In the following exercises you are to read the statements and write what you would say. Second, you are to read the response choices and indicate whether they are:*

+ = assertive response
– = aggressive response
N = nonassertive response

First Statement

"I'm not going to pay that amount of money."

Write what you would say: _____

_____

_____

_____

_____

_____

Identify the following

_____   a. "You will or I'll throw your butt in jail."

_____   b. "I will require that you pay that amount of money."

_____   c. "It's out of my hands. I'm sorry, there's nothing we can do."

Second Statement

"I don't have an alcohol problem. Why do I have to go to AA?"

Write what you would say: _____

_____

_____

_____

_____

Identify the following

_____ a. "Look, I'm just trying to do my job. Why don't you make it easier on both of us and go?"

_____ b. "You've gotta be kiddin'—with your DWI record! You drunks are all alike—full of bull."

_____ c. "I will require that you attend and I will insist that you bring me a signed statement indicating your attendance each week."

Third Statement

"I work from 7:00 A.M. to 7:00 P.M. I can't report or I'll lose my job."

Write what you would say: _____

_____

_____

_____

_____

_____

Identify the following

_____ a. "I'm sick and tired of you people coming in here with excuses. You got yourself into trouble and now all you do is bitch."

_____ b. "I will require that you report each month and I will check with your employer to make sure you are here."

_____ c. "Maybe it would be better, I guess, to kinda let it slide for a while. We usually don't make exceptions."

Fourth Statement

"My wife is supposed to be sending those payments in for me."

Write what you would say: _____

_____

_____

_____

_____

_____

Identify the following

_____ a. "Don't give me that excuse. I've heard all the excuses and I'm not that stupid."

_____ b. "I'm sorry but we haven't gotten a payment yet. Maybe something went wrong. We have a lot of payments to keep up with, you know."

_____ c. "I insist that you submit your payments and I will directly check on these payments in the next three weeks."

Fifth Statement

"Are you through with me now?"

Write what you would say: _____

_____

_____

_____

_____

_____

Identify the following

_____ a. "Oh yes! Just a few more minutes. We won't keep you much longer."

_____ b. "You better get your attitude straightened out or you are going to have a lot of trouble. I'll tell you when I'm through with you when I am ready."

_____ c. "I will indicate when your meeting is over and what is expected of you in the meetings."

Sixth Statement

"Is there another officer I can have?"

Write what you would say: _____

_____

_____

_____

_____

_____

Identify the following

_____ a. "What do you think this is—a short-order restaurant?"

_____ b. "I just work here. I don't make the assignments. Making a switch would be too much trouble 'cause we're swamped with paperwork as it is."

_____ c. "I will be your officer. I will not make a change. I will insist that you report to me on time each month."

Seventh Statement

"You're not going to make me pee in that bottle, are you?"

Write what you would say: _____

_____

_____

_____

_____

_____

Identify the following

_____ a. "Stop stalling. You know what you are supposed to do."

_____ b. "Give me a break . . . I've had a really long day."

_____ c. "I require that you provide a urine specimen and I insist that you do it now."

Eighth Statement

"You can't make me go to AA. I'll start drinking again."

Write what you would say: _____

_____

_____

_____

_____

_____

Identify the following

_____ a. "I am requiring that you attend AA on a regular basis for six months. I will evaluate your case at that time."

_____ b. "Look! It doesn't make any difference to me. I'd just as soon throw you in jail anyway. I see you people day in and day out and I couldn't care less."

_____ c. "It's the system. Take it or leave it. It's not my idea."

Interview Challenge

How would you complete the following encounter? Keep in mind the concerns raised by the questions following the preliminary interview narrative.

You are a probation officer who is interviewing a forty-year-old male who is on probation for sexual abuse of a child. The probationer made his sixteen-year-old son have sexual intercourse with his mildly retarded wife in the motel where they are living. The probationer has had several prior sexual abuse incidents. Beginning the interview, the man says, "I don't need to be on probation because I have decided to live my life for the Lord. I have placed my life in his hands."

1. What skills will you need to get the interview started?

   _____

   _____

   _____

2. What will you want to ideally get accomplished in the interview?

   _____

   _____

   _____

3. How will you divide your interview time between official objectives and personal concerns in the interview (i.e., how closely will you stay with required questions)?

   _____

   _____

4. What do you anticipate the major segments of the interview to be?

   _____

   _____

   _____

5. What would be the most appropriate interview style to use in this situation?

_____

_____

_____

6. What will be some of the barriers to communication in the interview?

_____

_____

_____

7. What would you need to minimally accomplish in this interview for you to consider the interview successful?

_____

_____

_____

12

Skill Integration

Learning Objectives

Subject: Skill Integration

Objectives: After a period of instruction the student (trainee) will:

1. Identify how an interviewer can develop a personal style of interviewing.
2. Identify when an interviewer may need to return to a safe resource in an interview.
3. Explain how to cycle back to an earlier skill.
4. Explain how to stage subsequent action in an interview.
5. Identify the future trends in interviewing.

Learning domains:

a. Cognitive
b. Psychomotor

> When you interrogate somebody, it's all an act.
>
> Mark Baker
> *Cops* (1985)

Now that all the interviewing skills have been presented, the challenge of this book is to put the skills together to obtain mastery as an interviewer. Going through the skills one at a time is relatively easy compared to integrating the skills into a professional repertoire.

You may be concerned that there is so much to remember and that the skills are quite complex. Fortunately, most of the skills are interrelated and meaningful in day-to-day experiences so they will become more natural as you "live" with and use them. In addition, when you master the skills in the preceding chapters, integration of the skills will come to you naturally. On the other hand, your skill as an interviewer will not be achieved by reading alone. This book can be successful only when you take the skills out of each chapter and practice them in criminal justice interviewing situations.

In this chapter, we focus on how you can integrate the skills that have been presented in previous chapters. In order to do this we examine the concepts of safe recourse, skill decisions, and cycling back. The ultimate integration of interviewing skills is demonstrated only in real interviews with real impact and effect on an interviewee. This "reality testing" is encouraged and reinforced in this chapter. Finally, the future trends of interviewing are discussed.

Systematic Training Model

The skills training model presented in this book is a structured, systematic approach to interviewing training. An overview of these skills is presented in Figure 12.1. As a trainee you moved from the simplest skills, such as empathy, to more complex ones, such as confrontation. It is crucial that you master the simpler skills, for the more complex skills are based on them. Systematically moving through the sequence of skills allows you to both evaluate where you are in the program and also acquire a method of interviewing.

The interviewing training model has been presented in a logical, step-by-step fashion. However, using the skills in the model is not as neat and clean as the model presents. Using the skills in the sequence would be very rigid and mechanical in actual criminal justice interviews. Therefore, we want to look at how the skills model can be incorporated into actual professional interview sessions.

Developing a Personal Style

Experienced interviewers seldom think about what they are going to say. They integrate the interviewing skills into a smooth personal style. To achieve your personal style, it is important that you take the

Empathy: Interpersonal Sensitivity	The interviewer accurately understands another person's thoughts, feelings, and behaviors.
Speed and Pacing	The interviewer skillfully uses silence, control, speed, and pacing in an interview.
Summarization	The interviewer summarizes both cognitive and affective information in an interview.
Immediacy	The interviewer is aware of the relationship between themselves and the interviewee. They really said what was going on in the interview.
Concreteness	The interviewer is precise, exact, and specific about actions, thoughts, feelings, and intentions.
Confrontation	The interviewer is skillful in pointing out discrepancies in an interview.
Assertion	The interviewer can make responsible directive and protective statements in an interview.

Figure 12.1   Overview of Criminal Justice Interviewing Skills

skills of interviewing and integrate them in your own way. This can be assisted by looking at flexibility and coordination.

Flexibility

Even though the training model presented in this book is logical and systematic, it can be applied too rigidly. The interviewer needs to remain flexible in the application of the skills because interviews don't always happen as neatly as the training sequence or examples would suggest. In order to maintain flexibility, the interviewer needs to avoid:

- Moving mechanically from one skill to another. As we have seen in the use of protective assertion, for example, the interviewer needs to use the appropriate skills as the occasion arises. The sequence of skills presented represents an ideal that is rarely followed in real interviews.
- Assuming that understanding always precedes action skills. Law enforcement and corrections officers frequently have to exert control and give directions before attempting to gain understanding. Interviews conducted in crises situations frequently call for immediate action regardless of whether the officers have subsequent time to conduct a full interview. They do not often have the luxury of prior understanding before taking action. In this case, the skills model, because of the gravity of the situation, takes on the appearance of:

PREDICTION–ACTION–UNDERSTANDING

ACTION–UNDERSTANDING–PREDICTION

  In the first sequence, the officers made a quick prediction as to what action should be taken. In some cases, the officer may not find out later whether the action was appropriate. For example, a parolee might disappear and the officer would not know if he/she had been arrested in some other state or were simply living a law-abiding life—but still a fugitive. In the second sequence, the officer took action, gained understanding after the action, and predicted what should be done in the future. For example, the officer may have taken an action that was a mistake but he/she will know what to do in similar future interview situations.

- Spending too much time on a specific skill. Effective interviewers have a wide repertoire of skills and use them in a socially intelligent way. They don't specialize and dwell on any one skill. For example, they don't overuse confrontation or assertion. Effective interviewers are flexible and spontaneous.

Coordination

As a beginning interviewer, you can expect to experience some awkwardness as you learn the interviewing skills. Using the skills in a smooth and coordinated way can be accomplished by practice and experience. Using the following procedures, suggested by Egan (1994), you will become more coordinated in the use of interviewing skills.

- *Modeling of extended interviews by skilled interviewers.* It helps to watch someone who can "put it all together." Live sessions, good films, and videotapes are all useful. You can read about interviewing, but you need to watch someone actually do it. "Modeling gives you the opportunity to have the 'ah-hah' experience in training—that is, as you watch someone competent, you say to yourself, "Oh, that's how it's done!" (p. 42).
- *Step-by-step supervised practice.* Watching someone else interview well will give you pictures in your mind of the interviewing skills, but it will not make you a coordinated interviewer. The next step is to learn and practice each skill under supervision. You need feedback from a supervisor so that you can determine what you are doing right or wrong. By gradually practicing interviewing skills under the condition of feedback, you will become more coordinated and confident.
- *Extended practice in interviewing skills outside the classroom.* You will become more coordinated in interviewing if you can practice interviewing in situations outside the classroom. If you can participate in a criminal justice internship or volunteer work, you will have an excellent opportunity to master the skills learned in the classroom.
- *Simulation.* Finally, the interviewing skills presented in this book will become more natural and coordinated if you practice interviewing situations that simulate the realities of actual criminal justice encounters. Interviews in the field are often not polite, reserved, or relaxed. Consequently, the more you have an opportunity to interview in crises and "heightened emotions" situations, the more confidence and coordination you will have. You want to be able to be smooth in pressure situations.

Returning to a Safe Recourse

The need for the skills in this training may arise at any point in the interview, but returning to *empathy* is a safe and recommended recourse if the interviewer encounters difficulty at any point in the interview. Empathy is a safe recourse because it is an honest reflection of human emotions that are usually very real. The risk is low because empathy does not involve threat, probing, or interpretation. The interviewer is simply responding, on a person-to-person basis, to what the interviewer sees and feels.

Immediacy

The interviewer may need to return to empathy after making an immediacy response in the interview. In other words, the relationship issue raised in the interview may precipitate very strong emotions on the part of the interviewee. Notice how the interviewer returns to empathy in the following conversation:

Interviewee: Look. I just gotta get out of these drug meetings. I just can't take it much longer. My old man's on my back. You're on my case. My kids are driving me crazy. I don't know what I'm gonna do . . . if I could just stay at home more at night.

Interviewer: You're under a lot of pressure. You're feeling squeezed and trapped and you're very dependent on me right now. (Immediacy of relationship)

Interviewee: (sobbing) I told him it wouldn't work . . . you wouldn't be able to excuse me. He's gonna kill me when I get home.

Interviewer: You feel scared, frightened, and cornered.

Because of the depth and extent of the interviewee's emotional response in this situation, the interviewer chose to return to empathy rather than follow the relationship issue of dependency or ask any concrete questions. These can come later.

Confrontation

As was pointed out when the skill of confrontation was presented, confrontation is preceded and followed by empathy. In addition to this, the interviewer may need to stay with empathy after a confrontation if the confrontation elicits a particularly strong emotional reaction by the interviewee. Since confrontation is a particularly strong skill, this is likely to occur. Notice how the interviewer returns to empathy in the following conversation:

Interviewee: (angrily) I don't need to come to see you at this stupid probation department. I'm not a criminal and I don't need you people. This is wasting my time and your time so let's forget my visits. I'll just call you when you want me to.

Interviewer: You feel disgusted, angry, embarrassed, and fed up. I even sense you're rather angry at me. (Immediacy of relationship)

Interviewee: Yes! No! Oh hell, I don't know. I'm so confused I don't know what's what.

Interviewer: I sense you are very confused and humiliated, and I'm a little concerned also, because on one hand, you insist you don't want to come here, and on the other hand, you made an agreement with the judge to come here faithfully. In fact, you were very willing and thankful to have this option. Can you clear this up for me?

Interviewee: (Silence, but looking very dejected and burdened)

Interviewer: (Silence)

Interviewer: My mentioning this has really hit you very hard and you're feeling very overwhelmed.

Interviewee: (crying angrily) You just don't know how I've messed my life up. My family? My husband? My job? I've been through hell for years . . . and now look at me . . . a common thief at the probation department. It's too much . . . I can't take it much longer.

Interviewer: You're frightened, scared, and desperate almost to the point of doing something very drastic.

In this situation, the interviewer made the choice to come back to empathy. The interviewer could have immediately made an assertive statement (and may have to later). Instead, the interviewer returned to empathy because of the intensity of the situation.

Assertion

It is also likely that an interviewer may choose to return to empathy after making an assertion. Notice how the interviewer returns to empathy in the following interview segment:

Interviewer: You're feeling very desperate and I will recommend that you enter a drug treatment program.

Interviewee: (Silence)

Interviewer: How does the idea sound to you?

Interviewee: Well, uh, I guess so.

Interviewer: You're pretty overwhelmed by the idea. Perhaps a little torn. On one hand, you feel desperate to take care of your addiction, but on the other hand, you are frightened about whether you can pull it off.

Interviewee: Yeah!

Interviewer: I can sense that you are very frightened and scared.

Once the interviewer has made an assertive statement, he/she may choose to respond with empathy. As long as the subsequent response does not erode the firmness of the assertive statement, returning to empathy is a safe and recommended recourse.

These are only a few of the situations where the interviewer returns to empathy. A safe recourse may also be needed after the skills of concreteness and immediacy. In any case, returning to a safe recourse is an important option for the interviewer because it is very difficult to "script" an entire interview. The interviewer needs the flexibility of safe options.

Making Skill Decisions

Putting together the skills means the interviewer is competent to use the appropriate skill when the occasion arises. Rarely does the interviewer have the time or resources to think through the decision to use a particular skill. Making choices at points of decision is one way in which interviews differ from structured and written questionnaires. A written questionnaire does not provide for dialogue based on what the respondent writes on the form, whereas an interviewer can follow leads or change the direction of the interview. The written, structured questionnaire can only go in one direction.

Choices

The competent interviewer has choices of which skills to use and these choices will affect the direction and outcome of the interview. For example, notice the choices and how they could affect the direction of the interview in the following interviewee statement:

Interviewee: He comes home late at night. We have a fight. He's drunk and it scares the kids. I don't know how much longer I can take it. What should I do?

Interviewer: Choice 1: You feel terrified, trapped, and desperate. (Empathy)

Interviewer: Choice 2: You feel very dependent on me right now. (Immediacy)

Interviewer: Choice 3: What do you mean "you have a fight"? (Concreteness)

Each one of these responses will have the effect of changing the direction of the interview. The interview will either tend to focus on feelings, facts, or relationships. Figure 12.2 presents an illustration of the possibilities for these choices.

Points of Decision

Figure 12.2 also illustrates the possible points of decision at which the choices can be made. Typically, all of the skills, except summarization, can serve as a point of decision. Whether the interviewer makes a particular choice at a point of decision will be affected by the purpose of the interview, the time allotted, and the interviewee's reaction in the interview.

Time Limitations

The amount of time available in an interview affects the use of skills. This includes the amount of time both for each interview and for the number of subsequent interviews. It is impossible to say how much

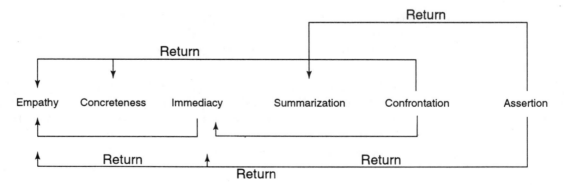

Figure 12.2 Cycling Back

of the interview is devoted to using specific skills. Criminal justice interviews vary from agency to agency and within an agency. In some situations the skills can be used only a little but in others a great deal. It depends on many other variables, the most important being the subject of the interview and the setting. Sometimes decisions are made external to the interviewer so there is very little time to conduct the interview. For example, the chief supervisor may limit interview time. Or, the number of interviews can limit the time available.

Some skills can be used in a shorter time span than others; concreteness skills are relatively brief, whereas relationship skills tend to consume more time. If time is very limited, then the interviewer will probably have to lean toward obtaining specific factual information. If more time is available, he/she can lean toward developing skills that take more time to apply. The challenge of the competent interviewer is to make choices as to which skills to use that are consistent with the availability of time. In so doing, the interviewer is optimizing effectiveness.

Cycling Back

The systematic interviewing skills model illustrated in this book is not a linear formula. It is a cyclical approach that is also illustrated in Figure 12.2. This cyclical process involves the insight of knowing when to return to earlier skills.

Returning to Earlier Skills

As has already been indicated, the interviewer may need to return to empathy. In addition, the interviewer may decide to cycle back to other skills depending on the demands of the interviewing situation. Figure 12.2 illustrates some of the cyclical return paths available to the interviewer. For example, the interviewer may want to summarize rather extensive or technical directive assertions to ensure that the interviewee has understood what has been said. He/she may also want to do this as a reinforcement to the directions.

When to Cycle Back

The interviewer will want to cycle back to an earlier skill whenever the interview situation demands. Specifically, the following conditions would cause consideration to cycle back:

- Whenever there are unexpressed feelings in the interview.
- Whenever there is incomplete information in the interview.
- Whenever an unresolved relationship issue is subverting the interview.
- Whenever clarification is needed.
- Whenever discrepancies continue to exist in the interview.
- Whenever the interviewer or interviewee (primarily the interviewer) is uncomfortable with the outcome of the interview.

Cycling back is needed whenever there is any unfinished business in the interview, especially if the interviewer has concerns that are not resolved.

Staging Subsequent Action

The skills sequence presented in this training can also serve as effective staging and groundwork for subsequent action in an interview. This subsequent action can be either a spinoff from all of the skills or a natural and logical extension of the entire sequence. Both types will be discussed and illustrated so that you can get a clear idea of how this staging develops. (The possibilities are infinite so just a few of the more frequently used extensions of the skills will be mentioned.)

Referrals

Frequently, an interviewer will need to refer the interviewee to another professional, program, or office. The skills sequence makes this very easy and more effective. Once the interviewer has staged the referral by establishing a need for the referral through the use of concreteness skills, the referral can follow the summary. Notice the following conversation:

Interviewee: I'm not doing very well. I think I'm gonna mess up on drugs again. You gotta do something or I'll be in jail for sure.

Interviewer: You're scared, worried, and desperate. If I can find you a drug program you will be relieved and not as worried. You're very dependent on me. If I don't find you a program you might do something drastic and frightening. Is that about the way it is? (Summary)

Interviewee: Yeah!

Interviewer: Okay! I'm going to refer you to an excellent drug program because you do seem to be at the point of getting into trouble. Let me tell you about this program and how you can get into it.

In this conversation, the interviewer, through concreteness of intentions—"What if I can?", "What if I can't?", and "How much time do we have?"—has established that a referral needs to be made. The referral can proceed from the summary, and, if, at any time, the interviewee begins to waver from the original commitment of attending the program, the interviewer may need to cycle back to confrontation or concreteness skills.

Contracts

The skills sequence can stage the development of a contract in an interview by spinning off from *concreteness of intentions*. Note how this is done in the following interview:

Interviewee: These visits to you twice a month are killing me. It's a long way across town and my old car isn't in very good shape. I need a break.

Interviewer: You're feeling very strung out and hassled. (Empathy)

Interviewee: Oh, you don't know the half of it. Every agency in this town has me and my wife going to some kind of meeting. It's almost every night of the week—AA on Monday, drug program on Tuesday, and a parents group on Thursday. On top of that, I gotta come see you twice a month. It's a wonder I can keep my job.

Interviewer: What would happen if I wasn't able to reduce your visits? (Concreteness of intentions)

Interviewee: I don't know, but I can't go on like this much longer. This schedule is running me ragged.

Interviewer: What would happen if I could reduce your visits?

Interviewee: It would be a great relief to me.

Interviewer: How much time do I have to work this out before you do something rash? (Concreteness of intentions)

Interviewee: Well, we can go on for a little while—a week or two.

Interviewer: If I can get your visits reduced, would you be willing to sign a contract that would increase your time in the drug program, which is closer to where you live, in exchange for fewer visits to me? (Contract)

Interviewee: You mean make an agreement?

Interviewer: A written agreement that I will be checking on to ensure you have complied with your part. (Assertion)

Interviewee: Yes! It would be better than what I have to do now.

In the above sequence, the interviewer presses for a contract at the point of *concreteness of intentions*, which leads with "What if I can?"

Information

Sometimes the interviewer may need to simply and straightforwardly provide the interviewee with information such as rules, procedures, directions, or laws. This is illustrated in the following interview segment:

Interviewee: You're not going to get any trouble out of me. I just want to stay clean and out of court. I don't want to be back here again and I sure don't want to go to jail.

Interviewer: You feel determined and almost frightened.

Interviewee: You're right! Once in court was enough for me.

Interviewer: Okay. Let's go over your rules of probation so that you are very clear as to what the court expects of you.

In this sequence, the interviewer sets the stage for giving the interviewee information with empathy. Criminal justice interviewers provide a lot of information on a day-to-day basis. Police, probation, parole, and correctional officers are frequently called on to provide information. The skills in this training sequence can stage this practice quite easily.

Some of the other interview actions that also follow this connection of staging are:

- Problem solving
- Disciplinary action
- Job termination
- Counseling
- Employment
- Performance appraisal

Interviewing involves skills that are vital for effective communication in face-to-face criminal justice interviews. Mastery of these skills will not only help the criminal justice professional become a better interviewer, but will also help them live more effectively when communicating with others in daily life. The goal was to blend training and education in a fashion that allows the two endeavors to complement each other. Buerger (2004) indicates that we need increased dialogue that addresses the needs of the law enforcement profession and the capacities of the academic field. Hopefully, this text has been a part of this needed dialogue.

Applying Theories, Techniques, and Practices

Now that the student/trainee has mastered the theories, techniques, and practices based on the basic skills model, it is appropriate to view the application possibilities of these skills. Interviews are conducted in both the criminal and juvenile justice systems in a wide variety of community and institutional settings. Figure 12.3 presents a visual representation of the variety of interview settings. Beginning with police interviews with victims, witnesses, and suspects, juvenile and adult offenders are interviewed at multiple points as they flow through the juvenile or criminal justice system. They can also leave the system at various points, and additional interviews would not occur unless they have future contact with the system. These interviews are conducted by some of the following:

- Police officers
- Victims' advocates
- Attorneys
- Mental health workers
- Detention workers
- Teachers
- Volunteers
- Probation officers
- Priests and ministers

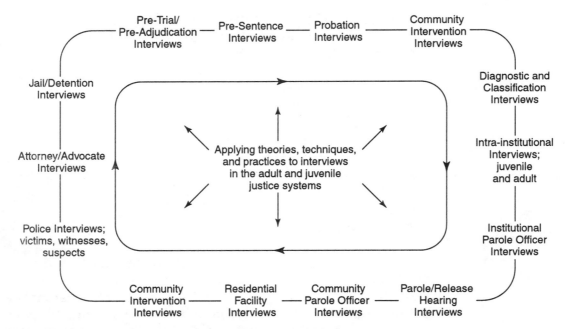

Figure 12.3   System Interview Flow Chart: Juvenile and Adult

- Social workers
- Substance abuse counselors
- Sex offender treatment providers
- Parole officers
- Psychologists
- Drug and family court workers
- Family shelter workers

The conclusion to be made from this list and visual representation is the assertion made in the first chapter that the juvenile and criminal justice systems are interview-driven with a multitude of settings that require interpersonal communication skills.

Future Trends in Interviewing

Interviews provide a wealth of information about individuals involved with the criminal justice system. What is the present state of the art and science of interviewing? What are the future trends in interviewing? These questions lead to some interesting, if not prophetic, answers. Predicting the future is always risky, but several trends seem to be developing.

State of the Art and Science

In the last ten years, there has been a rapid expansion in the knowledge of interviewing, interrogation, deception, mulitcultural competencies, and basic communication skills. This rapid expansion has led to an information or *technology transfer gap* in the field. Previously, most of what we know about interviewing and interrogation emerged from antedotal or personal case reports provided by experienced and perceptive professionals working in the field. There was not much other information available. Recently, in the United States and Europe, researchers have conducted creative and elaborate studies that have provided a wealth of information on interviewing and interrogation. The results of these studies have created a gap between what we know and what is being used in criminal justice agencies. Several factors have led to the gap and are likely to perpetuate the gap for some time:

■ The criminal justice system is conservative and slow to change and more subject to political forces than scientific knowledge.

■ The criminal justice system is more concerned with what a specific person is doing or going to do, and less concerned with the rates or percentages that groups of people will do. Consequently, research results are interesting, but in specific cases, are not very helpful.

■ Thousands of law enforcement officers in the United States have already been trained in questionable techniques that have very little empirical support. The technology transfer gap is likely to continue until there is unlearning and relearning by officers who are confident in their current procedures.

Currently, a large quantity of available research results are found in esoteric and highly technical books and scientific journals. Most of these sources are not read by individuals working in the field.

The purpose of this text was to provide a small solution to the technology transfer gap by presenting the research in a form that can be used by a wider audience in the criminal justice system.

Future Trends

Currently, in the United States, police are permitted by law to engage in trickery and deceit during an investigation and an interrogation. It is not clear about where to draw the line between unacceptable and acceptable police interview tactics (Memon & Bull, 1999). It will be a slow process, but interrogation in the United States is likely to change, as it has in other countries. In England and Wales, for example, specific legislation prohibits police use of deceit, coercion, and oppression. Specific safeguards are in place during police interviews that tend to reduce the interrogative pressure in the interview and increase the likelihood of active legal representation in the interview (Medford et al., 2003). The technology transfer gap is narrower in these countries because the courts recognize research on interviewing and interrogation and how susceptible individuals are to manipulation. As evidence mounts, the compelling need for the U.S. criminal justice system to change will be overwhelming.

The literature of interviewing and interrogation has followed the pattern of first and second waves. The *first wave* consisted of the literature appearing in the latter years of the twentieth century. This interviewing and interrogation literature was primarily based on personal experiences and was not *evidence based.* Evidence-based practices are based on controlled scientific studies and the carping critics of the scientific community. The books and manuals appearing in the first wave were very valuable, not because they necessarily got the techniques correct, but because their contributions led to research to determine if they had gotten the techniques correct. Consequently, the literature of the first wave had a valuable *heuristic value.* The *second wave* of interviewing literature, appearing at the beginning of the twenty-first century, has been evidence based and, in many cases, a study of the interviewing and interrogation assertions made in the first wave. The unanswered question for the second wave concerns the degree to which the research results of the second wave will gain the extensive popularity and implementation of techniques generated in the first wave.

Interviewing permeates all facets of contemporary life and this trend is likely to increase in the criminal justice system. Computer surveys, computer assessments for substance abuse, and computer diagnosis of minor medical problems have been in place for some time. Mann and Stewart (2004) identify the future of interviewing in cyberspace. They mention electronic interviewing through e-mail surveys, Web-page-based surveys, and computer-mediated communication in both public and semi-private arenas. This means that now and in the future, interviewers can access virtual interviewees from across the globe or from a local agency. With electronic communication the possibilities for interviewing seem limitless. Computer-assisted interviews (CAI) are currently being used to survey the extent of drug use in the United States. Lessler, Caspar, Penne, and Barker (2000) found that CAI:

- increased the reporting of drug use
- allowed respondents to correct inconsistencies in their responses
- eased the task of responding for poor readers and educationally challenged respondents

Finally, a promising and innovative interviewing training technique has been developed using computer technology. This technique uses *interrogative virtual reality* training to teach interviewers how to detect deception. Computer-controlled virtual humans are used to simulate deceptive behaviors. Trainees respond to virtual humans who exhibit a variety of cues for deception. They are then trained and evaluated in a virtual environment. The complex training tasks require interviewers being trained to make judgments and decisions based on the training tasks. Cues that may lead to aggressive, high-risk, or hostile behavior are emphasized in the training (McKenzie, Scerbo, Catanzaro, & Phillips, 2003). This technique holds considerable potential for interviewing in situations where quick decisions have to be made in dangerous situations (Forsythe, 2004).

Conclusions and Recommendations

Interviews play an important role in the operation of the criminal justice system. The need for interviewing training in criminal justice is supported by the importance of obtaining complete and accurate information in all components of the system. By improving interview techniques, the functioning of the entire system can be improved since the system relies heavily on information gathered in face-to-face encounters.

The question remains: How effective are training programs for forensic interviewers? Powell (2002) suggests that training programs are not very effective. Research findings suggest that training programs are effective in teaching interviewers what they should do, but the knowledge is not being transferred to their actual interviewing practices. To reduce this training transfer problem, Powell recommends three critical elements that should be included in all training programs.

- Clear translation of recommendations, based on research, into training guidelines and practice.
- A variety and repetition of opportunities to practice specific interviewing techniques that are accompanied by critical feedback.
- Trainers participating in the evaluation of training.

The need for additional research on the effectiveness of interviewing techniques is critical. Interviewing training must be transferred to practice in the fields of law enforcement, corrections, and the courts. Hopefully, this text will assist in making this transfer, not only because the training information is research based, but also because it is presented in a practical, "user-friendly" format and curriculum design.

Frank and Feeley (2003) have made some specific recommendations for training professional lie catchers in light of the difficulty of the task mentioned in earlier chapters. Their recommendations were that law enforcement professionals should be trained:

- In situations that are relevant to the ones that professionals face during interrogation. The situations should be similar to real-world situations.
- In high-stake situations with specific behavioral clues. It would seem useless to train professionals on clues that do not generalize across high-stake situations and a period of time in the future.
- In techniques and information that will teach them how to detect lies after ample practice and feedback.
- In learning situations that are evaluated by accessing pre- and posttest performance.
- So that the effects of training persist over a period of time. Old habits return easily and booster training may be needed in order for the skills to persist.

The question remains as to whether we can train professionals to accurately detect truth and lies, but Frank and Feeley do not think we have looked at the question thoroughly. They assert that we may be better than we have been if we train effectively.

The importance of believing a lie or disbelieving the truth having such a profound impact on a person's life demands that we have better training programs. Greater understanding about the processes that are associated with deception and how this might affect liars' responses are critical skills for police officers (Vrij & Taylor, 2003). Consequently, the recommendation logically follows that law enforcement officers at the local, state, and federal levels have training programs consistent with the previous recommendations. From a broader perspective, the following recommendations are also offered to improve interviewing in the criminal justice system:

- Formal training should be introduced at both the entry level and in-service level in criminal justice agencies.
- Courses in interviewing should be a part of the required curriculum in undergraduate criminal justice programs in colleges and universities.
- Courses in advanced communication, which would include theories of confessions, suggestibility, and deception, should be offered as electives in graduate programs in criminal justice and forensic psychology.
- Basic human relations, communication skills, or interpersonal skills training should be the foundation for interviewing training.

The body of knowledge in the science, art, and theory of criminal justice interviews has been expanding rapidly in recent years. This book is evidence of this expansion. Hopefully this book has given an appreciation of where we've been, where we are, and where we need to go in this exciting and important area of criminal justice.

Summary

Interviewers can integrate all of the skills by developing a personal style, knowing when to return to a safe recourse, making decisions, cycling back, and staging subsequent actions. Integration also means having a perspective of the future trends in interviewing and the possibilities for professional improvement. Interviewers need to be minimally competent in integrating all of the skills in the interviewing training model.

Now that you have completed the entire interviewing skills sequences, you may want to complete the final Assessments 12.1 and 12.2 and then finish with the final Interview Challenge. After the assessments are completed, you may find it revealing to compare the results with the assessment results in Chapter 4.

Study Questions

1. How can a personal style of interviewing be developed?
2. Why is returning to empathy a safe recourse?
3. What are some of the conditions that would necessitate cycling back in an interview?
4. Explain what the technology transfer gap is in interviewing.
5. What is CAI?
6. What is interrogative virtual reality training?
7. How effective are training programs for forensic interviewers?
8. What are the differences between first wave and second wave interviewing procedures and practices?
9. Explain what evidence based means in interviewing research.
10. What is meant by interviewing procedures having heuristic value?

Assessment 12.1

Communication Posttest

Now that you have completed the interviewing skills sequence, you may wish to complete the communication posttest and compare your results with those obtained on the pretest in Chapter 3.

*Below are five statements. You are to read each statement as if it were being said to you. In the space to the left of each response, indicate whether the response to the statement is a **TURN-ON, TURN-OFF,** or **STAY WITH** response.*

First Statement

I don't understand why they always let that old man do the job when they know I can do the job better. I can't stand being messed over.

Show Ratings Here:

_____ 1. All this bitching isn't going to get you anywhere. You have to start thinking more positively.

_____ 2. You feel cheated and ignored.

_____ 3. Don't worry. Someday you will get your chance.

_____ 4. That's the way the system works. You know that.

Second Statement

I can't understand why the old lady won't let me have custody of my kids. She doesn't give a damn about those kids.

Show Ratings Here:

_____ 1. You feel furious, cheated, and perhaps very hurt because it's very painful to be separated from your children.

_____ 2. You feel upset and confused.

_____ 3. Why do you feel this way?

_____ 4. I know how to get them back. Just listen to me and I'll fix it for you.

Third Statement

I really need to write a letter to my wife but I don't know what to say. I'm afraid I'll just make things worse by saying the wrong thing. I'm not very good at writing letters.

Show Ratings Here:

_____ 1. How many times have you written her so far?

_____ 2. You sound pretty upset.

_____ 3. Don't look at me. I sure couldn't do it.

_____ 4. Well, somebody your age sure ought to be able to write a letter. You sound to me like a wimp.

Fourth Statement

I just got a letter from my wife. It was some more bad news . . . my son is on drugs. He's quit school and probably getting into trouble. She can't do a thing with him and I'm stuck in here.

Show Ratings Here:

_____ 1. You feel trapped and worried.

_____ 2. How old is your son?

_____ 3. Yeah, that's all I ever get is bad news!

_____ 4. You're feeling lost, helpless, and tortured because it's so hopeless when your family is in trouble.

Fifth Statement

My people called the parole board and were told I'd be released Monday but I can't go home. I have to go to a funky halfway house.

Show Ratings Here:

_____ 1. What a ripoff. I can understand your attitude.

_____ 2. Just a minute. The parole board is just trying to do what's right. You're very lucky to be getting out.

_____ 3. You are really caught in a bind. On one hand, you want to go home and that makes you excited, but on the other hand, you are steamed about the halfway house.

_____ 4. That's the system—take it or leave it.

Finally, you may wish to complete the *Post-Interviewing Self-Rating Assessment* that you completed previously in Chapter 4. Once you have scored the "last interview" portion of this form, you can refer to the form in Chapter 4 and make a comparison of the numbers on the "first interview" portion to see how you now feel about interviewing and how much your attitude has changed. If this program in interviewing has been successful, your scores should be much lower.

Assessment 12.2

Postinterviewing Self-Rating

Rate yourself from 1 to 10 on each item.

1 = not like you
10 = much like you

FIRST INTERVIEW	LAST INTERVIEW	
_____	_____	I would hate to do the wrong thing.
_____	_____	I can't imagine myself being a successful interviewer.
_____	_____	I worry about being observed by my instructor/trainer.
_____	_____	It makes me nervous to be in front of the class/group.
_____	_____	A video recorder bothers me.
_____	_____	I talk too much in the interview.
_____	_____	I want to get the interview over as soon as possible.
_____	_____	I'm afraid I might forget what to say in the interview and almost panic.
_____	_____	I feel a lot of pressure to keep the interview going.
_____	_____	When the interviewee gets upset I want to smooth things over.
_____	_____	It is difficult for me to confront the interviewee.
_____	_____	I'm afraid I will be too shy and not talk loud enough in the interview.
_____	_____	There are certain topics I feel uneasy about discussing in the interview.
_____	_____	If the interviewee stops talking, total silence scares me.
_____	_____	I can't imagine conducting an interview without notes in my hand to look at.
_____	_____	Interviewing an offender who has committed a terrible crime makes me nervous.
_____	_____	I don't think I could interview victims of crimes.

(continued)

FIRST INTERVIEW	LAST INTERVIEW	
_____	_____	I wouldn't know what to do if I suspected the interviewee of lying.
_____	_____	I don't feel comfortable interviewing in serious situations.
_____	_____	I don't think I can handle interviews with people of different cultural backgrounds than my own.

Interview Challenge

How would you complete the following encounter? Keep in mind the concerns raised by the questions following the preliminary interview narrative.

You are a caseworker in an adult correctional institution for women. An inmate tells you, "My husband has filed a motion with the court to have my parental rights severed on the grounds that I'm an unfit mother. He'd do anything to hurt me and I can't do anything about it. I don't have any reason to go on if I lose those kids."

1. What skills will you need to get the interview started?

    _____

    _____

    _____

2. What will you want to ideally get accomplished in the interview?

    _____

    _____

    _____

3. How will you divide your interview time between official objectives and personal concerns in the interview (i.e., how closely will you stay with required questions)?

    _____

    _____

    _____

4. What do you anticipate the major segments of the interview to be?

    _____

    _____

    _____

5. What would be the most appropriate interview style to use in this situation?

_____

_____

_____

6. What will be some of the barriers to communication in the interview?

_____

_____

_____

7. What would you need to minimally accomplish in this interview for you to consider the interview successful?

_____

_____

_____

References

Aiding people in conflict. (1988). National Mental Health Association, Alexandria, VA.

AINSWORTH, P. B. (2002). Psychology and policing. Cullompton, Devon, UK: Willan Publishing.

ALBERTI, R. E., & EMMONS, M. L. (1986). *Your perfect right.* San Luis Obispo, CA: Impact.

ALLEN, B. P. (1990). *Personal adjustment.* Pacific Grove, CA: Brooks-Cole.

ANDREWS, D. A., & BONTA, J. (1995). *LSI-R: Level of Service Inventory* (Revised). Toronto: Multi-Health Systems.

ARNOFF, K. M. (1999). *A psychosocial manual for cross-cultural communications between Hispanic and Anglo-American populations in the work place.* Unpublished doctoral dissertation, University of Michigan, Ann Arbor.

Arrestee drug abuse monitoring program (ADAM). (2001). Washington, DC: National Institute of Justice.

BAKER, M. (1985). *Cops.* New York: Pocket Books.

BANAKA, W. H. (1971). *Training in depth interviewing.* New York: Harper & Row.

BARONE, J. T., & SWITZER, J. Y. (1995). *Interviewing art and skill.* Boston: Allyn & Bacon.

BARTOL, C. R. (1983). *Psychology and American Law.* Belmont, CA: Wadsworth Publishing Company.

BASCH, M. F. (1983). Empathic understanding: A review of the concept and some theoretical considerations. *Journal of the American Psychoanalytic Association, 31,* 101–126.

BAUMGARTEN, E., & ROFFERS, J. (2003). Implementing and expanding on Carkhuff's training technology. *Journal of Counseling and Development, 81*(3), 285–291.

BAXTER, J. S., JACKSON, M., & BAIN, S. A. (2003). Interrogative suggestibility: Interactions between interviewees' self-esteem and interviewer style. *Personality and Individual Differences, 35,* 1285–1292.

BENJAMIN, A. (1981). *The helping interview* (3rd ed.). Boston: Houghton Mifflin.

BENNETT, M., & HESS, J. E. (1991, March). Cognitive interviewing. *FBI Law Enforcement Bulletin, 60*(3), 8–10.

BENSON, R. (2000). *Ragnar's guide to interviews, investigations, and interrogations.* Boulder, CO: Paladin Press.

BERENSON, B., & MITCHELL, K. M. (1974). *Confrontation: For better or worse.* Amherst, MA: Human Resources Development Press.

BERNE, E. (1964). *Games people play: The psychology of human relationships.* New York: Grove Press.

BLOOM, B. S. (Ed.). (1956). *Taxonomy of educational objectives.* New York: Longman, Green.

BOOK, H. E. (1988). Empathy: Misconceptions and misuses in psychotherapy. *American Journal of Psychiatry, 145*(4) 420–424.

BOON, J. C. W., & BAXTER, J. S. (2000). Minimizing integrative suggestibility. *Legal and Criminological Psychology, 5*(2), 273–284.

BOSHEAR, W. C., & ALBRECHT, K. G. (1977). *Understanding people: Models and concepts.* La Jolla, CA: University Associates.

BRAMMER, L. M. (1979). *The helping relationship: Process and skills.* Englewood Cliffs, NJ: Prentice-Hall.

BRENNER, S. L., HEAD, S. B., HELMES, M. J., WILLIAMS, R. B., & WILLIAMS, V. P. (2003). A videotape module to teach assertion skills. *Journal of Applied Social Psychology, 33*(6), 1140–1152.

BRILL, N. I. (1973). *Working with people: The helping process.* Philadelphia: Lippincott.

BROWN, F. L., AMOS, J. R., & MINK, O. G. (1975). *Statistical Concepts: A Basic Program,* Second Edition. New York: Harper & Row.

BUCHER, R. D. (2004). *Diversity consciousness: Opening our minds to people, cultures, and opportunities* (2nd ed.). Upper Saddle River, NJ: Pearson/Prentice-Hall.

BUERGER, M. (2004, January). Educating and training the future police officer. *FBI Law Enforcement Bulletin, 73*(1), 26–32.

BURGOON, J. K., & BULLER, D. B. (1994). Interpersonal deception III: Effects of deceit on perceived communication and nonverbal behavior dynamics. *Journal of Nonverbal Behavior, 18*(2), 155–184.

BURKE, B. L., ARKOWITZ, H., & MENCHOLA, M. (2003). The efficacy of motivational interviewing: A meta-analysis of controlled clinical trials. *Journal of Consulting and Clinical Psychology, 71*(5), 843–861.

BUTLER, E. A., EGLOFF, B., WILHELM, F. H., SMITH, N. C., ERICKSON, E. A., & GROSS, J. J. (2003, March). The social consequences of expressive emotion. *Emotion, 3*(1), 48–67.

CARKHUFF, R. R. (1969). *Helping and human relations: Selection and training* (Vol. 1). New York: Holt, Rinehart and Winston.

CARKHUFF, R. R. (1971). *The development of human resources.* New York: Holt, Rinehart and Winston.

CARKHUFF, R. R. (1987). *The art of helping* (6th ed.). Amherst, MA: Human Resource Development Press.

CARKHUFF, R. R., & BERENSON, B. G. (1977). *Beyond counseling and therapy.* New York: Holt, Rinehart and Winston.

CARTER, J. A. (1997). *A systematic development of a video-based self-instructional interview training package.* (Doctoral dissertation, University of Michigan). Ann Arbor, MI: UMI Microfilm.

CHANG, V. N., & SCOTT, S. T. (1999). *Basic interviewing skills: A workbook for practitioners.* Chicago: Nelson-Hall.

CHERRYMAN, J., & BULL, R. (2001). Police officers' perceptions of specialist investigative interviewing skills. *International Journal of Police Science and Management, 3*(3), 199–212.

CHRISTIE, R., & GEIS, F. L. (1970). *Studies in Machiavellianism.* New York: Academic Press.

CHUNG, R. C., & BEMAK, F. (2002). The relationship of culture and empathy in cross-cultural counseling. *Journal of Counseling and Development, 80,* 154–159.

CINNAMON, K. M., & MATULEF, N. J. (1979). *Assessment and interviewing.* Kansas City, MO: Applied Skills Press.

CLEAR, T. R., CLEAR, V. B., & BURRELL, W. D. (1989). *Offender assessment and evaluation: The presentence investigation report.* Cincinnati, OH: Anderson.

CLEDE, B. (1990). *Police officer's guide.* Harrisburg, PA: Stackpole Books.

CODERONI, G. R. (2002). The relationship between multicultural training for police and effective law enforcement. *FBI Law Enforcement Bulletin, 71*(11), 16–18.

COHN, A., & UDOLF, R. (1979). *The criminal justice system and its psychology.* New York: Van Nostrand Reinhold.

COLLINS, R., LINCOLN, R., & FRANK, M. G. (2002, April). The effect of rapport in forensic interviewing. *Psychiatry, Psychology, and Law, 9*(1), 69–78.

COLWELL, K., HISCOCK, C. K., & MEMON, A. (2002). Interviewing techniques and the assessment of statement credibility. *Applied Cognitive Psychology, 16,* 287–300.

COMMUNITY JUSTICE ASSISTANCE DIVISION (CJAD). (1991). *Strategies for Case Supervision.* Austin, TX: Texas Department of Criminal Justice.

CONNELLY, M. (2001). *Angels flight.* New York: Warner Books.

CORMIER, W. H., & CORMIER, L. S. (1979). *Interviewing strategies for helpers.* Monterey, CA: Brooks-Cole.

CRAIG, R. J. (2003). Assessing personality and psychopathy with interviews. In J. R. Graham & J. A. Naglieri (Eds.), *Handbook of psychology: Vol. 10. Assessment psychology.* Hoboken, NJ: Wiley.

D'AUGELLI, A. R., D'AUGELLI, J. F., & DANISH, S. J. (1981). *Helping others.* Monterey, CA: Brooks-Cole.

DANIELS, T. (1985). *Microcounseling: Training in skills of therapeutic communication with R.N. diploma-program nursing students.* Unpublished doctoral dissertation, Dalhousie University, Nova Scotia.

DANISH, S. J., & HAUER, A. L. (1973). *Helping skills: A basic training program.* New York: Behavioral Publications.

DEJAGER, C. (1992, Winter). Adventures in science and cyclosophy. *Skeptical Inquirer, 16*(2), 167–172.

DEL CARMEN, R. V. (2001). *Civil Liabilities for Probation/Parole Officers and Supervisors* (3rd ed.). Washington, DC: U.S. Dept. of Justice, National Institute of Corrections.

DILLARD, J. M., & REILLY, R. R. (Eds.). (1988). *Systematic interviewing: Communication skills for professional effectiveness.* Columbus, OH: Merrill.

DOWLING, J. L. (1979). *Criminal investigation.* New York: Harcourt Brace Jovanovich.

DOWNS, C. W., SMEYAK, G. P., & MARTIN, E. (1980). *Professional interviewing.* New York: Harper & Row.

EDELWICH, J., & BRODSKY, A. (1980). *Burnout: Stages of disillusionment in the helping professions.* New York: Human Sciences Press.

EGAN, G. (1975). *The skilled helper: A model for systematic helping and interpersonal relating.* Monterey, CA: Brooks-Cole.

EGAN, G. (1976a). *Interpersonal living: A skills/contract approach to human-relations training in groups.* Monterey, CA: Brooks-Cole.

EGAN, G. (1976b). *The skilled helper: A systematic approach to effective helping* (4th ed.). Monterey, CA: Brooks-Cole.

EGAN, G. (1994). *The skilled helper: A problem-management approach to helping.* Pacific Grove, CA: Brooks/Cole.

EKMAN, P. (1986). *Telling lies: Clues to deceit in the marketplace, politics and marriage.* New York: Berkley Books.

EKMAN, P. (2001). *Telling lies: Clues to deceit in the marketplace, politics, and marriage.* New York: Norton.

EKMAN, P. (2003). *Emotion revealed: Recognizing faces and feelings to improve communication and emotional life.* New York: Times Books/Henry Holt.

EKMAN, P., O'SULLIVAN, M., & FRANK, M. G. (1999). A few can catch a liar. *Psychological Science, 10*(3), 263–266.

ELLIOTT, W. N. (2002). Managing offender resistance to counseling—The "3 R's." *Federal Probation, 66*(3), 43–49.

ERB, E. D., & HOOKER, D. (1967). *The psychology of the emerging self.* Philadelphia: F. A. Davis.

EVANS, D. R., HEARN, M. T., UHLEMANN, M. R., & IVEY, A. E. (1989). *Essential interviewing: A programmed approach to effective communication* (3rd ed.). Pacific Grove, CA: Brooks-Cole.

FALS-STEWART, W. (1993, April). Neurocognitive defects and their impact on substance abuse treatment. *Journal of Addictions and Offender Counseling, 13*(2), 46–57.

FENLASON, A. F., FERGUSON, G. B., & ABRAHAMSON, A. C. (1962). *Essentials in interviewing.* New York: Harper & Row.

FISHER, G. L., & HARRISON, T. C. (2000). *Substance abuse: Information for school counselors, social workers, therapists, and counselors* (2nd ed.). Boston: Allyn & Bacon.

FISHER, R. P., & GEISELMAN, R. E. (1992). *Memory-enhancing techniques for investigative interviewing: The cognitive interview.* Springfield, IL: Charles C. Thomas.

FISHER, R. P., GEISELMAN, R. E., & AMADOR, M. (1989). Field test of the cognitive interview: Enhancing the recollection of actual victims and witnesses of crime. *Journal of Applied Psychology, 74*(5), 722–727.

FISHER, R. P., GEISELMAN, E., & RAYMOND, D. S. (1987). Critical analysis of police interview techniques. *Journal of Police Science and Administration, 15*(3), 177–185.

FORSYTHE, C. (2004). The future of simulation technology for law enforcement: Diverse experience with realistic simulated humans. *FBI Law Enforcement Bulletin, 73*(1), 19–23.

FRANK, M. G., & FEELEY, T. H. (2003, February). To catch a liar: Challenges for research in lie detection training. *Journal of Applied Communication Research, 31*(1), 58–75.

GARCIA, J. G., WINSTON, S. M., BORZUCHOWSKA, B., & CARTWRIGHT, B. (2003). A transcultural integrative model for ethical decision making in counseling. *Journal of Counseling and Development, 81*(3), 268–277.

GARRETT, A. (1972). *Interviewing: Its principles and methods* (2nd ed.). New York: Service Association of America.

GEISELMAN, R. E., & FISHER, R. P. (1985, December). Interviewing victims and witnesses of crime. *National Institute of Justice: Research in Brief.* Washington, DC: U.S. Department of Justice.

GEISELMAN, R. E., & PADILLA, J. (1988, November 4). Cognitive interviewing with child witnesses. *Journal of Police Science and Administration, 16,* 236–242.

GEISELMAN, R. E. (1999). Commentary on recent research with the cognitive interview. *Psychology, Crime, and Law, 5,* 197–202.

GELLER, W. A. (1993, March). Videotaping interrogations and confessions. *National Institute of Justice: Research in Brief.* Washington, DC: U.S. Department of Justice.

GILBERT, S. V. (2004). *Interviewing and Interrogation: The discovery of truth.* Belmont, CA: Wadsworth/Thomson Learning.

GLADSTEIN, G. A. (1983). Understanding empathy: Integrating counseling, developmental, and social psychology perspectives. *Journal of Counseling Psychology, 30*(4), 467–482.

GLUCKSTERN, N. B., PACKARD, R., & WENVER, K. (1989). *Conflict prevention skills* [Videotape]. North Amherst, MA: Microtraining Associates.

GOFFIN, R. D., JELLY, R. B., & WAGNER, S. H. (2003). Is halo helpful? Effects of inducing halo on performance rating accuracy. *Social Behavior and Personality, 31*(6), 625–636.

GORDON, R. L. (1975). *Interviewing: Strategy, techniques and tactics.* Homewood, IL: Dorsey Press.

GOZNA, L. F., VRIJ, A., & BULL, R. (2001). The impact of individual differences on perceptions of lying in everyday life and in a high stakes situation. *Personality and Individual Differences, 31,* 1203–1216.

GRAHAM, M., & MILLER, D. (1995). Cross-cultural interactive preferences profile. *The 1995 annual: Volume 1, training.* San Diego, CA: Pfeiffer.

GRANHAG, P. A., & STROMWALL, L. A. (2002, February). Repeated interrogations: Verbal and non-verbal cues to deception. *Applied Cognitive Psychology, 16,* 243–257.

GRANHAG, P. A., STROMWALL, L. A., & JONSSON, A. (2003). Partners in crime: How liars in collusion betray themselves. *Journal of Applied Social Psychology, 33*(4), 848–868.

GREEN, T. M. (1997). Police as frontline mental health workers: The decision to arrest or refer to mental health agencies. *International Journal of Law and Psychiatry, 20*(4), 469–486.

GUBRIUM, J. F., & HOLSTEIN, J. A. (2003). From the individual interview to the interview society. In J. F. Gubrium & J. A. Holstein (Eds.), *Postmodern interviewing* (pp. 21–49). Thousand Oaks, CA: Sage.

GUDJONSSON, G. H. (1989). Compliance in an interrogative situation: A new scale. *Personality and Individual Differences, 10*(5), 535–540.

GUDJONSSON, G. H. (1992). *The psychology of interrogations, confessions and testimony.* New York: Wiley.

GUDJONSSON, G. H. (2001). False confession. *The Psychologist, 14*(11), 589–591.

GUDJONSSON, G. H. (2003). *The psychology of interrogation and confessions: A handbook.* West Sussex, UK: Wiley.

HACKNEY, H. (1978). The evolution of empathy. *Personnel and Guidance Journal, 57*(1), 14–18.

HADLEY, R. G., & BRODWIN, M. G. (1988, November). Language about people with disabilities. *Journal of Counseling and Development, 67,* 147–149.

HAILS, J., & BORUM, R. (2003, January). Police training and specialized approaches to respond to people with mental illness. *Crime and Delinquency, 49*(1), 52–61.

HAKANSSON, J., & MONTGOMERY, H. (2003). Empathy as an interpersonal phenomenon. *Journal of Social and Personal Relationships, 20*(3), 267–284.

HANEY, H., & LEIBSOHN, J. (1999). *Basic counseling responses: A multimedia learning system for the helping professions.* Pacific Groves, CA: Brooks/Cole, Wadsworth.

HARRIS, T. A. (1969). *I'm Ok, You're Ok.* New York: Harper and Row.

HAYES, P. A. (1996). Addressing the complexities of culture and gender in counseling. *Journal of Counseling and Development, 74,* 332–338.

HERMANS, H. J. M., FIDDELAERS, R., de GROOT, R., & NAUTA, J. F. (1990, November-December). Self-confrontation as a method for assessment and intervention in counseling. *Journal of Counseling and Development, 69*(2), 156–162.

HOLLIN, C. R., & PALMER, E. J. (2003). Levels of service inventory—Revised profiles of violent and nonviolent prisoners. *Journal of Interpersonal Violence, 18*(9), 1075–1086.

HOLMBERG, V. Z. C. (2002). Murderers and sexual offenders: Experiences of police interviews and their inclination to admit or deny crimes. *Behavioral Sciences and the Law, 20,* 31–45.

HOLMES, W. D. (2002). *Criminal interrogation: A modern format for interrogating criminal suspects based on the intellectual approach.* Springfield, IL: Charles C. Thomas.

HUGGINS, M. K., HARITOS-FATOUROS, M., & ZIMBARDO, P. G. (2002). *Violence workers: Police torturers and murderers reconstruct Brazilian atrocities.* Berkeley: University of California Press.

HUGHES, J. N. (1988). Interviewing children. In J. M. Dillard & R. R. Reilly (Eds.). *Systematic Interviewing: Communication skills for professional effectiveness* (pp. 90–113). Columbus, OH: Merrill Pub.

INBAU, F. E., Reid J. E., & BUCKLEY, J. P. (1986). *Criminal interrogation and confessions* (3rd ed.). Baltimore: Williams & Wilkins.

IVEY, A. E. (1971). *Microcounseling: Innovations in interviewing training.* Springfield, IL: Charles C. Thomas.

IVEY, A. E. (1994). *Intentional interviewing and counseling: Facilitating client development in a multicultural society* (3rd ed.). Pacific Grove, CA: Brooks-Cole.

IVEY, A. E., & AUTHIER, J. (1978). *Microcounseling: Innovations in interviewing, counseling, psychotherapy and psychoeducation.* Springfield, IL: Charles C. Thomas.

IVEY, A. E., & GLUCKSTERN N. (1984). *Basic influencing skills.* North Amherst, MA: Microtraining Associates.

IVEY, A. E., & GLUCKSTERN, N. (1982). *Basic attending skills.* North Amherst, MA: Microtraining Associates.

IVEY, A. E., & GLUCKSTERN, N. B. (1984). *Basic interviewing skills.* North Amherst, MA: Microtraining Associates.

IVEY, A. E., & LITTERER, J. (1979). *Face to face: Communication skills in business.* North Amherst, MA: Amherst Consulting Group.

JOHNSON, D. W. (1981). *Reaching out: Interpersonal effectiveness and self-actualization* (2nd ed.). Englewood Cliffs, NJ: Prentice-Hall.

JOHNSON, E. S. (1981). *Research methods in criminology and criminal justice.* Englewood Cliffs, NJ: Prentice-Hall.

JONGEWARD, D., & JAMES, M. (1973). *Winning with people: Group exercises in transactional analysis.* Reading, MA: Addison-Wesley Publishing Company.

JOURARD, S. M. (1974). *Healthy personality.* New York: MacMillian.

JUNG, J. (2001). *Psychology of alcohol and drugs: A research perspective.* Thousand Oaks, CA: Sage.

KADUSHIN, A. (1990). *The social work interview* (3rd ed.). New York: Columbia University Press.

KAPPELER, V. E., SLUDER, R. D., & ALPERT, G. P. (1994). *Forces of deviance: Understanding the dark side of policing.* Prospect Heights, IL: Waveland Press.

KASDORF, J., & GUSTAFSON, K. (1978). Research related to microcounseling. In A. E. Ivey & J. Authier (Eds.), *Microcounseling: Innovations in interviewing, counseling, psychotherapy and psychoeducation* (2nd ed.). Springfield, IL: Charles C. Thomas.

KASSIN, S. M., & FONG, C. T. (1999). "I'm innocent!": Effects of training on judgments of truth and deception in the interrogation room. *Law and Human Behavior, 23*(5), 499–516.

KASSIN, S. M., GOLDSTEIN, C. C., & SAVITSKY, K. (2003). Behavioral confirmation in the interrogation room: On the dangers of presuming guilt. *Law and Human Behavior, 27*(2), 187–203.

KASSIN, S. M., & McNALL, K. (1991). Police interrogations and confessions: Communicating promises and threats by pragmatic implication. *Law and Human Behavior, 15*(3), 233–251.

KELTNER, D., & EKMAN, P. (2000). Facial expressions of emotion. In M. Lewis & J. M.

Haviland-Jones (Eds.), *Handbook of emotions* (2nd ed.,). pp. 236–249 New York: Guilford Press.

KELTNER, D., EKMAN, P., GONZAGA, G. C., & BEER, J. (2003). Facial expression of emotion. In R. J. Davidson, K. R. Scherer, & H. H. Goldsmith (Eds.). *Handbook of affective sciences* (pp. 415–432). New York: Oxford University Press.

KERCHER, G., SHADDOCK, J., BARRUM, J., & SHEARER, R. (1978). *Mentally handicapped offender training program for law enforcement*. Huntsville, TX: Criminal Justice Center.

KIERULFF, S. (1988). Sheep in the midst of wolves: Personal-responsibility therapy with criminal personalities. *Professional Psychology: Research and Practice, 19*(4), 436–440.

KIM, B. S. K., & LYONS, H. Z. (2003). Experiential activities and multicultural counseling competence training. *Journal of Counseling and Development, 81*(4), 400–408.

KING, P. (2003). *Multicultural competencies of probation officers*. Unpublished doctoral dissertation, Sam Houston State University, Huntsville, TX.

KING, P., & SHEARER, R. A. (2004). A multicultural training curriculum for probation officers. *Executive Exchange*, pp. 16–17.

KNIGHT, H., & STEVENSON, W. (1976). *Communication for justice administration: Theory and skills*. Cincinnati, OH: Anderson.

KOHNKEN, G. (1998). A phased approach to interviewer training. In C. P. Thompson, D. J. Herrmann, J. D. Read, D. Bruce, D. G. Payne, & M. P. Toglia (Eds.), *Eyewitness memory: Theoretical and applied perspectives* (pp. 89–106). Mahwah, NJ: Erlbaum.

LASSITER, G. D., GEERS, A. L., HANDLEY, I. M., WEILAND, P. E., & MUNHALL, P. J. (2002). Videotaped interrogations and confessions: A simple change in camera perspective alters verdicts in simulated trials. *Journal of Applied Psychology, 87*(5), 867–874.

LEO, R. A. (1996, Winter). Inside the interrogation room. *Journal of Criminal Law and Criminology, 86*, 266–303.

LERNER, K., ARLING, G., & BAIRD, C. (1986). *Client management classification: Strategies for case supervision*. Madison, WI: National Council on Crime and Delinquency.

LESSLER, J. T., CASPAR, R. A., PENNE, M. A., & BARKER, P. (2000). Developing computer assisted interviewing (CAI) for the national household survey on drug abuse. *Journal of Drug Issues, 30*(1), 9–34.

LIEBERMAN, D. J. (1998). *Never be lied to again*. New York: St. Martin's Griffin.

LINK, F. C., & FOSTER, D. G. (1989). *The kinesic interview technique*. Riverdale, GA: Interrotec Associates.

LOFTUS, E., & KETCHAM, K. (1994). *The myth of repressed memory*. New York: St. Martin's Press.

LONG, L., PARADISE, L. V., & LONG, T. J. (1981). *Questioning: Skills for the helping process*. Riverdale, GA: Brooks-Cole.

MADINGER, J. (2000). *Confidential informant: Law enforcement's most valuable tool*. Boca Raton, FL: CRC Press.

MacHOVEC, F. J. (1989). *Interview and interrogation, A scientific approach*. Springfield, IL: Charles C. Thomas.

MANIS, L. G. (1998). *Assertion training workshop: Leader's guide*. Holmes Beach, FL: Learning Publications.

MANN, C., & STEWART, F. (2003). Internet interviewing. In J. F. Gubrium & J. A. Holstein (Eds.), *Postmodern interviewing* (pp. 81–105). Thousand Oaks, CA: Sage.

MANN, S., VRIJ, A., & BULL, R. (2002). Suspects, lies, and videotape: An analysis of authentic high-stake liars. *Law and Human Behavior, 26*(3), 365–376.

MASTERS, R. E. (2004). *Counseling criminal justice offenders* (2nd ed.). Thousand Oaks, CA: Sage.

McGRATH, R. J. (1990, December). Assessment of sexual aggressors. *Journal of Interpersonal Violence, 5*(4), 505–519.

McKENZIE, F. R., SCERBO, M., CATANZARO, J., & PHILLIPS, M. (2003). Nonverbal indicators of malicious intent: Virtual reality training. *International Journal of Human–Computer Studies, 59*, 237–244.

MEDFORD, S., GUDJONSSON, G. H., & PEARSE, J. (2003). The efficacy of the appropriate adult safeguard during police interviewing. *Legal and Criminological Psychology, 8*, 253–266.

MEISSNER, C. A., & KASSIM, S. M. (2002). "He's guilty!" Investigator bias in judgments of truth and deception. *Law and Human Behavior, 26*(5), 469–480.

MELOY, J. R. (1992). *The psychopathic mind.* Northvale, NJ: Jason Aronson.

MEMON, A., & BULL, R. (Eds.). (1999). *Handbook of the psychology of interviewing.* Chichester, UK: Wiley.

MEMON, A., VRIJ, A., & BULL, R. (2003). *Psychology and law: Truthfulness, accuracy, and credibility* (2nd ed.). Chichester, UK: Wiley.

MILLER, K. R. (2001). Interpreting in an alternate universe: Texas prison vernacular. *Views, 18*(10), 13–15.

MILLER, S., WACKMAN, D., NUNNALLY, B., & MILLER, P. (1988). *Connecting: With self and others.* Littleton, CO: Interpersonal Communications Programs.

MILLER, W. R., & ROLLNICK, S. (1991). *Motivational interviewing: Preparing people to change addictive behavior.* New York: Guilford Press.

MILNE, R., & BULL, R. (1999). *Investigative interviewing: Psychology and practice.* Chichester, UK: Wiley.

MOLYNEAUX, D., & LANE, V. W. (1982). *Effective interviewing: Techniques and analysis.* Boston: Allyn & Bacon.

MYREN, R. A., & GARCIA, C. H. (1989). *Investigation for determination of fact: A primer on proof.* Pacific Grove, CA: Brooks-Cole.

NANCE, S. (2001). *Conquering deception.* Kansas City, MO: Irvin-Benham Group.

NARDINI, W. (1987). The polygraph technique: An overview. *Journal of Police Science and Administration, 15*(3), 239–249.

National Mental Health Association (1988). *Aiding people in conflict: A manual for law enforcement.* Alexandria, VA: National Mental Health Association.

National Research Council. (2003). *The polygraph and lie detection.* Washington, DC: National Academies Press.

NEIL, T. C. (1980). *Interpersonal communications for criminal justice personnel.* Boston: Allyn & Bacon.

NELSON, D. B., & LOW, G. (1981). *Personal skills map.* Corpus Christi, TX: Institute for the Development of Human Resources.

NELSON, D. B., & PIERCE, N. T. (1988). *Personal achievement skills system.* Corpus Christi, TX: Institute for the Development of Human Resources.

NELSON-JONES, R. (1990). *Human relationships: A skills approach.* Pacific Grove, CA: Brooks-Cole.

NEWTON, T. (1998). The place of ethics in investigative interviewing by police officers. *Howard Journal of Criminal Justice, 37*(1), 34–52.

OFSHE, R. J. (1992, July). Inadvertent hypnosis during interrogation: False confession due to dissociative state, misidentified multiple personality and the satanic cult hypothesis. *International Journal of Clinical and Experimental Hypnosis, XL,* 125–126.

O'SULLIVAN, M. (2003). The fundamental attribution error in detecting deception: The boy-who-cried-wolf effect. *Personality and Social Psychology Bulletin, 29*(10), 1316–1327.

PALMIOTTO, M. J., BIRZER, M. L., & UNNITHAN, N. P. (2000). Training in community policing: A suggested curriculum. *Policing: An International Journal of Strategies and Management, 23*(1), 8–21.

PARKER, L. C., MEIER, R. D., & MONAHAN, L. H. (1989). *Interpersonal psychology for criminal justice.* New York: West.

PEARSE, J., GUDJONSSON, G. H., CLARKE, I. C. H., & RUTLER, S. (1998). Police interviewing and psychological vulnerabilities: Predicting the likelihood of confession. *Journal of Community and Applied Psychology, 8,* 1–21.

PEDERSON, D. (2000). *A handbook for developing multicultural awareness* (3rd ed.). Alexandria, VA: American Counseling Association.

PEDERSON, D. B., & IVEY, A. (1993). *Culture-centered counseling and interviewing skills: A practical guide.* Westport, CT: Praeger.

PEKERTI, A. A., & THOMAS, D. C. (2003). Communication in intercultural interaction: An empirical investigation of ideocentric and sociocentric styles. *Journal of Cross-Cultural Psychology, 34*(2), 139–154.

PERLS, F. S. (1971). *Gestalt therapy verbatim.* New York: Bantam Books.

PERSKE, R. (2000, December). Deception in the interrogation room: Sometimes tragic for persons with mental retardation and other developmental disabilities. *Mental Retardation,* pp. 532–537.

PHELPS, S., & AUSTIN, N. (1975). *The assertive woman.* San Luis Obispo, CA: Impact.

PINE, J. C. (Ed.). (1974). *Interpersonal communication: A guide for staff development.* Athens: Institute of Government, University of Georgia.

POLCIN, D. L. (2003). Rethinking confrontation in alcohol and drug treatment: Consideration of the clinical context. *Substance Use and Misuse, 38*(2), 165–184.

PORTER, S., WOODWORTH, M., & BIRT, A. R. (2000). Truth, lies, and videotape: An investigation of the ability of federal parole officers to detect deception. *Law and Human Behavior, 24*(6), 643–658.

POWELL, M. B. (2002). Specialist training in investigative and evidential interviewing: Is it having any effect on the behaviour of professionals in the field? *Psychiatry, Psychology, and Law, 9*(1), 44–55.

RABON, D. (1992). *Interviewing and interrogation.* Durham, NC: Carolina Academic Press.

RAKOS, R. F. (2003). Asserting and confronting. In O. D. W. Hargle (Ed.), *The handbook of communication skills* (2nd ed., pp. 289–319). New York: Routledge, Taylor & Francis.

REESE, H. (2003, November). The keys to quality interview techniques. *Law and Order, 51*(11), 66–69.

REID, J. E., & Associates. (2000). *The Reid technique of interviewing and interrogation.* Chicago: Author.

REID, J. E., & Associates, Inc. (1995). *Seminar schedule.* Chicago: Author.

REULAND, M., & MARGOLIS, G. J. (2003). Police approaches that improve the response to people with mental illness: A focus on victims. *The Police Chief, 70*(11), 1–9.

REYNOLDS, J., & MARIANI, M. M. (2002). *Police talk: A scenario-based communications workbook for police recruits and officers.* Upper Saddle River, NJ: Prentice-Hall.

RICHARDS, H. J., & PAI, S. M. (2003). Deception in prison assessment of substance abuse. *Journal of Substance Abuse Treatment, 24,* 121–128.

ROZELLE, R. M., DRUCKMAN, D., & BAXTER, J. C. (2003). Non-verbal behavior as communication. In O. D. W. Hargle (Ed.), *The handbook of communication skills* (2nd ed., pp. 67–102). New York: Routledge, Taylor & Francis.

RUFFIN, J. L. (2002). Law enforcement perspectives and the use of trickery and deceit during the interrogation process. *Dissertation Abstracts International, Section A, Humanities and Social Sciences, 63*(1-A), 339.

RYALS, J. R. (1991, March). Successful interviewing. *FBI Law Enforcement Bulletin, 60*(3), 6–7.

SANDERS, M. (2003). Building bridges instead of walls: Effective cross-cultural counseling. *Corrections Today, 65*(1), 58–59.

SANDOVAL, V. A. (2003). Strategies to avoid interview contamination. *FBI Law Enforcement Bulletin, 72*(10), 1–12.

SCHRAMM, W. (Ed.). (1960). *The process and effects of mass communication.* Urbana: University of Illinois Press.

SCHUBERT, M. (1971). *Interviewing in social work practice: An introduction.* New York: Council on Social Work Education.

SCHUTZ, W. C. (1973). *Elements of encounter.* Big Sur, CA: Joy Press.

SEGAL, D. L., & COOLIDGE, F. L. (2003). Structured interviewing and DSM classification. In M. Hersene & S. M. Turner (Eds.), *Adult psychopathy and diagnosis* (pp. 72–103). Hoboken, NJ: Wiley.

SEITER, R. P., & WEST, A. D. (2003). Supervision styles in probation and parole: An analysis of activities. *Journal of Offender Rehabilitation, 38*(2), 57–75.

SHARPLEY, C. F., HALAT, J., RABINOWICZ, T., WEILAND, B., & STAFFORD, J. (2001, December). Standard posture, postural mirroring, and client-perceived rapport. *Counseling Psychology Quarterly, 14*(4), 267–280.

SHAW, M. E., CORSINI, R. J., BLAKE, R. R., & MOUTON, J. S. (1980). *Role playing: A practical manual for group facilitators.* San Diego, CA: University Associates.

SHEARER, R. A. (1989). *Interviewing in criminal justice.* Acton, MA: Copley.

SHEARER, R. A. (2001). Strategic alignment in community supervision of offenders. *Perspectives, the Journal of the American Probation and Parole Association, 25*(3), 18–21.

SHEARER, R. A., & KING, P. (2004). Multicultural competencies in probation: Issues and challenges. *Federal Probation, 68*(1), 3–9.

SHEARER, R. A., & MOORE, J. B. (1978). *Personality dimensions of probated felons.* Paper presented at the annual meeting of the American Society of Criminology, Dallas, TX.

SHENOUR, E. A. (1990, Spring). Lying about polygraph test. *Skeptical Inquirer, 14*(3), 292–297.

SHUY, R. W. (1998). *The language of confession, interrogation, and deception.* Thousand Oaks, CA: Sage.

SIEGMAN, A. W., & POPE, B. (Eds.). (1972). *Studies in dyadic communication.* New York: Pergamon Press.

SILBERMAN, C. E. (1978). *Criminal violence, criminal justice.* New York: Vintage Books.

SILVER, I. (1986). *Police Civil Liability.* New York: M. Bender.

SINCOFF, M. Z., & GOYER, R. S. (1984). *Interviewing.* New York: Macmillan.

SKOPEC, E. W. (1986). *Situational interviewing.* New York: Harper & Row.

SMITH, M. J. (1975). *When I say no, I feel guilty.* New York: Bantam Books.

STEINMETZ, M. (1995, May/June). Interviewing children: Balancing forensic and therapeutic techniques. *NRCCSA News, 4*(3).

STEWART, C. J., & CASH, W. B. (1985). *Interviewing principles and practices* (4th ed). Dubuque, IA: William C. Brown.

STROMWALL, L. A., & GRANHAG, P. A. (2003). How to detect deception: Arresting the beliefs of police officers, prosecutors, and judges. *Psychology, Crime and Law, 9,* 19–36.

TARVER, M., WALKER, S., & WALLACE, P. H. (2002). *Multicultural issues in the criminal justice system.* Boston: Allyn & Bacon.

TCU INSTITUTE OF BEHAVIORAL RESEARCH (2002). *TCU/Brief Intake Interview.* www.ibr.tcu.edu.

TWGEYEE (Technical Working Group for Eyewitness Evidence). (1999). *Eyewitness evidence: A guide for law enforcement.* Washington, DC: U.S. Department of Justice, Office of Justice Programs.

TWGEYEE (Technical Working Group for Eyewitness Evidence). (2003). *Eyewitness evidence: A trainer's manual for law enforcement.* Washington, DC: U.S. Department of Justice, Office of Justice Programs.

Texas Department of Criminal Justice. (1999). *Institutional parole case summary.* Huntsville, TX: Texas Department of Criminal Justice.

TIMERMAN, J. (1981). *Prisoner without a name, cell without a number.* New York: Vintage Books.

TOCH, H. (1977). *Living in prisons: The ecology of survival.* New York: MacMillian.

TOMM, K. (1987a). Interventive interviewing part I: Strategizing as a fourth guideline for the therapist. *Family Process, 26,* 3–13.

TOMM, K. (1987b). Interventive interviewing part II: Reflexive questioning as a means to enable self healing. *Family Process, 26,* 167–183.

TOUSIGNANT, D. D. (1991, March). Why suspects confess. *FBI Law Enforcement Bulletin, 60*(3), 14–18.

TROWBRIDGE, B. C. (2003). Suggestibility and confessions. *American Journal of Forensic Psychology, 21*(1), 5–23.

TRYON, G. S. (Ed.). (2002). *Counseling based on process research: Applying what we know.* Boston: Allyn & Bacon.

VAUGHN, M. S. (1992). The parameters of trickery as an acceptable police practice. *American Journal of Police, XI*(4), 71–95.

VERNON, M., RAIFMAN, L. J., GREENBERG, S. F., & MONTEIRO, B. (2001). Forensic pretrial police interviews of deaf suspects: Avoiding legal pitfalls. *Journal of Law and Psychiatry, 24,* 43–59.

VRIJ, A. (2000). *Detecting lies and deceit.* New York: Wiley.

VRIJ, A. (2003). "We will protect your wife and child, but only if you confess": Police interrogations in England and the Netherlands. In P. J. van Poppen & S. D. Penrod (Eds.), *Adversarial versus inquisitorial justice: Perspectives on criminal justice systems,* pp. 55–79. New York: Kluwer Academic/Plenum Press.

VRIJ, A., EDWARD, K., ROBERTS, K. P., & BULL, R. (2000, Winter). Detecting deceit via analysis of verbal and nonverbal behavior. *Journal of Nonverbal Behavior, 24*(4), 239–263.

VRIJ, A., & MANN, S. (2001). Telling and detecting lies in a high-stake situation: The case of a convicted murderer. *Applied Cognitive Psychology, 15,* 187–203.

VRIJ, A., & TAYLOR, R. (2003). Police officers' and students' beliefs about telling and detecting trivial and serious lies. *International Journal of Police Science and Management, 5*(1), 41–49.

WALTERS, S. B. (2000). *The truth about lying: How to spot a lie and protect yourself from deception.* Naperville, IL: Source Books.

WALTERS, S. B. (2003). *Principles of kinesic interview and interrogation* (2nd ed.). Boca Raton, FL: CRC Press.

WALSH, A. (1997). *Correctional assessment, casework and counseling* (2nd ed.). Lanham, MD: American Correctional Association.

WALTMAN, J. L. (1983). Nonverbal communication in interrogation. *Journal of Police Science and Administration, 11*(2), 166–169.

WAMBAUGH, J. (1970). *The new centurions.* New York: Dell Books.

WAMBAUGH, J. (1972). *The blue knight.* New York: Dell Books.

WAMBAUGH, J. (1973). *The onion field.* New York: Dell Books.

WAMBAUGH, J. (1975). *The choirboys.* New York: Dell Books.

WEITEN, W., & LLOYD, M. A. (2003). *Psychology applied to modern life* (7th ed.). Belmont, CA: Wadsworth Thompson Learning.

WHITEHEAD, J. T. (1989). *Burnout in probation and corrections.* New York: Praeger.

WHORF, B. (1956), *Language, thought and reality.* Cambridge, MA: MIT Press.

WICKS, R. J., & JOSEPHS, E. H., Jr. (1977). *Techniques in interviewing for law enforcement and corrections personnel: A programmed text.* Springfield, IL: Charles C. Thomas.

WILLIAMS, B. (2003). The worldview dimensions of individualism and collectivism: Implications for counseling. *Journal of Counseling and Development, 81,* 320–374.

WILLIAMS, E. (1989). The mind of the sexually abused child: Factors impinging upon interview structure. *Police Journal, LXII*(3), 226–233.

WILSON, C., & POWELL, M. (2003). A guide to interviewing children: Essential skills for counsellors, police, lawyers, and social workers. *Applied Cognitive Psychology, 17*(2), 249.

WOLF, R., MESLOH, C., & CHERRY, B. R. (2002). *Constitutional issues surrounding police interviews and interrogations.* Orlando: University of Central Florida/Pearson Custom Publishing.

WONG, Y. S. (2003). Evaluation of sociocultural competency training in enhancing self efficacy among immigrant and Canadian-born health sciences trainees. *Dissertation Abstracts International, Section B. The Physical Sciences and Engineering, 63*(8-B), 3980.

WRIGHT, B. S. (2000). Policing in a multicultural society. In W. G. Doerner & M. L. Dantzker (Eds.), *Contemporary police organization and management: Issues and trends,* pp. 229–250. Boston: Butterworth-Heinemann.

WRIGHT, K. N. (1985). Developing the prison environment inventory. *Journal of Research in Crime and Delinquency, 22*(3), 257–277.

WRIGHTSMAN, L. S. (1987). *Psychology and the legal system.* Monterey, CA: Brooks-Cole.

WRIGHTSMAN, L. S. (1991). *Psychology and the legal system* (2nd ed.). Pacific Grove, CA: Brooks-Cole.

YESCHKE, C. L. (2003). *The art of investigative interviewing: A human approach to testimonial evidence* (2nd ed.). New York: Butterworth/Heinemann.

YOUNG, M. E. (1992). *Counseling methods and techniques: An eclectic approach.* New York: Merrill.

YUILLE, J. C., MARYSEN, D., & COOPER, B. (1999). Training investigative interviewers: Adherence to the spirit, as well as the letter. *International Journal of Law and Psychiatry, 22*(3-4), 323–336.

YUILLE, J. C., TOLLESTRUP, P. A., MARXSEN, S. P., & HERVE, H. F. M. (1998). An exploration on the effects of marijuana on eyewitness memory. *International Journal of Law and Psychiatry, 21*(1), 117–128.

ZULAWSKI, D. E., &. WICKLANDER, D. E. (1993). *Practical aspects of interview and interrogation.* Boca Raton, FL: CRC Press.

Index

Page numbers followed by *f* indicate figures.

333